PEGLER

ANGRY MAN OF THE PRESS

BY OLIVER PILAT

> Some day somebody should take the
> hide off Peg because the stuff inside
> is so much better than the varnished
> surface which blinks in the sunlight
> of public approval.
>
> HEYWOOD BROUN—1939

BEACON PRESS   BOSTON

By OLIVER PILAT

Sea-Mary, a novel
The Mate Takes Her Home, a novel
Sodom By The Sea, with Jo Ranson
The Atom Spies

DEDICATION

Almost a quarter of a century ago, several meetings at the Riverside Drive apartment of Ferdinand Lundberg led to the organization of a secret anti-Communist caucus in the New York local of the American Newspaper Guild. Those present included David Davidson, Victor Riesel, Fred Woltman, Sidney Hertzberg, Harry Lopatin, and Mr. and Mrs. Lawrence Delaney.

I have been in contact recently with Davidson, now national chairman of the Writers Guild of America; Riesel, a syndicated labor columnist; Woltman, the Pulitzer prize-winning journalist now living in retirement in Florida; Lundberg, whose latest book is *The Coming World Transformation*; and Delaney, currently Democratic Leader of Suffolk County, New York. Memory being a creative faculty, there is no agreement between them (and me) as to who were the other founding fathers of that controversial group.

Through the courtesy of Larry Delaney, I have seen a couple of rare early issues of *The Guild Progressive*, the newspaper published by the caucus when it became strong enough to discard secrecy. Those who dared union expulsion by listing themselves as sponsors of this subversive publication included William Burgess, Herman Dinsmore, Ralph J. Frantz, James Kelly, Ted Poston, Jo Ranson, Samuel Romer and Paul Sann.

The caucus soon established representatives on the various Guild-affiliated publications in New York. Among them were Thelma Boozer and Carl Lawrence, *Amsterdam News*; Morton Coates, George Wells, *Associated Press*; Arthur Rosenstock, *Bronx Home News*; Peggy O'Reilly, T. Norman Palmer, *Brooklyn Eagle*; Harry Berkowitz, Pearl Wiesen, *Daily Forward*; Gerald Browne, Robert Conway, *Daily News*; John Chamberlain, *Fortune*; Lewis Gannett, Robert Stern, Carl Levin, McIlvaine Parsons, *Herald Tribune*; Leon Racht, Syd Boehm, *Journal American*; Frank McMaster, *Long Island Press*; Richard H. Rovere, *Nation*; Mary Ellison, *New Republic*; Hilda Loveman, *Newsweek*; Angeline Leibinger, *New York Times*; Leo Margolin, James A. Wechsler, *PM*; Al Cusick, Marvin Berger, Maureen McKernan, Margo Fein,

Edward Hunter, *Post*; Walter Randall, *Standard & Poor's*; Max Danish, Harry Crone, Will Chasen, Dan Bell, Morris Iushewitz and others from the labor press; Calvin Fixx, Robert Cantwell, Joseph Kastner, Gilbert Cant, Kay Walsh and a whole procession of other lovely girls, most of them with red hair and names like Jean, Peggy and Ruth, from *Time*.

Obviously, this is an impossible task. Omitted names are already thrusting themselves forward accusingly from the vanished years—names like Sylvan Pollack, Donald Robinson, Thurston McCauley, George Reaney, William Ucker, Leonard Smith, Walter Engels and a hundred more.

We took ourselves so seriously then; but the task *was* serious. We did what we started out to do; we played a leading role in routing the Communist-influenced leadership of the American Newspaper Guild in 1941, and in the New York local some years later. To all of us, named and unnamed, I affectionately dedicate this volume about a former Guildsman whose instincts were for the underdog but whose fixed modes of thought made him a company man.

January 10, 1963   O. P.

CONTENTS

1. THE TRUE CRUSADER 1

2. RIDING THE UMPIRE 10

3. EXCELSIOR 24

4. CUB IN CHICAGO 40

5. ON HIS OWN 52

6. FOREIGN CORRESPONDENT 67

7. THE ROMANCE IN HIS LIFE 81

8. SPORTSMAN 95

9. HEAD OF THE FAMILY 110

10. COUNTRY SQUIRE 127

11. THE SHORT ESSAY 142

12. OVER THE TOP 158

13. WAR GARDEN 172

14. TURN TO THE RIGHT 186

15. OUT IN THE DESERT 192

16. SETTLING AN OLD SCORE 203

17. BANSHEE AT BAY 219

18. MISOGRAMMARIAN 232

19. MAN OF THE UNDERWORLD 245

20. THE BROTHELIAN PRESS 263

   BIBLIOGRAPHY 281

   INDEX 283

1. THE TRUE CRUSADER

Here was a writer who reached instinctively for an opponent's throat. His urge to humiliate and kill, felt through the filter of newsprint, made him the nation's outstanding controversialist in the twentieth century. "Journalism's angry man," they called him. Indignant would have been a better adjective, since his brief essays were usually inspired by a strong but elemental sense of justice. In Robert Burns's phrase, he was an "unco' righteous" fellow.

Poorly educated, non-intellectual, not even sophisticated—despite the Broadway-wise cynicism he affected—he found it easier to grapple with an enemy than with an idea. He became as deadly a duelist with words as Alexander Dumas with a sword at Versailles, or Aaron Burr with a pistol at Weehawken.

For focusing his highly obtrusive pique in a readable way, he was rewarded with wide attention, a Pulitzer prize and lesser journalistic medals, a biography in *Who's Who* and an income exceeding that of the President of the United States.

Despite frequent insinuations that he must be unbalanced, he was sane by ordinary medical and legal standards. The emotional intensity of his columns provided an excellent form of catharsis. By his own standards, he was incorruptible, honorable and sincere, but sincerity is only an effort to gauge reality and conform to it, and his tools for that effort were inadequate.

He remained uncomfortable no matter where he lived. Usually separated from his followers by distance, he felt conscious of unfriendly eyes, ears and voices close to him. He had a weakness for wanting to make history, yet he could not help realizing that the tide ran adversely. In such a mood, he once remarked that the late Henry L. Mencken, a lesser insurgent, "never lived an hour in the bitter loneliness of the True Crusader of the Press." This was his preferred self-image: "the reporter who tells the truth and walks alone," the True Crusader of the Press.

Once upon a time, it was possible for many millions of Americans, not all of them dunderheads, reactionaries and bigots

1

by any means, to open their newspapers with a little quickening of the pulse, wondering whom Westbrook Pegler would clobber that day. They read him as many televiewers now watch fights, enjoying the feel of conflict without knowing too much about the background of the fighters or caring too much about the outcome.

Pegler began newspaper work in 1910, but it was not until 1933 that he emerged permanently from the toy department (as he termed sports writing) and began to sell notions upstairs.

In both fields, his chief asset was a crowd-pleasing style. As a commentator, he at first favored epithets that were more noisy than damaging. His column abounded in exploding paper-bag phrases like "blood-thirsty bull twirp" for A.A. Berle, Jr., an Assistant Secretary of State, "China Boy" and "pi-yu" for Henry Luce, the Far Eastern-oriented publisher, and "little padrone of the Bolsheviki" for Fiorello H. LaGuardia, a reform Mayor of New York.

Those under attack usually found some means of retaliation. Even when the contestants were poorly matched, the atmosphere of a sporting event persisted. An invisible bell would sound. The fighters would advance to ring center and touch gloves. Pegler would call Elsa Maxwell "a professional magpie," and she would shout back that he was a "duck-billed platypus" because "he hated all the other birds so much that the last one died the other day because of chronic ruffling of the feathers." Or he would dismiss J. Edgar Hoover as "a night-club fly-cop," and the FBI chief would reply that his critic suffered from "mental halitosis." He would call Walter Winchell "a gents-room journalist," and Winchell would snarl in reply: "louse in the blouse of journalism . . . feelthy log-roller . . . exponent of grouch journalism."

Judged as one-round bouts, the decision in these exchanges usually went to Pegler.

Harold L. Ickes, the ex-Bull Mooser from Chicago who served four terms as Franklin D. Roosevelt's Secretary of the Interior, became a favorite opponent. "Ickes is my man," crowed Pegler. "I can take that LaGuardia, too, any time, because he is a bulldozing four-flusher and he will tin-can it and back away, squealing like a pig under a gate if you carry it right to him and never let go. . . ."

Ickes married money, sneered Pegler, but he was stingy.

"Hey, Ickes, you penny-ante moocher, tell us about the two times you put yourself away in the Naval Hospital in Washington for three dollars a day all contrary to law, and you a rich guy able to pay your way in regular hospitals as all other sick civilians have to do. Why you cheap sponger, you couldn't rent a hall room in a pitcher-and-bowl fleabag in Washington for three bucks a day. You know who paid the overhead on your hospital bargain, don't you? Well, I did! And George Spelvin [Pegler's Everyman]. We paid it . . ."

And Ickes, who had asked publisher Eugene Meyer of the Washington *Post* to cancel his subscription because he could no longer "endure the stench of that awful column," replied: "I would no more think of reading Pegler than I would of handling raw sewage."

An even round, full of action.

Pegler's intensifying determination to win, regardless of how many Marquis of Queensberry rules he fractured in the process, was illustrated during the 1940 presidential campaign. The columnist accused Clifton Fadiman, a New Deal literary expert, of being a Communist, on the unconvincing ground that Fadiman once contributed to a *New Masses* forum. With the suavity of a skilled master of ceremonies disposing of a heckler, Fadiman expressed regret that he had only one hundred thousand dollars worth of insurance; if it were twice that amount, enough to take ample care of his family, said Fadiman, he would surely slay Pegler and go willingly to the chair. The columnist returned to the attack with references to "killer Fadiman, the Union Square quarterback and bull-butterfly of the literary teas."

At this point, unfortunately, Hendrik Willem Van Loon decided to intervene. Van Loon was a brilliant, cantankerous and sentimental Dutchman who had produced thirty historical works, some of them best-sellers. If only because of his bulk—he stood six foot three and weighed nearly three hundred pounds—he had been a conspicuous member of an exurbanite intelligentsia located in Fairfield County and Pound Ridge on either side of the Connecticut-New York border. This group was led by Heywood Broun, a columnist with whom Pegler had been engaged for several years in a running feud of considerable significance. After Broun's death, the crowd had turned almost to a man against Pegler, but Van Loon had not been one of the more partisan members. At any rate, he issued a mild statement in defense of

3

Fadiman to the effect that young men frequently showed an abnormal interest in national problems without intending to take
any precise political stand.

Like a pugilist sensing an opening, Pegler pounced on the
word "abnormal." For millions to read, he wrote in his syndicated
newspaper column: "Any man so possessed would be bored by
normal men. Now that Mr. Van Loon mentions it, I realize that
this could have been why I have always felt a robust aversion to
this moist and buxom continental with his lacy mannerisms and
his flouncing aversions . . ." He was no authority on "queeries,"
Pegler ground on, whereas Van Loon had "great opportunity to
study his specialty in the circle of his friends and particularly in
the field of introspection."

Van Loon, a man in his sixties with only a few years left to
live, became critically ill. For days, he lay motionless in bed.
Word issued from his hotel suite that his doctors had forbidden
him to move, even to smile. The historian was a married man,
with two grown children by the first of his four marriages, and a
host of friends, but as he began to recover he showed a distaste for people. He preferred the company of his dogs—Noodle
II, a dachshund, and Mingo, a huge black Newfoundland named
after Sir Walter Scott's pet. Convalescence progressed gradually to a point at which Van Loon was willing to discuss his attitude with a visitor. After reading the Pegler column, he said, he
came to the conclusion that he would have to challenge the writer
to a duel and kill him. His standards, however, permitted dueling
only with equals. It was therefore frustration rather than the
original insult, he said, which had laid him low.

Pegler probably lost that round on a foul. Having discovered, however, the devastating effect of a more or less veiled
imputation of effeminacy, the columnist employed it against
scores of well-known Americans ranging from Woodrow Wilson
to Frank Sinatra.

Though Sinatra subsequently became a masculine sex symbol of a familiar Hollywood sort, as well as an actor, he was
known in those days solely as a crooner with a frail physique.
Friends claimed they could see through him—he was so thin.
Jokers turned off electric fans when he entered a room lest he be
blown away. Sinatra endured these cracks, since, like the early
Ford jokes, they constituted free advertising. He even tolerated
the prearranged swooning of bobbysoxers at his performances,

4

but he was unwilling to take the Pegler purple treatment without retaliation.

One evening in the fall of 1944, Sinatra went hunting for the columnist at the Waldorf Astoria in New York. Orson Welles, the director and Shakespearean actor, accompanied Sinatra as guide and native gun-bearer. Welles said that they went to Pegler's room and that Pegler wasn't there. He might have been "hiding under the bed," Welles declared in a radio interview; they had failed to look there. Either way, said Welles, Pegler was lucky, since Sinatra was tougher than he looked—he knew how to handle his fists—and "nobody could be as tough as Westbrook wrote."

The "he's agin" columnist—so christened by Jack Alexander in a *Saturday Evening Post* profile—was aghast. His version, promptly relayed to the customers in a tone of fury, was that Sinatra paid a visit to the CIO Political Action Committee—"headquarters of the disguised Communist Party"—where he had a few drinks before returning to the Waldorf to "kick up an hysterical row."

"A house detective used force to subdue Sinatra," said Pegler stoutly. "Had he come to my room, I would have thrown him out!"

Fifteen years later, the columnist was still reworking the incident in print. "Let me tell you that when he (Sinatra) got drunk and boasted that he had gone to my room in the Waldorf to slug me on the night that Roosevelt licked Tom Dewey," he wrote in 1959, "I chased the ratty bum clear up to Canada and made him admit that he hadn't gone anywhere near my quarters. And if he had I would have thrown him down the stairwell. That still goes."

Sinatra ignored him. Back in 1944 he had apparently won what he wanted. While he was still on the prowl, representatives of the two men arranged a meeting, according to the Broadway grapevine, and an agreement was reached. Pegler retained the right to fuss at Sinatra on miscellaneous grounds, but he had to discontinue any suggestions of effeminacy. In return, so the story went, Sinatra promised to end his physical pursuit.

Pegler did not forget Orson Welles. In due time, he found occasion to describe the director as a "dear, roguish boy . . . [whose] whole nature seems to chitter and cheep in the language of the elves," and whose activities could best be judged by adjectives like "cute," "exquisite," "delicious" and "precious."

Orson Welles managed to overlook this slur on his manhood; he was then married to Rita Hayworth.

Under the American system, a social critic may legitimately be allowed the widest latitude in writing, even when his views would be considered in poor taste if uttered publicly, or criminal if translated into action.

Writing is twice-removed from life itself. No bones are broken by calling a man a camel in the French manner, a bloody fool in the British tradition or a son-of-a-bitch in the beloved, somewhat outmoded American style. Delivering an unsmiling insult in person is once-removed from physical consequences, though it can cause a fight if nobody intervenes. Typing the same insult or voicing it for publication is still another step away from action, since it adds time and space and opportunity to reconsider. Threatening to kill is not killing, and putting homicidal threats on paper is only a shadow of a felony.

There must always, to be sure, come a point when the laws against slander and incitation to violence operate. Pegler's contribution to controversy in his time was to keep pushing outward this point of no return. He developed a grotesquerie of affront and an implacability in pursuing grudges which dwarfed the efforts of contentious contemporaries.

To a certain extent, floating hostility and a sly lust for blood always colored his writing. Back in the 1920s, what set him apart from other debunkers of sports was a savagery which seemed more instinctive than contrived. For several years at the height of the anti-Semitic agitation during the late 1930s, he sent out a message of his own composition about the Jews instead of a routine Christmas card. The theme was that those who blame everything on the Jews would discover, the day after all Jews vanished, that they still faced identical problems. The thing was well written and obviously well meant. The bulk of the message, however, consisted of an extremely graphic description of an imaginary massacre at sea "of the last few hundred thousand Jews" which turned the stomachs of some recipients.

As he gained in experience as a controversialist, Pegler became rougher. He promoted Ickes from "house dick of the New Deal" to "the little Joe Goebbels of the New Deal." After years of referring almost tolerantly to Henry A. Wallace, Roosevelt's naïve Vice-President, as "Old Bubblehead," he shifted to "slobbering snerd," which was purely abusive.

6

In the early 1940s, Pegler accused Treasury Secretary Henry Morgenthau of "theft and larceny" for a ruling on the withholding tax. He brushed off David Dubinsky and Sidney Hillman as "dialect unioneers." He characterized Supreme Court Justice James F. Byrnes as dishonest, committed to highway robbery and unfit for the bench because he had held in a decision that the federal anti-racketeering statute did not apply to a case brought against the Teamsters Union. He sideswiped Supreme Court Justice Frank Murphy as "an emotional if not a mental case" for another decision which displeased him.

The columnist found excuses for race riots, assassinations, lynchings and bombings. He urged the police to "club on sight" juvenile delinquents, punks, tinhorns, bums and rats. Ordinary citizens, he maintained, should join with strikebreakers "in the praiseworthy pastime of batting the brains out of pickets." He was hardly ever remote from violence. Even an offbeat column about the rescue of cats from trees might erupt in a sudden demand that the animals be blown to bits. During the 1948 presidential campaign, he denied rumors that he was ghost-writing speeches for Governor Thomas E. Dewey, the Republican candidate. "Dewey cuts them up," he explained, "whereas my method would be to belt them down . . . I would finish them and leave the muggs for dead."

Deliberate unprovoked rudeness can be more shocking than a slap in the face. Again and again Westbrook Pegler proved his mastery over this technique in dealing with women. When Mary Pickford, once a fan of his, made a displeasing comment on radio, he wrote about her as "Mary Pigfoot." When Helen Gahagan Douglas, a former actress, was praised widely for a speech at the 1944 Democratic National Convention, Pegler dissented. The "cheesecake glamor" of Representative Douglas, he declared, had "turned to senescent limburger." He admired Clare Boothe Luce at one time; after they fell out he insinuated that her birthplace was not Riverside Drive in New York, as recorded, but a roadhouse. When Mrs. Luce was serving as the American Ambassador at Rome, the columnist implied that her prolonged seclusion after a supposed case of arsenic poisoning from the murals in the Embassy was merely a cover-up for a face lift.

Late in 1947, Westbrook Pegler decided to demolish Corliss Lamont, a freethinking, presumably unaffiliated radical—which to the columnist meant Communist. Lamont was also a doctor of philosophy, a humanist with several books to his credit and

7

a record of teaching at Columbia, Harvard, Cornell and the New School for Social Research. A series of offensive columns was duly constructed around the theme that his father, Thomas W. Lamont, might be a magic name in 'Wall Street as chairman of J. P. Morgan and Company, but did not carry much weight at home. The financier, said Pegler, was ruled "with a whim of iron" by his wife, "a left-winger living on the right side of the street" who encouraged her boy Corliss (then forty-five) in his political derelictions. The elder Lamont, added the columnist, ought to straighten out his wife "with a punch in the snoot."

What about Corliss himself? Well, recalled Pegler, a Mayor of Galway named Lynch under similar circumstances "once hanged his kid . . ." In February, 1948, while the family lawyers were still debating what to do about Pegler, Thomas Lamont died. Mrs. Lamont, a mildly liberal but retiring woman interested in such organizations as the American Association for the United Nations, the New York Women's Trade Union League and the *Journal of Philosophy*, decided to let the matter drop.

Winthrop Aldrich, president of the Chase National Bank, was the chief financial backer of the 1952 drive to gain the Republican presidential nomination for General Dwight D. Eisenhower. In covering the Republican National Convention in Chicago that year as a partisan of the more conservative Senator Robert A. Taft of Ohio, Pegler focused his anti-Ike ire on Aldrich. In his syndicated copy, he declared that the banker, who was "so old that he could stand on his head until he died," had quarters in the Hilton Hotel "containing more bugs than Paddy's flop in the old days." It required subsequent columns for readers to understand that the bugs were microphones planted secretly by the Taft forces. Aldrich, then sixty-six, was far from senile. Instead of remaining upside down until he died, as suggested, Aldrich went on to serve an active and useful term as Ambassador to the Court of St. James.

Sporadically, the columnist would reach out for some relatively unknown person, promote him to national prominence overnight through a series of critical columns, and then allow him to return to obscurity. Arthur James Deutch, forty, a former government official who annoyed the oil lobby in 1947, and Theodore Brameld, a New York University professor who had the misfortune in 1955 to prepare a report on an academic conference on "anti-intellectualism," were two among many in this category.

These victims were like hunters clawed in the woods by a

8

bear. After a brief exposure to publicity, they dropped out of the newspapers. The public was never told whether they recovered from their wounds or not.

Over the years, some readers of Westbrook Pegler have speculated over the possible relation of his attacks to the deaths of columnist Heywood Broun, labor racketeer Mike Carrozzo and President Roosevelt's wartime Secretary of the Navy, Colonel Frank Knox. Though this notion deepened the aura of deadliness surrounding Pegler, the list was based on the dubious assumption that words could be cast like molten metal into bullets—and shot straight into the heart of an enemy.

2. RIDING THE UMPIRE

A boy who never learns to talk back to his father will want terribly to sass other people when he is older. If he comes from a really authoritarian home he dares not discharge his internal turbulence at any target unsanctioned by his father or by the regents he chooses for his father's authority. By common consent of almost everybody's father, however, the most diffident citizen may snipe at a baseball umpire, a tax collector or a President. Of the three, the most obvious target in the country is offered by the White House.

Though the late H. L. Mencken used to boast that he never wrote a single commendatory word about a sitting President, the boy who became known as Westbrook Pegler could make no such claim. He said kind words on occasion about Franklin D. Roosevelt, Harry S. Truman, Dwight D. Eisenhower and John F. Kennedy, the chief White House tenants during his extended term as a commentator. Nevertheless, he went farther than any other American writer, farther perhaps than *Pravda* or any other foreign publication, in insulting these men in high office.

Westbrook Pegler's earliest political memory involved standing on the bar rail of Frank Hawkins' saloon in Excelsior, Minnesota, soon after the turn of the century when he was not yet nine and listening to his father denounce President Theodore Roosevelt. A half-century later, when he had become the severest critic of a fifth cousin of Theodore named Franklin, Westbrook concluded that the Roosevelts were "a sinister breed" which might yet complete the destruction of the country by foisting a third member of the clan on the White House.

There was nothing tentative about his ultimate rejection of Franklin D. Roosevelt, yet on two occasions Westbrook Pegler gave him whole-hearted support: after Pearl Harbor, which dramatized the President's role as commander-in-chief of the armed forces; and earlier in 1932, when Roosevelt stood for the presidency as a champion of those opposed to prohibition (it was noteworthy that Westbrook's father was a fervid patriot who as long as he lived—and he lived to be almost one-hundred—

would fight to the death over his right to a daily quota of drinks).

Many of the epithets coined by the columnist for monotonously regular use against the President—like "Little Lord Fauntleroy" and "Mama's Boy"—had nothing to do with politics. They were out of tune with Roosevelt's perseverance and bravery in the face of crippling physical disability. The inevitable conclusion was that Pegler was projecting the difficulties of his own childhood. The most moving articles he ever wrote concerned cruelty to children.

The columnist had plenty of help in his repetitious campaign against the Roosevelts. Leaders of the Liberty League and journalistic isolationists like Colonel Robert R. McCormick and William Randolph Hearst were always willing to provide ammunition. Fairly early in the New Deal, Colonel McCormick dismissed F.D.R.'s whole ancestry as "un-American." The Chicago publisher asserted that "great-grandfather James was a Tory," and that "a Southern connection, James Bulloch, would have destroyed the Union." Years later, Westbrook Pegler went baying along this stale trail to such good effect that he had to apologize in print for saying that Rufus Bulloch, "the scalawag Governor of Georgia," was "the great-grandfather of the Empress Eleanor." The wrong Bulloch was being gored.

Nothing about the Roosevelts was too trivial to escape the notice of the great controversialist. Did Eleanor Roosevelt knock over the front gate of her estate when she was learning to drive as a girl? Did "Mama's Boy" row on the varsity or class crew at Harvard? What was the color of the band on *McCall's* magazine when it accepted a column of monthly comment by Mrs. Roosevelt? Sure enough, it was *red!*

After President Roosevelt's death, Westbrook Pegler relaxed only briefly before returning to the attack. He called F.D.R. "the feeble-minded fuehrer," "Moosejaw" and, occasionally, "the Spook." Mrs. Roosevelt became "the Gab," "La Boca Grande," and "the Widow." On one occasion, she was asked why she did not allow her sons to horsewhip Pegler. "He is such a little gnat on the horizon, he cannot touch my husband's memory," she replied.

Naturally, her exhibition of indifference drove the columnist to new furies. On the formal side, he did a takeoff of Mrs. Roosevelt's column, "My Day," which ranked as one of the three best literary spoofs of his career, the others being parodies of the columns of Arthur Brisbane and O. O. McIntyre. On the informal side, he distributed among his friends two hundred copies of a

11

privately printed book of poems about somebody called "Lady I." [*] W. C. Fields, the humorist, was so delighted by the gibes at Mrs. Roosevelt that he promised to leave one million dollars in his will to Pegler (so the columnist reported), but he forgot his promise. In the course of a radio interview, Mrs. Roosevelt remarked that she and Franklin "had a lot of queer friends" during their early married life. By queer, she meant unconventional or eccentric. Pegler, however, emphasized the remark in the context of a jeering analysis of Roosevelt's efforts as Assistant Secretary of the Navy during World War I to cope with homosexuality among American sailors.

"It is not cynicism to wonder whether the Empress Eleanor was being naïve or imposing on the naïveté of the public when she said on the air that she always had lots of queer friends. She certainly is a woman of the world and, some of her associates considered, can hardly expect to be regarded as an ignoramus in such matters. Queer was right!"

Toward the end of his life, the columnist carried his hatred for F.D.R. everywhere he went. After viewing the statue of the late President in Grosvenor Square in London, he suggested to readers that if they were touring Europe it "might be a good idea" to get drunk and desecrate the statue. During a visit to Moscow in 1959 with Vice-President Nixon's party, Pegler picked up a three-volume biography of Roosevelt at the American Fair. He was reminded of the unsuccessful effort of a lunatic to kill President-elect Roosevelt in Miami on February 15, 1933, in the course of which Mayor Anton Cermak of Chicago was fatally shot. The "devil's advocate" in him was aroused, the columnist confessed, and he mused over "what sort of a world we might have had now had Joseph Zangara been a better shot that day in Bayfront Park, Miami, when Tony Cermak was called to his reward."

Shortly after 2:00 P.M. on November 1, 1950, Griselo Torresola and Oscar Collazo, two Puerto Rican nationalists, strolled toward Blair House with the intention of killing President Truman. Blair House is just across Pennsylvania Avenue from the White House. The Trumans had moved in there temporarily because the weight of Margaret Truman's grand piano, used daily for vocal exercises, had cracked a cellar beam and required ex-

[*] *Lady I*, printed in 1942 in New York at the Sign of St. Christopher, is available for inspection in the rare book room of the New York Public Library.

tensive repairs and alterations to the historic home of Presidents.

When Special Officer Leslie Coffelt stepped out of a sentry box at the entrance to Blair House, the assassins drew their revolvers and shot him dead. Another guard ran up and fell to the pavement with bullet-shattered knees, but he continued to fire, back from the ground. A third guard opened fire from behind a parked car.

Awakened from an early afternoon nap by the clatter of small-arms fire, President Truman hurried to a second-story front window and peered down as Collazo collapsed under a rain of bullets near the door. Torresola was already dead. The national reaction to the attempt on the President's life was one of horror mingled with relief, though John O'Donnell, Washington Bureau chief of the New York *Daily News*, grumbled in his column that three Republican Presidents—Lincoln, Garfield, and McKinley—had been killed, whereas two Democrats, Roosevelt and Truman, escaped without a scratch. Commenting on O'Donnell's attitude, *The New Yorker* wrote that it did not seem possible "for any American except Westbrook Pegler" to go further than that.

Pegler did go further. The curious thing is that out of some boyhood memory he had originally been a strong Truman supporter. In 1947, the columnist spoke warmly of the President as a real man, one who could "get tough without nastiness." He indicated that he was reminded of his father who was, as he wrote frequently, "a hell of a fighter."

For a while, Pegler had the run of the White House. Johnny Maragon, his old friend from the baseball training camps down South, was making himself useful to Major General Harry Vaughan, the President's military aide. In the absence of the Trumans, the columnist came around several times to see Maragon, who had graduated from tipster to fixer. Though Johnny went to jail eventually for lying about his relationship with a company which sent gifts of black-market perfume to the wives of cabinet members, Pegler obtained a number of lively columns from the association.

A discovery that Truman fully shared F.D.R.'s attitude on trade unions and other matters led Westbrook Pegler to reconsider his earlier enthusiasm. The President, he decided, was a familiar type out West ". . . thin-lipped, a hater, a bad man in any fight. Malicious and unforgiving and not above offering you his hand to yank you off balance and work you over with a chair leg, pool cue or something out of his pocket."

13

The assassination column was distributed by King Features for use November 7, but it was withdrawn on the eve of publication. Excerpts leaked to the public on November 14 through a story in the New York *Post*. Subsequently the column became an historic document through insertion in the Congressional Record.

Pegler had disparaged "all this emotion over an absurdly non-dangerous and futile attack on the life of a man who happens to be President. If it takes this much to remind us that no President is a holy person, the cost is great but the result is worth it . . . I wasn't shocked, I wasn't horrified, and I believed that most of those who wrote and said that they were, were liars." He deplored the "stupid attack on the policemen guarding the house where President Truman lives," Pegler continued, but "nowhere near as much" as he condemned attacks "by union goons of Truman adherents" on the wives of non-strikers in Butte, Montana.

While in favor, the columnist said, of shooting Joseph Stalin, he gave a reprieve to the President. "As to Harry S. Truman, at the present stage of the game, I am willing to settle for the impudence, the scare and the reminder of the scene at the Blair House."

Pegler usually had a point, a kernel of indignation in his mind around which phrases gathered like ants around a dead bee. In this case, he was focusing on a relatively obscure strike or lockout dating back four years. There had been ten days of tumult in April, 1946, in the Anaconda Company town of Butte, Montana. According to Robert S. Allen's book on municipal corruption, *Our Fair City*, the copper company asked for a display of force against the strikers on the ground that there had been threats and efforts to frighten the families of strikebreakers. Refusing to be stampeded, the local sheriff swore in one hundred union men as deputies. Though the union was not under Communist control, the company raised the cry of "Red" and secured an exclusive essay from Westbrook Pegler for the company-owned newspaper in Butte, the Montana *Standard*.

Pegler complained that the sheriff had evacuated the families of the strikebreakers instead of "tearing into the mob with guns and shooting them dead." Blaming all of Butte's complicated difficulties on Franklin D. Doosevelt, price-rationing and mass-picketing, he wound up: "The thing to do is blow their heads off." After the company ran this for the edification of its local readers, Pegler promised another special column, but he never got around to writing it. Not until the shooting at Blair House did his "point"

14

rear up in his mind, full-clothed in rhetoric and ready for syndication. Over a four-year period, however, there had been a shift in emphasis. Pegler now put the blame on President Truman instead of on the late President Roosevelt.

Overlooked at first among the various insulting remarks about Truman in the assassination column was an assertion that Margaret Truman was more of a screecher than a singer in any professional sense. This fact was not entirely unsuspected in musical circles. Margaret had a fair drawing room voice, but ever since her 1947 debut in Detroit critics had been expressing politely veiled doubts about its concert quality.

"When the President's daughter goes up and down the land squawking and blatting to the consternation of local critics who can't believe their ears," Pegler wrote, "the local Democratic organizations turn out high quorums with a blackjack for a gavel and the Secret Service pokes the taxpayers out of the hotel elevators and snoops upon them in the halls, all at their expense in dough and dignity, as though they would be found dead, unavoidably, in her presence."

Miss Truman's purpose seems to have been to establish her personality beyond the shadow of the White House. She was a charming girl, a particular favorite among newspapermen, from whose ranks she eventually chose a husband. Since she was smart enough to realize her vocal defects and to labor over them, her performances improved to some extent and it could be argued that those who paid to hear her sing were rewarded in other coin than the strictly musical. Unfortunately, the bootlegged column was reprinted in the *Congressional Record* on the eve of her most important concert to date. Official Washington, of course, reads the *Congressional Record* the way show people read *Variety*.

A capacity audience in Washington's Constitution Hall, including the President of the United States and his guest, Prime Minister Clement Attlee of Great Britain, seemed to enjoy Margaret's singing that night. Now that Pegler had broken the ice, however, the reviews could not be favorable. When Harry Truman read Paul Hume's piece in the Washington *Post* next morning at breakfast, he reacted not like a president but like a father defending his daughter's honor. Several erroneous versions appeared in newspapers but the correct version of the letter which he dashed off without consulting his secretariat, according to Paul Hume, who received it, appeared in *Time* magazine. It went as follows:

"Mr. Hume: I have just read your lousy review of Margaret's concert. I've come to the conclusion that you are an eight-ulcer man on four-ulcer pay. It seems to me that you are a frustrated old man who wishes he could have been successful. When you write such poppycock as was in the back section of the paper you work for, it shows conclusively that you're off the beam and at least four of your ulcers are at work. Some day I hope to meet you. When that happens you'll need a new nose, a lot of beefsteak for black eyes and perhaps a supporter below. Pegler, a gutter-snipe, is a gentleman alongside you. I hope you'll accept that statement as a worse insult than a reflection on your ancestry."

Harry S. Truman may go down in history as one of the most effective presidents, but this was not his most felicitous moment. His abusive letter was bound to leak out. It placed him in the position he least desired, that of helping to undercut his daughter's career. Only the restraint and good manners of Hume and Margaret saved the situation at all. Hume said for publication that a man bearing the burden of world crisis, including war in Korea, ought to be indulged in an occasional outburst of temper. Margaret, who had continued on tour to another city, remarked coolly that Hume was a fine critic who had every right to his opinion.,

Reached in New York City, Westbrook Pegler read a prepared statement to reporters. "It is a great tragedy in this awful hour," he intoned, "that the people of the U.S. must accept in lieu of leadership the nasty malice of a President whom Bernard Baruch, in a similar statement, called a rude, uncouth, ignorant man."

Instead of retiring to the kitchen with a broken heart, Margaret Truman accepted her new status as a minor national joke. She began making appearances on TV, where she could dilute her singing with bits of comedy and straight acting. The public liked her and the time came when she could concede casually during an appearance on a national network that her income exceeded that of the presidential piano-player who was her father. This was not surprising, she said. "Naturally an artist receives more than her accompanist."

The public was never told, but the night tables in the convention hotels were piled high with mysteriously deposited tracts referring to General Dwight D. Eisenhower as "a Swedish Kike" serving an international Communist conspiracy. That was 1948, when both the Republicans and the Democrats gathered in

Philadelphia. It was the same at each national convention. The leaflets were unsigned, but similar ones distributed · elsewhere bore the name of Gerald L.K. Smith's Patriotic Tract Society. Almost everybody knew that the General came of non-Jewish German-Swiss folk on both sides. After tracing the "Swedish Kike" phrase to a joke about Cadet Eisenhower in the 1915 Howitzer Yearbook of West Point, reporters covering the conventions, by mutual agreement which was not conspiratorial, ignored the matter.

Neither party nominated Eisenhower in 1948, but his name and personality remained in presidential speculation. Having no public outlet, the racist campaign against him flourished underground. It was particularly venomous in the little hate sheets, some of which had led a furtive existence since prewar isolationist days. Sooner or later most of these sheets found their way out to columnist Westbrook Pegler's home on the Arizona desert. He did not ask for them. They came free and without solicitation from racists who shared his antipathies and who sought his attention.

As the time approached for the nomination of presidential candidates in 1952, the Reverend Gerald B. Winrod, a professional bigot second only to Gerald L.K. Smith, produced a fresh version of an anti-New Deal pamphlet of the 1930s which had been called "Dru Deal." Both the original "Dru Deal" and Winrod's popularization of it asserted that a 1912 novel called *Philip Dru: Administrator* provided a conspiratorial program for world revolution.

Philip Dru: Administrator was a sleazy novel written by Colonel Edward M. House, a confidential advisor of President Wilson. Winrod described House as the representative of an international group of Jewish bankers who were secret Communists. This brought in the so-called "invisible government" fantasy, an American extension of the forged, discredited but never completely forgotten old *Protocols of the Learned Elders of Zion,* which had been devised by Czarists as an excuse for pogroms in the first decade of the 20th century and later incorporated by Hitler in *Mein Kampf.*

American rabblerousers on the far right loved that "invisible government" phrase. They did not need to explain it; their readers knew it meant Communist Jews.

During the 1940s, the inflammatory tag-line began to creep into public usage. Pegler made several references in his column to "the invisible government of the Harvard Law pro-Communist

17

anti-American cult." On May 29, 1950, Walter Trohan, the Washington correspondent of the *Chicago Tribune,* quoted an unidentified person "with the highest State Department connections" as identifying Supreme Court Justice Felix Frankfurter, former Secretary of the Treasury Henry Morgenthau, Jr., and Senator Herbert H. Lehman of New York as "the secret government of the U.S."

Every mass movement, Eric Hoffer once wrote, needs an explanation of the past "dynamic enough to move its following to fury." Hoffer added: "The explanation may be fuzzy at the edges; indeed, a little room for individualistic embroidery . . . never hurt any totalitarian doctrine. However, the explanation must be simple, easily if not completely understood and it must provide a scapegoat, a foreign devil or a domestic one with a foreign flavor."

This was precisely what Winrod was trying to provide with his 1952 exhumation of Philip Dru, who never existed. "Wilson failed them (the international Jewish bankers)" wrote Winrod. "Franklin Roosevelt served them to the end of his days. Harry Truman remains their pawn. Dwight Eisenhower is their choice in this, the catastrophic year of 1952! Their methods are different today than in the past but the objective remains the same— namely, the complete domination of mankind!"

The campaign by Winrod and other racists against Eisenhower in Chicago, the 1952 convention city, became too grimy to be ignored. Commentators from coast to coast carried exposés of the surreptitious pamphleteers.

Frank Conniff, a bellwether among Hearst columnists, declared that anti-Semitism was being employed brazenly at Chicago "in an effort to stymie Eisenhower's nomination." Senator Taft, the General's rival for the nomination, held a press conference to scoff specifically at Winrod's fairy tale and at "smearing tactics" generally. On July 6, 1952, the GOP adopted a civil rights plank starting: "We condemn bigots. . . ." When the Democrats took a similar stand, it looked as if the Dru fantasy had been laid to rest.

Westbrook Pegler tried to be tolerant toward President Eisenhower until he found that the President, with the full consent of a knowledgeable segment of the country's capitalists, was willing to accept domestic reforms of the New Deal and go on from there. As he got angrier, some of his comments were suppressed by King Features. Early in July, 1954, the columnist

18

charged flatly that his bosses "had been more interested in having a friend in the White House" than in permitting the truth to be told. Several days later, he brought up Philip Dru for the first time. In one of dozens of high-pitched columns on the same subject, he wrote on August 28, 1954: "During all these years since 1911 and 1912, by the secret evil design of one man, the government of this great republic has been corrupted and transformed. Both Hitler and Mussolini became the 'instruments' of a brutal scheme hatched by Colonel Edward Mandell House of Texas. In the U.S., Woodrow Wilson, Franklin D. Roosevelt and Harry S. Truman furthered the plot. . . ."

Pegler gave no credit to Winrod or the earlier "Dru Deal" pamphlet. He presented his political nightmare as a bit of original political research. However, Upton Close, one of the lesser fringe agitators, was malicious enough to point out in his personal magazine, *Closeups*, that the House book had been previously brought to Pegler's attention.

The odd thing was that Colonel House never played as big a political role—even in the Wilson administration—as he imagined. By the time the New Deal arrived, he exercised so little influence of any kind that Edgar Eugene Robinson, in *The Roosevelt Leadership 1935-1945* saw no need to mention him. Edward Mandell House—who was not Jewish, despite a middle name conferred on him by his father out of respect for a local shopkeeper—does not appear anywhere in the published reminiscences of James A. Farley, F.D.R.'s chief political mechanic during most of the New Deal. During his first term, Roosevelt did talk vaguely for a while about finding "some sort of a job for old Colonel Mouse"—as he called the old wire-puller—but nothing suitable was ever found.

George E. Sokolsky, King Features columnist who began to move ahead of Pegler in syndicate sales during the 1950s, and who was one of the few newspaper people respected by Pegler, wrote in 1958 that Colonel House "never replaced President Wilson in matters of judgment." For his colleague's benefit, Sokolsky added that House served Wilson as "a legman. He had to compete with more able men such as Herbert Hoover, Bernard Baruch, Robert Lansing, Newton Baker, etc. In the end, Wilson dropped House."

After seven years of peddling this theory which the Anti Defamation League of B'nai B'rith has compared to the earlier Protocols of Zion, Pegler disposed of it nonchalantly one day during a discussion of other matters. "E. M. House, the soap-wrapper colonel from Texas," he wrote on March 22, 1961, "undoubtedly did hypnotize Woodrow Wilson, but he overplayed his hand and anyway he was just a cheap adventurer who flagrantly double-crossed and mocked Wilson among the English aristocracy and wound up as nothing."

"True, Frank Roosevelt did pay him homage in a pilgrimage to his home at Magnolia, Massachusetts, after Roosevelt's first nomination, but the little that we have credibly learned about that meeting amounts to no substantial historical importance."

Joseph P. Kennedy, a politically minded financier and philanthropist, stepped up to Westbrook Pegler on Park Avenue in New York one day in 1945 and introduced himself. He had recognized Pegler from the rather saturnine sketch used with the column, while the columnist recognized Kennedy from pictures circulating during his term as Ambassador to the Court of St. James.

After an exchange of pleasantries, Pegler mentioned a problem. A woman in Pawtucket, Rhode Island, had written to him about her granddaughter, a housebound cardiac patient who was losing ground in her education because her only teaching came during an occasional hour with a nun from a nearby convent. What could be done? Joe Kennedy's idea was that the physical condition of the child might be improved. That very day he phoned Dr. Frank Lahey of the Lahey Clinic in Boston, who sent an ambulance down to Pawtucket for the girl. Thereafter the columnist and the financier became friendly.

In 1952, Pegler mentioned another problem. His protégé, Senator Joe McCarthy, was sick and embarrassed by lack of funds for his reelection campaign in Wisconsin. Joseph P. Kennedy promptly asked the columnist to transmit a three thousand dollar campaign contribution. Pegler did not wish to appear as intermediary, so the money was conveyed to McCarthy through a mutual friend of Kennedy and Pegler.

Not long afterward, Joseph P. Kennedy asked Pegler to persuade Joe McCarthy to stay out of Massachusetts where John F. Kennedy, the former Ambassador's son, was making his first race for the Senate. With General Eisenhower as a popular and high-level presidential candidate, the Republican party believed that Henry Cabot Lodge, its Senatorial candidate in Massachusetts, could be put across by a couple of demagogic McCarthy appeals

20

in South Boston. Westbrook Pegler had no particular use for Lodge; so he told Joseph P. Kennedy he would do what he could.

In several columns appearing about this time, Pegler predicted that Joe McCarthy, the hottest and most influential GOP orator in the country, would not come to the aid of his fellow Republican in the Bay State. As McCarthy's semi-official spokesman, he noted that Lodge was less sympathetic to the Wisconsin Senator than John Kennedy, a Democrat. He gently wrapped McCarthy's mantle around Kennedy.

"Kennedy wouldn't put on a gas-mask or a clothespin if Joe McCarthy should offer to go up there and strike a few blows in his name," he wrote. "Kennedy is anti-Red, though a Democrat . . . and he will agree with anyone who argues, as Joe McCarthy does, that you can't tangle with a skunk and come out smelling like a barbershop. Kennedy would be glad to embrace McCarthy on a platform in South Boston and the only consideration that prevents that is Joe's party loyalty, not any hypocrisy on Jack's part. . . ."

Privately, Pegler urged McCarthy to forget about Massachusetts and go out to Indiana to help "a real Republican, Senator William Jenner." McCarthy followed this advice. John Kennedy survived politically that year and went on, eventually, to greater things.

For a columnist so sensitive to the ethical shortcomings of others, all this maneuvering was highly dubious. Moreover, it involved a basic miscalculation. Since he dealt entirely with Joseph P. Kennedy, who made no bones about having become anti-Roosevelt and anti-New Deal, the columnist appraised the son in the father's image. It was a great shock to discover that John F. Kennedy had a political philosophy of his own.

By the time Senator Kennedy ran for President, he was being hotly pursued by the columnist. Among other things, Pegler wrote that Jack Kennedy, as he called Joe Kennedy's son, was Walter Reuther's "stooge" and Eleanor Roosevelt's "captive." Kennedy once "studied Communist international finance under the prophet, Harold Laski, in London" and once "posed unashamed" for a photograph with James Roosevelt. According to Brooklyn *Tablet* standards on issues like medicare for the aged, his religious principles were "non-Catholic if not, indeed, anti-Catholic" and according to Barry Goldwater, he had "neither principles nor guts." (Senator Goldwater denied making the statement, but Pegler said he had the notes to prove it.)

Obviously the real bone in the columnist's throat was the fact that Kennedy had made clear his distaste for McCarthyism well in advance of the 1960 election. Coming several years after McCarthy's death from a man who Pegler believed owed his first Senatorial election to McCarthy, this repudiation, Pegler wrote, was "the most sordid act of the kind in all experience."

Immediately after the election, Pegler wrote that the popular vote showed every second voter in the country opposed to "Kennedy"—no longer Jack!—"many of them to the degree of absolute hatred for the heartless personal nature which he revealed in his betrayal of Senator Joe McCarthy. . . ."

In view of Kennedy's friendliness with Frank Sinatra and his "rat pack," the columnist continued, there was "a plain social commitment between the presidential family circle and an element which ramifies into the underworlds of Las Vegas, Los Angeles, New York and Florida." He expressed fear lest the White House be "given over to bongo, expresso and weird characters wearing Castrovian beards."

Considering the fact that J.F.K. had not yet been inaugurated, that was a running head-start for a record-breaking campaign of abuse against the Kennedy administration. For some reason, the campaign did not develop. During the next two years, relatively few scurrilities about the First Family appeared in the column. Those that did appear were of a sort which might have eluded a not-too-alert censor. The columnist, for example, used George Spelvin to snicker that the purpose back of all that touch football in the Kennedy circle was to make passes at each other's wives.

On another occasion, long after he had seemingly abandoned his Dru Deal of presidential conspiracy, he slid the following lines into print during a discussion of the Versailles peace treaty: "Colonel House had a son-in-law named Gordon Auchincloss, who was working for him in the Crillon. I have been meaning to run him down and report whether he was a relation of the Auchinclosses who are Jacqueline Kennedy's step-kin. But that must wait . . ."

Wait for what? The Hearst papers had changed since William Randolph Hearst's death in 1951. As supporters of the Kennedy administration, they were censoring unfriendly references to the President or to any member of his family.

Pegler liked to say that there were many strong and diverse personalities in his own family but never a trace of scandal. He

22

was disproportionately gleeful when he discovered scandal on the family tree of an enemy. He found that the President's grandfather, John F. (Honey Fitz) Fitzgerald, a Boston mayor around the time of the First World War, was once removed as a Congressman by an investigating committee because his supporters stuffed ballot boxes in several Boston precincts, yet he could not manage to slide this delectable tidbit into print. When the blowup with his King Features syndicate finally came in the late summer of 1962, the columnist promptly cited censorship of the Honey Fitz incident as primary and sure proof that he had been unfairly treated by the Hearst management.

3. EXCELSIOR

Arthur James Pegler, father of the True Crusader, dated back to the romantic pre-social security days of journalism. By-lined reporters were then greatly admired and poorly paid. One of these front-page heroes, David Graham Phillips, who also wrote feminist fiction, asserted proudly that he would "rather be a reporter than President." Though Pegler performed prodigies of valor, he scorned the cheerful daredevils of the camel-corps phase of foreign correspondence. He belonged among the domestic misanthropes in the business, men like Victor Watson, most ruthless of Hearst exposé artists; Colonel John Cockerill of the St. Louis *Post-Dispatch*, who "seemed to dwell in a perpetual fury"; and Charles E. Chapin, the granitic tyrant of the New York *Evening World* city desk who wound up in Sing Sing for killing his wife.

Arthur Pegler's contempt for his fellows developed out of early struggles as a boomer. The boomers were a hard-working, hard-drinking tribe of nomads. Like the beatniks of the middle years of the twentieth century, they may have represented an unconscious reaction to laissez-faire business operation. Telegraphers, printers, and reporters alike, they drifted from employer to employer and from town to town as resentment, whim or the iron bite of necessity dictated.

Many boomers wore out and died early, but Arthur Pegler settled down and lived to be ninety-nine. Since his journalistic renown had faded during a quarter of a century of retirement, the wire service obituaries were brief when he died in Arizona on March 7, 1961. Except for the fact that he was the father of Westbrook Pegler, his death might have gone unnoticed.

If biographical details about Arthur James Pegler were often in conflict, it was due to his habit of revising his adventures to suit himself and his momentary audience. Some things were definitely known: he was born in 1862 in Staines, England; he received "too little education to mention," and he left home at a tender age. For the benefit of a *Time* interviewer in the 1930s, he said he worked for the London *Daily Telegraph* before he was twenty, emigrated to the United States in 1884 and rode the range in Iowa and the Dakotas for three years before returning to journalism with the Sioux City, Iowa *Times*. According to a later account approved for the *Saturday Evening Post*, he was running copy for Fleet Street reporters when his father, to prevent him from becoming a newspaperman, sent him to the United States to learn the cattle business. In this more light-hearted version, Arthur said he abandoned ranching because he could not learn to stay on a horse. He tried farming too, but he gave that up because clod-hopping hurt his feet.

Arthur James Pegler spent the last few years of his life at Rancho Toda La Vista, a Tucson sanitarium. In 1956, when he was deaf, almost blind and very feeble, he indulged in some relatively inglorious reminiscences. He revealed, among other things, that his work experience in England had been confined to two years as a potboy in Stone's, an alehouse on Panton Street near Leicester Square, London. To his visitor, who was his son Westbrook, he described how at the age of seventeen he bought a ticket on the Epsom Derby. Out of the eighty pounds which he won he purchased a farewell gift for his mother and transatlantic passage for himself on the four-masted sailing ship *Assyrian Monarch*.

From New York he proceeded by rail to Le Mars, Iowa to join a colony of three hundred English lads who were "studying farming" under Captain Ronald Moreton, a former British naval chaplain. There he was known as "Chicken" because of his jerky walk and scrawny neck. It required two years of peonage, during which he received only twenty dollars in cash at the end of each harvest season, for Chicken to muster up courage to quit.

There was a gap in authentic reminiscence at this point. Arthur James Pegler apparently held various casual jobs, including one at eight dollars a week as a laborer on the slag-heap of a Jones and Laughlin steel plant. To judge from his subsequent sentimentality about hoboes, who shared with boomers a preference for free rail travel, he might have been a knight of the road for a while. Certainly it was during this period of exploitation and poverty that he developed his fierce hatred of the rich.

How Arthur Pegler got into newspaper work in the United States is unclear. His first major story was a murder trial in Sioux City, which he covered for a local newspaper. Because of its sensational aspect—a brewer had shot a Methodist minister who was leading a Sioux City campaign for prohibition—the case attracted big-city correspondents from as far away as Omaha and

Chicago. Always a strong defender of man's right to tipple, Arthur Pegler could not conceal his exultation when the brewer was acquitted on grounds of economic self-defense.

The expendable nature of boomers was illustrated by an experience of Arthur Pegler's in 1892. He wrote a series of articles for a St. Paul, Minnesota, newspaper exposing the Rice Street gang of thieves. Soon thereafter he was waylaid by gang members, who smashed his right cheekbone with a rock and tossed him off a steep bank into a river.

He came to in a hospital. Newspapers then did not generally meet expenses for disability in line of duty or keep an ailing reporter on the payroll, so Arthur hurried back to work. He dismissed his necessary heroism as "the rub of the green," but he could no more forget the niggardliness of his boss than he could erase the scar from his cheek. Though ordinarily he relished executions, he declined the invitation passed on to him by the city desk to witness the hanging of two members of the Rice Street gang. When he got on his feet financially, he shifted to another St. Paul newspaper.

Out of his hardships, Arthur James Pegler developed a harsh and domineering presence. "He was tall and gaunt and hard-faced," according to a description of him during this period taken from Robert J. Casey's *Such Interesting People*. Casey continued: "He was short of temper to everybody outside the newspaper business and so assured of himself that no secretary then alive was to take the responsibility for keeping him out of august presences. He had a trace of an English accent and a voice like a dull file."

It was Robert Casey, incidentally, who made the famous remark—later pirated by Walter Winchell and others—that the most interesting persons encountered by newspapermen were usually other newspapermen. Casey was thinking of Arthur Pegler at the time. However, Pegler won no popularity prizes among his colleagues in general. He was often surly and unpleasant in the office and he developed an uncomfortable habit of barroom brawling. He and an associate, according to one typical story, dropped into a Washington Avenue saloon one snowy winter afternoon to warm their hands. After a few drinks, Pegler launched into loud denunciation of a local alderman until an abrupt and ringing challenge came from an adjoining bar stool.

The reporter gulped at the size of his rough-looking opponent but he obediently peeled off his overcoat. To his surprise, the other man dropped his hands. "It's a dude!" he said, pointing to Pegler's vest and spats. "I wouldn't wanna hurt a dude." Pegler really tried to unleash war then, but he was hustled to safety. The tough bystander, he learned later, was an off-duty cop.

Arthur Pegler covered strikes and lockouts, lynchings, underworld murders, political assassinations and casual homicides. Once he traveled all the way to Victoria, British Columbia, on the trail of a woman named Belle Guinness, who had fled from her "murder farm" in Indiana after slicing off the heads of nine Swedish swains. He had followed the wrong woman; the fugitive he tracked down turned out to be Belle's mother's sister-in-law. Even so, she provided some information about Belle's earlier eccentricities which he could use. Another time Arthur Pegler went to report a riot in Rock Island, Illinois. The trouble subsided before he got there, so he set off a brace of giant firecrackers under the Mayor's window at midnight to justify a quick dispatch about a mysterious attempt at intimidation by bombing. When authentic news became scarce, he was always willing to liven up the scene with a little judicious fakery.

Some reporters blamed Pegler for pretending to be an Englishman. That he actually came from England did not occur to them. They were right in sensing something spurious, but his real masquerade was more far-reaching and subtle—he believed that discerning observers recognized him as "an Oxford man." There was no evidence that he ever saw the town of Oxford.

Nevertheless, his hard black derby, yellow gloves, fancy vest, and stick were his conception of what an Oxford man wore and he encouraged the notion that he was a university graduate by using an oddly inflated vocabulary. Thus he invited friends to have a "libation" instead of a drink. If they failed to buy in their turn they were "parsimonious" rather than stingy. He once called his city editor an "ineffable screw." Except for his pugnacious stance and his creative fluency with a supplementary language of obscenity and abuse, he would have been laughed out of the business.

Arthur Pegler's chief contribution to journalism, on the authority of Ben Hecht and others, was the invention of "the Hearst style." This combination of blood-and-thunder rhetoric, trick idiom and colorful phrases was best illustrated by the famous line about "fifteen foul fiends dancing on the grave of this fair white girl tonight." Like the consciously heightened tone of voice used in later years by radio commentators, the Hearst style reached out for attention. Back around the turn of the century it sold newspapers to semi-illiterates and immigrants fumbling for understanding in a strange tongue. It may have provided some low-brow readers with a temporary substitute for beauty and culture, but with the passage of time, this particular kind of over-writing became sheer atrocity.

Eventually Arthur Pegler felt obliged to repudiate his stylistic child. In a magazine article on yellow journalism during World War I, he likened a Hearst newspaper to a "screaming woman running down the street with her throat cut." The metaphor was faulty by Hearst standards, since it failed to specify whether the woman was disheveled, partially disrobed or naked.

At any rate he was promptly fired by the Hearst paper in Chicago for which he was then working.

Besides the Hearst style, Arthur Pegler left another artistic monument, a tear-jerking melodrama about white slavery entitled *Little Lost Sister*. Under urging from Charles Washburn, an experienced playwright, he dashed off three acts on three successive evenings in 1913, based on his own exposé of urban prostitution. This put him in the select company of Laura Jean Libbey and Harry Clay Blaney as a writer of the Ten-Twenty-Thirties, as old-fashioned melodramas were then called. For twenty years, *Little Lost Sister* ran in stock, on showboats and in repertory shows in the Cumberland Mountains, where it was second in popularity only to *The Trail of the Lonesome Pine*. It was revived as late as 1940.

Arthur Pegler had no claim on the earnings of his play, since he had waived royalties in favor of three hundred dollars in cash to pay for an immediate operation on his wife. Though he gave up booming, he never acquired much moss. During his fifty-four years in journalism, he was often unemployed and chronically in debt. His salary never exceeded one hundred dollars a week.

Francis W. Pegler was born August 2, 1894, in Minneapolis. His family could be described as middle-class respectable. His mother went regularly to church and his father, as temporary head of the Minneapolis *Journal* sports department at twenty dollars a week, could inscribe "editor" in the space reserved for father's occupation on the birth record.

Actually, no class label applied closely to the Peglers. They were a restless family, rarely resident long enough in one spot to put down identifiable roots. Their 1894 address, 2838 Eighth

Avenue South, was in a good neighborhood, though slightly less desirable than the one at 2717 Grand Avenue South, where an older boy, John A. Pegler, was born February 6, 1893. Their earlier neighborhood was one of the few in Minneapolis boasting both street pavements and brick sidewalks while retaining the old-fashioned charm of large shady elms and huge front lawns.

Westbrook Pegler does not seem ever to have mentioned publicly or written that he started life as Francis. No trace of that now-vanished Christian name can be found in the columnist's uncollected works or in the philippics and panegyrics about him. Neither he nor any relative has explained why the name Francis was dropped. The nearest Westbrook himself came to an explanation was to tell some neighbors many years later as a joke on himself that he had trouble covering Gertrude Ederle's swim across the English Channel in 1926 because the State Department expected him to be a girl.

The birth certificate still on file in Minneapolis helps to explain the mistake. Dr. A. J. Murdock, the obstetrician, was a careless penman. In filling out the certificate he scrawled Frances Pegler, the mother, and Francis Pegler, the son, exactly alike. Since the mother could not be a man, the State Department reasoned in its old-fashioned way that the child must be a girl. Eventually the State Department corrected its record and by inference acknowledged its mistake.

The decision to eliminate Francis was undoubtedly made by Arthur Pegler. One of his beliefs was that boys must be manly little men. Originally he had humored Frances Pegler's desire for a daughter or a boy named after herself but he soon ruled out Francis as a name because of possible imputations of effeminacy. Since he had already bestowed his first name as a second name for his first son, his middle name of James became the inevitable formal substitute for Francis. Arthur Pegler made no secret of his impatience with another inspiration of his wife—that lace-curtain name of Westbrook—but he concluded that canceling this would cause too much fuss. He compromised by calling Westbrook "Bud."

At the age of five, Westbrook was exposed to what modern pyschologists call a traumatic experience. He got lost during a Sunday afternoon walk with his father in Minneapolis. Arthur encountered an acquaintance with whom he wished to consider some of the leading issues of the day. For greater convenience, they adjourned to a nearby saloon.

Left to his own devices, the boy strayed off. Eventually his tear-streaked countenance attracted the attention of a policeman. After the customary candy-and-ice cream-cheer-up at the police station where he had by this time been reported missing, Westbrook was driven home in a squad car. Arthur whooped with delight when he saw his son ride up in grandeur. "Bud always did hanker for a trip in the paddywagon!" he declared. "Imagine scaring us all to death for a free ride!" Abruptly and unreasonably, Westbrook found himself a hero. He did not object, though he remained shaken. Only considerably later, when he told the story privately to his mother, was he allowed the luxury of more tears. The family always held that Bud got lost on purpose.

A couple of years after the episode of the paddywagon, Westbrook was brought to the newspaper office in the late afternoon to escort his father home. Glancing idly out of the wide second-story front window of the city room, he saw a horse take fright, bolt through the snow with a sleighload of milk, and finally capsize the sleigh. *Here was life in the raw!* Westbrook shouted frantically across the cityroom to his father, who grabbed hat and coat and tore downstairs. Breathless at the window, as in a box at a play, the child watched his father surge through slush and milk to get the vital details. Spelling out the story later under his father's by-line, he seemed already in anticipation to be a newspaperman.

Arthur James Pegler had a brass press badge with red enamel letters which was kept in the drawer of the heavy mission table in the living room. As a special favor, Westbrook and Jack were allowed to take turns pinning his badge on their shirts and admiring themselves in the mirror. Since they often heard how he rushed through fire lines to rescue old ladies and babies from the flames before moving nonchalantly to phone the facts to his newspaper, the badge entitled them to perform similar feats in their imaginations.

Even an ordinary father seems larger than life to his children. The extraordinary Arthur James loomed so large at home that he almost blotted out the horizon. The Governor, as the boys were taught to refer to him English style, required quick obedience, a flawless performance of chores and no back talk. At an early age, Westbrook and John understood that they must hold down part-time jobs. They were earning spending money long before they got out of grade school.

Arthur Pegler had fashioned such a dour mask for the world

30

that he had trouble softening it at home. He was quick to take offense; when annoyed, he would swing at the boys with a wide open palm or belabor them with systematic cuffs to the back of the head. Worse yet was his roaring and glaring. Even in calm moods he showed no kindness to his sons and little enough to his wife. She was a slim, pleasant-looking woman, freckled and red-haired, a native of Canada who had been working as a waitress in Minneapolis in 1889 when she met and married him. Naturally, Arthur Pegler did not mention to his wife that he had once been a potboy in a London bar, subject to orders from bar maids. If he had, it would probably not have changed their relationship. She was a sweet, normally submissive woman who stood up infrequently to her husband, and then only on vital issues like religion and money.

As a Catholic, Frances Nicholson Pegler wanted her boys brought up in her own faith. When she broached the subject her husband growled about "damn Papists and low Connemaras" —the last phrase being in reference to the natives of County Galway in Ireland, from which her parents had emigrated. Sometimes he growled for comic effect and sometimes he was in earnest. Though officially a member of the Church of England, he showed no interest in corresponding American denominations and generally regarded church-going as a bore.

Family quarrels over money ran deep and bitter. In addition to a salary ranging from twenty to thirty dollars a week which he received in turn from five or six St. Paul and Minneapolis newspapers during this period, Arthur Pegler was able to make two to five dollars more a week in cash by slipping into print the names of selected sportsmen, business leaders and politicians.

Newspapers winked at the practice, since it reduced the pressure for higher salaries. By a similar process, reporters could acquire suits, groceries, cases of beer, and even railroad passes worth thousands of miles of travel. Arthur Pegler enjoyed a newspaper expense account on top of everything else, but this solved no problems, since he considered expensive clothes and liquor among the essentials of life. Mrs. Pegler got along on what was left.

Though he ruled harshly over a discordant house, Arthur Pegler recognized his basic obligations. He did not desert his family nor cease trying to pay the bills. When the boys were quite young he used to read aloud to them an hour or more at a

31

time in the evening from the Bible, Shakespeare, Milton, and Dickens. He gave up hearing the boys' lessons because it made him too irritable, but he sometimes assigned special compositions in English. Jack always finished first; Westbrook was a terribly slow writer.

What set Arthur Pegler apart from ordinary fathers was the excitement he brought home. His carefully sharpened anecdotes concerned strange and threatening persons in the outside world who had to be placated, outfaced or outwitted. For domestic consumption he wrestled with the forces of evil in a debonair fashion, but his suppressed tension could not help emerging from his manner and creeping like smoke into the ears of his young listeners.

A characteristic out-of-town adventure of Arthur Pegler began when he was caught in a snowstorm near Selby, Iowa. He knocked at the door of a farmhouse and was admitted by a woman. After the two had become acquainted, the woman asked him to sit up with her husband's body while she went off to arrange for a coffin.

For an hour or so the reporter sat there dozing. Suddenly he realized that the corpse's eyes had opened. They were blue. "You're dead," Arthur Pegler reminded the corpse.

"Hell, no," replied the corpse, raising its head. "It's just my epileptic fits! The old woman tried to bury me three times before this."

With guffaws for commas, Arthur Pegler brought his narrative to a climax by describing how he and the corpse drank together companionably after their eerie discourse. Then his face sobered. "In the name of God, boys," he said, "do anything else but don't be a newspaperman!"

Growing up in the shadow of a person like that involved handicaps as well as advantages, but his sons perceived only the good side. "Of all the dumb, wonderful luck that any newspaperman ever had," Westbrook wrote for a later syndicate blurb about himself, "I think mine has been the best since I was the son of a newspaperman and writer who always talked newspaper around home. Every story he ever covered seemed to him and, naturally, to me, the greatest story that ever happened."

Having become increasingly annoyed at living conditions in the city, Arthur James Pegler moved in 1901 to Excelsior, a lakeside resort nineteen miles west and slightly south of Minneapolis. He had fallen in love with Excelsior's fresh air, sparkling water and festive atmosphere during a holiday visit. The relative cheapness of year-round rentals and the prospect of vacations at no extra cost also impressed him.

Excelsior looked its best in Summer. The *Belle of Minnetonka*, a coal-burning sidewheeler which could carry up to fifteen hundred passengers, tied up there with a half dozen other quite large excursion boats. Some of these boats went in for minstrel shows, others had bands for dancing. There were scores of smaller boats, most of them no larger than trolley cars, hundreds of flat-bottomed boats and canoes for fishing and romance. Excelsior doubled in size during the summer as city folk poured into available small cabins and cottages to take advantage of the boating and the Coney Island carnival type of shore attractions, but when the warm weather ended, the town quickly contracted to its year-round core.

Making only routine inquiries about his future neighbors— the 850 to 900 storekeepers and others in the tourist business, pilots and crews from the boats, and their families who lived year-round in well-spaced frame houses inshore from Lake Minnetonka—Arthur Pegler proceeded to rent the largest house in town. More than half a century later, this house was still standing, in excellent condition, two stories high, with an oversized bay window and an elegant front porch. Comparatively new when the Peglers had it, it boasted coal furnace heat and indoor plumbing, and it offered the particular advantage of being diagonally across Water Street from the Milwaukee & St. Paul Railway depot, whose morning and evening trains made commuting possible.

Excelsior's year-round residents were non-intellectual lower–middle-class people, hidebound and clannish, decent enough on the whole but very different from the Peglers. Three saloons kept open year-round, and Arthur Pegler's willingness to take a drink should have counted in his favor among the black sheep, mostly boatmen, who defied the puritanical preaching of the town's Protestant leaders.

Most of the locals, however, were put off by the reporter's manner and accent. They accused him of "putting on airs like an English lord." Because he wore a vest even on hot summer days, he was assumed to be "snooty, too damn good for everyone else." On top of this he soon offended local sensibilities in an irrevocable fashion. He had shifted newspapers again, from the

33

Minneapolis *Journal* to the Minneapolis *Daily News*, and he was busy on a series about local Indian skirmishes. His final episode scooped the historians.

The tom-toms began beating, he wrote, when government troops marched to bring Chief Bugonaygaeship (known as Chief Old Bug) to Duluth to answer charges of illegally distilling liquor. The Chippewa braves of Chief Old Bug mobilized. In the subsequent Battle of Sugar Point—which allegedly never reached the history books because all the reporters covering it lost their scalps, according to Pegler—the Indians escaped without casualties but five American soldiers and a major were killed. Since all this supposedly happened at nearby Leech Lake, Minnesota, it caused a furor until letters to the newspaper demonstrated that it was fictional.

Arthur Pegler was a prolific writer, capable of banging out four or five columns of lively copy in the course of a single day at the office. He was also easily bored. It displeased him that the Indians always lost the skirmishes in the history books. Passing off a tall tale about Chief Old Bug the Bootlegger—to give the Indians one small victory out of all those defeats—seemed like a good idea at the time. Since he took no back talk from the boys at the office, Arthur was not going to listen to gripes from a lot of dumb boatmen. After one explosion in a bar, Excelsior decided to stay away as much as possible from this opinionated stranger who seemed to go wild without warning.

Frances Pegler made a smoother adjustment to the community. She didn't visit much with her neighbors, but she was thought to be well-educated and well-bred. Nobody bridled at the report that as Frances Nicholson, a young girl in her teens from Canada, she had worked as a waitress in Minneapolis; honest labor needed no excuse in Excelsior. She looked frail and she complained about her health, but she did her own housework. When the groceries were delivered from the Samson Brothers' store, she often chatted with James Goodnow, the delivery boy, about the fox terrier pup she had given him. She did not bother with a garden, and there were no flowers or bushes on the Pegler property, but her boys kept the yard neat.

According to local gossip, Mrs. Pegler "took quite a bit" from her husband. Though Excelsior had three churches—Methodist, Congregational and Episcopal—the nearest Catholic church was located three miles away at Chanhassen, Minnesota. The Peglers did not own a horse and buggy. After working hard all week

Arthur Pegler was not inclined on a Sunday to rent a hack from the local livery stable to attend a church which was not his own. Domestic debate over the propriety and expense of such trips usually overflowed into the vexing area of family finance.

The disciplinary power of Arthur James Pegler's name was displayed one evening after a band concert. Since band concerts were big events in Excelsior, the boys overlooked the family curfew. Mrs. Pegler searched for them frantically. Finding them at last, she warned in loud tones that their father would be furious. In sudden alarm, Jack refused to return home until he was assured that his father had missed the evening train and was staying overnight in Minneapolis. Westbrook didn't say a word.

At the age of eight or nine Westbrook had an oddly negative personality. A chunky fellow with sandy-reddish hair and conspicuous freckles, he seldom laughed, cried, or even spoke. Though he impressed adults as being well-behaved and polite, he seemed colorless and mediocre to other boys. Neighbors noted that he did what he was told in an abstracted way. "Westbrook was an almost ideal boy," recalled one woman who lived near the Peglers in Excelsior, "but sometimes I felt as if he weren't there."

Jack, aggressive, talkative and something of a charmer, made a more distinct impression. He had the freedom which came from adjusting to his role as chief lieutenant of his father. The effect of this was to impose on Westbrook two fathers instead of one.

The Excelsior Grade School, which both boys attended, was a four-room frame building. It burned down soon after the family arrived, and was replaced by a smaller brick building. Miss Stratton, a kindly woman known for reciting poems and orations to her classes, taught Westbrook's favorite subject—English—but neither she nor any other teacher found him remarkable. Westbrook stayed close to his brother in school to avoid the hazing invited by his shyness. Even outside school he tagged along after Jack, since he lacked friends and Jack did not mind sharing his. When he wasn't with Jack or playing with the Pegler dogs, who enjoyed a great local reputation for killing cats, he was reading. "I never could get Bud's nose out of a book," Jack once complained affectionately.

To please his father, Westbrook tried desperately to master baseball. Though he was left-handed, he learned to throw with either hand. In pickup games he baited the umpire vigorously from the sidelines. Yet as an adult he confessed: "When I was a

35

kid, I was a punk ball-player. I just wasn't any good. Football the same. Skating the same. Maybe this is what makes me so mean."

Throughout his boyhood he avoided fights. He was a stranger in town, different in background from the other boys, not a fighter, not a talker, not strong or well-coordinated or skillful at sports. On top of everything else, he had a shameful secret, a hidden name resembling that of his mother! No wonder he wrote in one column that youthful experiences "involving courage or the lack of it" would be too painful and humiliating for him to describe or for the public to read. That was one reason advanced by him for putting off writing of his autobiography. Another was a reluctance to dwell on the domestic squabbling of his parents. He noted that a son of Damon Runyon wrote "a fierce article about his childhood which painted a very bad picture of his mother." The columnist added: "If he had to do the story at all, the brave, honest thing was to write the truth, but would it not have been better to forget it?"

No doubt parental restrictions barred him to some extent from the common unconscious life of childhood. With all the teeming marine life of Excelsior at hand, local youngsters learned to swim before they could walk, but Jack and Westbrook, being unable to swim, were required to stay away from the water unless their father was present. Arthur Pegler also put out of bounds the town's two chief natural playgrounds: Solberg's Point, where coal was stored for the excursion boats along an M. & St. L. siding fronting on the lake, and the Town Pump, which was really a square where itinerant farmhands could pause for a drink and a rest in the shade on their way to or from the Dakota wheatfields.

A summons to the role of little merchant filled in spare time. At the urging of his father, Westbrook handled several Minneapolis newspapers. After shouting "wuxtry" from a horse-drawn wagon on Water Street, the chief street in town, he would jump on his bicycle to service outlying farm customers. He knew one farmer who would occasionally sell him four or five quarts of milk in a metal container which he could bring home with him. Sandy, the Negro chef at Hawkins' bar, was willing to pay twenty-five cents for a soup turtle out of Budd's Lake or Galpin's Lake. Westbrook often dreamed of catching some turtles for Sandy, but he resisted the temptation, since the lakes also were out of bounds.

When a newspaper circulation war developed in Minneapolis, Arthur Pegler's *Daily News* imported a gang of young sluggers from Chicago under the leadership of nineteen-year-old Billy Breslin who, under the name of Jack Britton, later became the welterweight boxing champion of the world. Breslin's flying fists cleared corner after corner of downtown Minneapolis. Excelsior remained quiet but there was always the possibility, of course, that the circulation war would reach there. Since he restricted his sales to the *Daily News* out of loyalty to his father, Westbrook worried for weeks lest the sluggers of the enemy waylay him along some quiet country road. Nobody bothered him.

Prohibition sentiment was rising in Excelsior.

The town's bluenoses sniffed at the idea of a boy under the age of ten being brought by his father into the evil atmosphere of a saloon. Westbrook sold papers in all three saloons, but his favorite was Frank Hawkins' place. There he kept his little merchant's receipts in a cup back of the bar. Once a week he was permitted to spend his pennies adult-fashion on lemon soda with onion-rich Western sandwiches prepared in the back room by Sandy. Standing with both feet on the bar-rail and munching away, the boy would listen to Hawkins and his father discuss politics over his head.

One Sunday afternoon, some of the sports in town staged a fight between a pair of mettlesome youngsters in an improvised ring while beer was sold to excited spectators in violation of Sunday closing rules. A county investigation placed the blame tentatively on a group from Hawkins' bar. The culprits were sufficiently close-mouthed to avoid prosecution, but the name of Arthur James Pegler—the newspaperman who brought his boy right into the bar with him—was prominently mentioned among the supposed promoters.

Since the Town Pump and its gracious shade trees were considered disreputable, the Pegler boys were required to slake their thirst at the Women's Christian Temperance Union booth two blocks away. There in the blazing sunlight a large tank, spigot and tin cup had been installed for the use of those who preferred to drink their water in respectable surroundings. One morning a scandalized town heard that a turtle and some fish had been discovered swimming in the WCTU tank. Once again the culprits were never satisfactorily identified, but another Pegler—Jack this time—was rumored to be the prankster.

That fall the three Protestant churches fought for approval

of a referendum which would close the three saloons. Several nights a week for about a month the churches staged free Anti-Saloon League magic-lantern shows. Since town entertainment was normally limited to free open-air band concerts and Town Hall card-trick magicians who charged twenty-five cents for adults and fifteen cents for children, this propaganda in the guise of entertainment was eagerly absorbed.

Somebody would sing "Where Is My Wandering Boy Tonight?" and a slide would show a white-haired mother gazing at a baby shoe. The next slide would reveal her derelict son sprawling over a table in a big-city saloon. According to these shows, one drink was enough to make a drunkard, and a drunkard's children, if any, were likely to be mental defectives. Prohibitionist propaganda for newspaper use was equally black-and-white. A homicide almost automatically was a whisky-murder. If a youngster out on the town took a swing at a cop, that became a whisky-reign-of-terror.

For an adult, some perspective was possible. The prewar prohibition movement was national in scope. It pitted fundamentalist religion against the saloon—"the church of the poor." It opposed middle-class morality and traditional folkways against a fast-changing technology. It represented the reaction of the rural mind against the rising power of the cities, immigration and the flourishing Roman Catholic community. All this background was absorbed naturally by the grownups, but all that Jack and Westbrook appreciated was that they and their family were in total disgrace.

Arthur James Pegler kept a case of beer in his cellar and a jug of rye in his cupboard. By definition that made him a drunkard and his family drunkards, too.

Arthur Pegler was going through a temporary period of joblessness and economic hardship which may have induced him to drink somewhat more than usual. Mrs. Pegler was one of the few Catholics in town. Since it was well known that Catholics had no religious scruples about intoxicants, she also felt the stigma of presumed alcoholism. In the school yard, classmates looked askance at Jack and Westbrook Pegler. To their horror the boys discovered that they were classified as the children of drunkards and as prospective drunkards themselves.

The drys gradually focused their ire on "the bums"—those few itinerant farm workers visiting the Town Pump who seemed to be the worse for alcohol. Several men were detained overnight in the two-cell jail not far from where the Peglers lived. Since the jail had no water, prisoners picked up on a Saturday night would be frantic with thirst by Sunday morning. Hearing their cries, Westbrook put a board against the outside wall and climbed up far enough for a glimpse through the barred window of unshaven men with cracked blue lips and bloodshot eyes. The boy went frantically to his mother for help. She tied a bottle of water to the end of a mop handle so he could shove the bottle to the window in drinking position. The men were pathetically grateful.

Shortly before election day, the prohibition campaign rose to an unexpected climax: a harvest hand locked up as a bum set fire to his mattress and suffocated in the smoke. The Rev. Mr. McKenzie, the local Methodist minister, arrived at the jail just in time, he said, to catch the sinner's dying words of repentance.

Before an enraptured audience, the minister prayed for the salvation of the poor man's soul—and for a thumping majority against the saloons at the polls! The resulting six-to-one victory for the drys left the Peglers feeling buffeted and alone in their own town.

4. CUB IN CHICAGO

Arthur Pegler reverted temporarily to his old practice of booming. Since he had exhausted the patience of the city editors of a half-dozen St. Paul and Minneapolis newspapers, he saw no future for himself in the Twin Cities area. Leaving his family as hostage for his debts on the dry and hostile shorefront of Lake Minnetonka, he went job-hunting to Chicago, fully prepared to go farther if necessary. Westbrook was only ten at the time, and the success of his father's adventure gave him a thrill he never forgot. Years later, he described the turning point in the family fortunes in these words: "My old man was absolutely flat more than a year and in hock to the loan sharks beyond the horizon, but he wangled a pass to Chicago on the old Northwestern and sent for us and went on to make a great reputation as a writer and reporter and as a rough-and-tumble fighter, too, wherever anyone called him out. I am proud to be an heir to all that . . ."

Arthur Pegler's manner of securing employment was almost predictably romantic. The first newspaper he visited was Hearst's Chicago *American*. The city editor there wanted a photograph of a girl involved in a front-page news story, but his staff reporters, using traditional deceptive tactics ranging from bribery to posing as the gas-meter inspector, had not been successful. Along came the boomer from Excelsior with an approach so radical that nobody had heard of it. He rang the doorbell at the girl's home, explained who he was, asked for the picture—and she gave it to him. Then he hurried back to the *American* to swap his prize for a twenty-five-dollar-a-week job.

It was understandable that the Pegler family in its first flash of relief should treat this story like an episode out of the Trojan War, but it was odd that Westbrook never lost his reverential tone in speaking about it. Over the years he devoted at least a dozen columns to his father's coup, adding details and citing Arthur's basic advice: "Always be sure, son, go to headquarters first for information!"

In his later treatments of the saga he often mentioned ways in which "we chased pictures in those days"—as if he had gained a generation on the Governor and were working simultaneously with him out of some timeless cityroom.

As every newspaperman knows, picture-scavenging is a low form of journalistic enterprise ordinarily reserved for cub reporters. Arthur Pegler was forty-two in the late fall of 1904, when he reached West Madison Street in Chicago on the trail of a job. Since he had been in the business almost twenty years, he could hardly be called a cub. On the other hand, a jobless middle-aged man with pyramiding debts, a frail wife and three children—Mrs. Pegler had just given birth out in Excelsior to her long-desired baby daughter—could not afford to be finicky. Whether he was offered a job before or after he went out for a picture was not too important. Suppose he did blow up a small, fairly sophisticated trade anecdote to unbelievable proportions? It served admirably to bolster morale at home and to disguise from others and possibly from himself any distress or humiliation over a humble start in the metropolis.

Chicago, a huge heaving place harder to pin down than an honest wrestler, scares many of the farm boys and girls and the smalltown folk who pour into it every week from all over the Midwest. To the Pegler boys, picking up preliminary impressions from nightly recitals of their father's adventures, it seemed ominous and overwhelming, although they did not immediately realize that it was the convention city of the nation, the hog butcher of the world, the candy bar center of the universe and the other impressive things catalogued by Carl Sandburg.

Sometimes a child trained to psychological slavery at home grows up in such a way as to throw off its effects. He may come into contact with decent playmates, kindly teachers or other significant figures who treat him affectionately as an individual.

Why this should happen to Jack and not to Westbrook was a minor mystery of personality. Jack seemed to have more inner bounce, more capacity for dealing with surprise on his own terms. At any rate, the difference between the boys became more pronounced in Chicago.

The family atmosphere was different than it had been in Excelsior if only because of another child in the house. Mrs. Pegler named her daughter Frances. As her affections focused on the girl bearing her name, she tended insensibly to withdraw some of the warmth formerly lavished on the boy who had been named Francis. Both Westbrook and his brother were too full of their

41

own problems of adjustment in Chicago, however, to worry over their relative share of mother love. That fall the Peglers' second son enrolled in the Chicago public school system as James Westbrook Pegler, officially and forever Poppa's boy.

The family settled on Kenmore Avenue in a row of three-story apartment houses. This was predominantly middle-class territory near the Loop on the well-groomed North Side, socially a notch above the South Side and several notches above the teeming West Side. Only a few intervening houses obstructed a view of Lake Michigan. Here and there near Kenmore Avenue vacant lots could still be found for playing games or for those personal combats which often prove to be milestones on a boyish road to self-respect.

The best local fighter in Westbrook's age bracket was a Negro named Willie White. Several of his bouts behind the signboard off Kenmore Avenue made an indelible impression on Westbrook's mind. Eventually Willie "got his ears pinned back by a little German with yellow corkscrew curls who wore a sort of pea-jacket with yellow buttons and cried bitterly all through a long bloody scrap that lasted until dusk. His father was something at the Bismarck Hotel and he knew absolutely nothing about fist-fighting but kept blasting away at Willie White and mauling away until Willie White 'gave licked' as the saying went."

In another homeric engagement, an older bully named Harry Eastman was upset by Manton (Matt) Eddy, later a General. Westbrook felt something akin to hero-worship for Matt Eddy, who was a couple of years ahead of him in school, but they could hardly be called friends. Westbrook could have used some friends during this period. Owing to the sharp separation of school grades by age in Chicago, he could no longer count on support from his brother Jack. Since he was disinclined to fight on his own behalf, he had to squirm out of trouble as best he could.

At the Horace Greeley grade school, which he attended for four years, Westbrook was a detached, almost invisible pupil. Judging from his ability in later life to rattle off the names of teachers and classmates, he developed an excellent memory, but no teacher struck fire in him and no subject, except possibly English, stirred his interest. Long division balked him completely. All he ever claimed for himself was that he did fairly well in the spelling bees, or spell-downs, as they were called. Lovelyn Miller, one of the few Negroes in the school, also performed creditably in the spell-downs. He and Lovelyn had little contact at the time, but they engaged in a desultory correspondence as adults after she became a columnist on the Chicago *Defender*.

Westbrook's chief recollection of the Greeley school was that once every year for three years he gave himself a dose of poison ivy. Every spring he went looking for the glossy, three-leafed sumach known to scientists as *rhus toxicodendron* and to most children as abomination. When he found it, he massaged his face, hands and forearms with the oily leaves. Soon ugly splotches betrayed his uneasy condition. His teacher would send him to the principal and the principal, under a Board of Education rule, had to excuse him from school for ten days.

As a grownup Westbrook demanded admiration for this sorry trick. All mothers kept remedies in their medicine chests, he said, which dried up the blisters in a day or two, thus leaving eight or nine days of the quarantine for a glorious unearned vacation. Encouraging poison-ivy infection year after year would seem almost incredible to anybody who ever experienced a severe dose. If it really happened, it could only be explained in terms of a morbid need for self-punishment. If it were fantasy—excluding a tall tale in his father's tradition—it certainly implied alienation, despair and an extreme distaste for the educational process.

After graduating without distinction from Greeley grade school, Westbrook went on to the Lane Technical School, a public institution devoted to manual training. Arthur James Pegler, as usual, made the family decision. He argued that a boy with a poor academic record might as well learn a trade. This reasoning made no sense, because Westbrook was unhandy. He had no aptitude for the course of study and no chance of mastering it.

One subject which attracted him at first was drawing. Unfortunately he encountered a teacher who ruled that the human body must be constructed like a house from the foundation up. Westbrook was an instinctive caricaturist; he wanted to start sketching catch-as-catch-can, with an ear or a nose. He and the instructor were simply incompatible. In math, Westbrook bought compasses and other equipment out of his own money and he struggled valiantly with the homework, but he could not

43

solve the problems. He took algebra three times and failed three times, winning promotion at last only because the school needed his desk.

Athletic prowess in or out of school would have provided some compensation for scholastic inadequacy but this also proved elusive. Westbrook was late in trying roller-skates and not good at skating. Despite his waterfront years in Excelsior, he could barely flounder across the first twenty-two-foot-wide public swimming pool he encountered in Chicago. Since classmates were thrashing triumphantly up and down the length of the pool, he soon avoided swimming. What he needed was a sport at which he could train secretly until the moment came to astonish the world, and he thought he had found it when a marathon-racing craze hit the school.

When his alarm went off at four o'clock in the morning, he arose and donned shorts, sports shirt and sneakers instead of his usual clothes for distributing newspapers. In company with another spindle-shanked youth from school he lumbered around the Graceland Cemetery, three laps to a mile, until legs and lungs rebelled. Trudging home frustrated, tired and uneasy in the quiet street, since the city was not yet awake, the boys realized that they were following a milkman on his route.

It was almost a matter of instinct to drop behind, wait a few seconds for the milkman to get out of sight, grab one bottle of milk from a doorway for drinking and another bottle to be smashed with a fine fury against an "El" pillar. In the exhilaration of the moment Westbrook's companion recalled that it was possible to pry open the locked wooden boxes on the sidewalks where wholesale bakery drivers deposited cinnamon buns and coffee rings and pies for delicatessen use. Though the boys did not go quite that far, they returned home with a warm feeling of deviltry, as partial compensation for athletic failure.

The before-and-after school jobs required by Arthur Pegler kept Westbrook busy without rounding out his character as fully as his father expected. Usually he got up early to distribute his quota of Chicago *Tribunes* before breakfast. He rolled the papers individually and tied them with string so they could be tossed like grenades up on back porches along the route.

Where a frozen wash on the line prevented this easy delivery the boy would stamp indignantly up the front stairs to drop his merchandise at the door. He also sold evening papers, hopping hazardously on and off street cars for a mere third of a cent profit per copy.

Handling the bulky Sunday papers required a little wagon. One wintry morning, Westbrook was shoving the wagon through the snow along the North Shore lakefront when a strong wind suddenly captured a dozen or more sections of paper. While he was chasing these his route book blew into the lake. Utterly defeated, the little merchant abandoned wagon, route book, papers and pride and went home. When his route boss called to pronounce a three dollar fine, the boy quit.

For a while thereafter he did chores in the Chicago stockyards. Finding the stockyards too coarse and smelly for his taste, he took a job setting up pins in a bowling alley. When that became intolerable because of the heat and the noise, he tried selling advertising on commission for a bowling alley publication, one of the most difficult and unrewarding things he ever undertook. The job he disliked least was jerking soda in a Wilson Avenue drugstore near his home. The pharmacist was willing to sell his stringy-looking freckled apprentice an occasional pack of illegal cigarettes and to permit himself to be addressed informally as "Doc." Despite these concessions, Westbrook found difficulty in relaxing as a soda jerk. He never did perfect the persiflage required for dealing with younger customers, particularly girls.

While Westbrook wrestled with discouragement, his father was becoming a success. Arthur Pegler had been known as a good general assignment man before he reached Chicago, but there he flowered.

Within a year after his arrival, his salary doubled. Robert J. Casey, who wrote an informal history of Chicago journalism, spoke of him as "a genius—easily the best reporter of his time." Gene Fowler hailed him as "Arthur the Great." Others used phrases for him ranging from "salty and verbally crackling" to "Olympian."

It was in Chicago that Arthur Pegler, who formerly wrote in longhand, acquired the ponderous Smith Premier typewriter which became his trademark. It had separate keyboards for small and large letters and it had to be turned up to see what was written. Nobody else, not even his sons, was allowed to use that machine, which was kept under padlock during its owner's absence from the office.

45

Arthur Pegler became a preferred witness at executions, which Chicago newspapermen collected like service medals. Before he finished he saw at least fifty of them. On out-of-town trials he was frequently attended by two telegraphers rather than the single one allotted to most correspondents. When a Governor mislaid his speech, it was Arthur who batted out a substitute text in short takes under the platform at the Fair Grounds. When an evangelist named Gypsy Smith arrived in town, it became Arthur's duty not only to cover the evening revivals but also to produce the lyrics for a daily hymn and the words for a daily front-page sermon in the Chicago *American*.

One summer a crusading new managing editor from the West took over affairs at the *American*. The editor, who liked to make history as a way of gaining circulation, was convinced of the guilt of a Chicago boarding house keeper who had been accused of poisoning her star boarder. The full weight of his determination to convict her fell on Arthur Pegler, who was handling the story during a spell of summer rewrite. The star boarder lay dead in the county morgue, unquestionably loaded with arsenic, but the prosecution could not find any container with even a trace of poison to provide the connecting link necessary for conviction.

According to a boastful story which Arthur Pegler told in later years to James Whittaker and other New York cronies, the reporter told a loyal photographer that they must somehow find the necessary evidence. Subsequently, a salt-cellar full of arsenic (obtained through photographic channels) was dramatically discovered at the boarding house by the *American*. Conviction of the woman resulted. When she was sentenced to hang on the basis of this manufactured evidence, however, the photographer began to brood, and Pegler was forced to confess to the managing editor. The editor had an immediate inspiration. The boarding house keeper was, after all, a WOMAN and a MOTHER —AN APPEALING SINNER! The front page was quickly cleared of competing news to make room for the *American*'s new mammoth mercy campaign. Sob-sisters, women's clubs, poets and pastors alike were enrolled in the crusade until a badgered Governor, in a room filled with magnesium smoke from photographers' flashes, signed the necessary papers commuting the woman's sentence to life imprisonment.

Though he told this story in later years to friends, Arthur Pegler did not include it in his reportage to his family. The stories he brought home had a clearer moral. Usually they relied heavily on stereotypes. Thus the police and the soldiers who were responsible for maintaining order were presumed to be brave and trustworthy. Shopkeepers were generally kind. Like many another new arrival in the United States, Arthur Pegler felt strongly patriotic, but at the same time he suspected those other immigrants who did not come already equipped with English. He associated himself strongly with Americanism, reserving his most bitter denunciations for foreigners and for anybody at home, in business or labor, who swindled the government. A skeptic in politics, he considered all politicians to be crooks or fakes. Judges were ward-heelers to him, reformers were do-gooders and radicals were bomb-throwers and traitors.

He moved warily in the midst of all these types. Once he toured Chicago art galleries in the guise of a British millionaire searching for a few choice new paintings. A spectacular exposé of fake masterpieces resulted. Another time, he entered a Chicago bank whose president had, in the oblique phrase of the day, gone to Canada. The examiners were already poring over the accounts when he walked in, laid stick and gloves on the board table, sat down and said: "Well, let us proceed to business, gentlemen."

Somehow the examiners thought he was the bank's lawyer and the bank's lawyer thought he was an examiner. Nobody questioned his presence until the time came for him to catch an edition. As he arose somebody inquired: "And whom do you represent, sir?" Arthur Pegler bowed slightly as he started out. "Hearst's Chicago *American!*" he replied.

Westbrook still came into occasional direct contact with newspaper work, more for his father's convenience than anything else. Once the elder Pegler allowed Jack and Westbrook to accompany him on a weekend assignment to cover an Indiana farm murder. The boys were supposed to be helping the *American's* photographer. Actually they scurried around in search of news tips as well as picture possibilities, but they did not manage to soften Arthur Pegler's bleak humor during the trip.

Another time fire broke out in a row of frame houses in a section remote from the Loop. The city editor had nobody handy to send out as a legman. Arthur Pegler, who was on rewrite, phoned home and ordered Westbrook to hustle out to the fire by streetcar. After a heart-breakingly slow trip the boy reached the scene of the disaster. Because of his youthful appearance he was jostled and abused by firemen, policemen and ordinary frantic citizens. By the time he reached the phone with some facts he was beside himself.

By this time, it was so late that the *American* wanted only the number of houses burned. Westbrook gave the number over the phone. "Hang up and go home," Arthur Pegler told him.

Westbrook could hardly believe his ears. "Hang up and go home!" roared his father. Westbrook hung up and went home. To Arthur Pegler it was just another anecdote. Imagine Bud trying to give details when all the paper wanted was the count!

Some of Westbrook's distress and uncertainty could be traced to the normal strains of adolescence. Lane was not coeducational, so he met no girls there; and the girls in his home neighborhood had their own social concerns. In tentative encounters with the other sex he came off poorly, since he was timid almost to the point of being tongue-tied, skinny and awkward.

In search of companionship Westbrook joined a fraternity at school. Most of the members were burly and profane youngsters from poorer sections of town who had been attracted to Lane by such courses as blacksmithing and foundry work. Their brash exuberance upset the new brother from Kenmore Avenue. Some of them would hop a streetcar, ring up fares on the hapless conductor who was inside tinkering with his coal stove, then jump off and run for their lives. They would use paper wads to extract a few pennies from slot machines or go on an evening binge of smashing street lights.

Two South Side lads belonging to the fraternity developed a depraved taste for Ramblers, Sampsons and chain-drive Queens cars. They would climb into an unguarded car, joyride around for awhile, then abandon it. Meeting this pair one evening on his way home from the Wilson Avenue drugstore, Westbrook was invited for a ride. He declined on the ground that it was too late and he was due home. Though he could not have borrowed a car himself in those days since he didn't know how to drive, he did a lot of worrying over the trouble he would have gotten into if he had gone with the other boys.

If he were caught, he wondered, would he be taken to the Town Hall police station to await the arrival of his raging father and his tearful mother? After a second offense, would he be incarcerated in the Pontiac Home for Juvenile Delinquents? Would

48

he continue downward step by step into the awful depths of crime to be jailed, perhaps executed, or would he emerge as one of those legendary mobsters already evident in Chicago who seemed able to defy the law with impunity?

In alternate visions, Westbrook pictured himself as a newspaper cartoonist in a large luxurious studio well equipped with female models. He admired the undemanding carefree life of the candy butcher on the Chicago-to-Peoria run who slept on cushions in a day coach during the layover. Such existences seemed to him almost as rewarding as that of an arch-criminal. Daydreaming, however, came abruptly to a close. Life at Lane could no longer be endured. Dropping out of classes, Westbrook grabbed the first available job, and became a filing clerk in an insurance office at twenty-five dollars a month.

In this emergency Jack came to the rescue. Under prodding from his father, Jack had applied for summer jobs with the *American* and the United Press. Partly, no doubt, because of Arthur Pegler's burgeoning reputation, he was accepted at both places. Preferring to work near his father at the *American*, Jack arranged to turn over the lesser UP spot to his younger brother.

As an office boy, Westbrook was responsible chiefly for preparing "books"—sandwiches of copy paper and carbons—for the rewrite men. In addition to this job, which soiled his hands and his clothes, he performed various minor chores ranging from the sharpening of pencils to the running of coffee and smokes for his elders. He stood around in readiness until the abrupt, impersonal cry of "Boy!" summoned him to specific duty. The coming and going of reporters, the joking and grumbling of rewrite men, the alternating concentration and boredom of the veterans on the rim of the copy desk and the occasional sharp conferences of editors mystified him until he came to realize that behind the clatter of typewriters, the jangle of phones, the shouting and confusion, stories were being ground out, unused notes spiked, headlines written, proofs corrected. Copy was flowing jerkily but irresistibly through human channels toward its final form of news. In this complex cityroom routine, Westbrook saw that he was performing a small but essential role, and he was thrilled; he was paid ten dollars a week but he would gladly, if necessary, have worked for nothing.

After several weeks' experience, Westbrook was allowed to "sing out the pony wire." This consisted in reading a prepared budget of news over a telephone circuit to small papers in nearby towns like Aurora, Joliet, Moline and Gary which could not afford the regular twenty-four-hour telegraphic service.

No extra pay was involved in this chore but young Pegler felt important as he rolled off the names of presidents, prime ministers, mayors and other celebrities involved in the news. He may have mispronounced a few names, particularly of foreign towns, but the stenographers in the subscribing newspaper offices who took down what he said in shorthand or directly on a typewriter were not inclined to be critical. An exception occurred when he was reporting the death of an American poet, Joaquin Miller. "That name is not 'Joe Quin,'" interrupted an educated voice at the Joliet *Herald*. "It is pronounced 'Wha-keen!'"

As a favor, Ed Conkle, the UP bureau manager, pinned a badge on Westbrook one day and told him to go out to the Morris plant at the stockyards, where Chief Horan and twenty-two of his firemen had been buried by a falling wall during a terrible fire the previous night. The firemen were still wetting down the ruins when Westbrook arrived. All the news service required by then was the names of the victims. A group of men would hoist a charred lump onto a stretcher, cover it with a tarpaulin from a salvage truck, scramble through the mud with it to an identification point, where the tarpaulin would be lifted and a policeman would roar out the name of the man and his company. Barely sixteen at the time the reporter felt faint from the combined smell of ham and human flesh but he would hurry tensely to a phone. After giving a name he would try to work in some details about the shrieks and moans of bereaved relatives, only to meet rebuffs. "Sh'dap," growled the bored rewrite man. "Get us the name of the next stiff!"

Since Westbrook was no longer in school he won permission that fall to remain in the littered, grim and exciting UP office. Within a few months he was allowed to write as well as sing out the pony wire, a promotion involving a six dollar raise which he spent largely on an effort to accustom himself to drinking beer.

The UP staff was not unduly impressed with its youngest recruit. He was too tense in a trade which favors the casual touch. He tried too hard. Discovering that Westbrook was easily upset by sudden noise when he was concentrating on composition of the pony wire, one of the reporters bribed a copy boy to whistle loudly and unexpectedly behind his chair. Westbrook

50

whirred up into the air like a quail. Since he was equally indisposed to shrug off the joke or push it to an open quarrel, variations of the game became inevitable. Even among the executives a disposition grew to write off Arthur Pegler's boy as a doubtful investment. Ed Conkle shook his head when asked for another raise. "If you want more money around here, Bud," he said, "you better go back to school."

On previous occasions, Mrs. Pegler had suggested a parochial school without success, but this time Arthur Pegler had no alternative to present.

Westbrook therefore went to Loyola Academy, a Jesuit institution, registering as J. Westbrook Pegler, which put the initial from his father first while retaining the middle name preferred by his mother. Though he reacted with his customary overemphasis to a new situation, Westbrook did well at Loyola. Serving Mass for the first time as an altar boy, he got confused about when he was supposed to ring the bell, so he rang it constantly until a priest took it gently from his hand. The error was attributed to excess enthusiasm. Westbrook studied a great deal of Latin at Loyola, including Julius Caesar's campaigns in Gaul, and he worked with unusual diligence in courses on drawing and English composition.

Father Seidenberg, the headmaster, showed considerable interest in the sobersided youngster. The pair could be seen walking about campus occasionally in deep conversation. Toward the start of his second term at Loyola, to his mother's incredulous delight, Westbrook talked seriously about becoming a priest.

That spring of 1912, the International News Agency, a competitor of the United Press, began to expand its Chicago staff in preparation for the scheduled Republican national convention there in June. Hearing about this opportunity from his father, Westbrook applied for a job. He was promptly accepted and never thereafter left newspaper work. Years later, when he was asked what he got out of Loyola Academy, which he had deserted in such a hurry, the syndicated columnist replied with a touch of his father's hauteur that he had "learned all three parts of Gaul."

5. ON HIS OWN

When Westbrook Pegler remarked, as he often did in later years, that the United States "began to go smash in Chicago in 1912," he based his belief on personal experience. He was there; he attended the stormy national convention that June which split the Republican party. It seemed obvious to him even as an untrained reporter that the Grand Old Party, which had monopolized federal government fairly steadily since the Civil War, would never be the same again, and that this applied also to the country.

To many older observers, social revolution seemed imminent in 1912. The safety valve of the frontier had been shut off. More than a third of the nation's farmers were no longer working their own acreage. Big factories already dominated the industrial scene under the spreading control of billion-dollar trusts. One per cent of the population had more money than the remaining 99 per cent. Wage-earners, women and minority groups, immigrants, farmers and small businessmen alike felt irritated and neglected. By the simplest gauge—the selection of scores of Socialists to local offices throughout the country—politicians in the major parties realized they were in trouble.

William Howard Taft sat in the White House. Whatever he attempted seemed to infuriate the liberals without pleasing the conservatives, so he did as little as possible. When Theodore Roosevelt returned from an extended tour abroad, during which he had shot rhinoceroses and hippopotamuses in Africa and dined with the crowned heads of Europe, he discovered that his handpicked successor as President was no longer inclined to take his advice and that millions of ordinary Americans were still looking to him for leadership.

Roosevelt—known to his admirers as Teddy or T.R.—was still bursting with energy at the age of fifty-four. Though he had announced he would not run again for President he was open to persuasion, since he had previously served only one elective term.

Sensing the roll of unrest under his feet, he worked out a political approach which he called the New Nationalism, from a phrase in Herbert Croly's book, *The Promise of American Life.* The New Nationalism sought wider powers for a more democratized government in order to restore individual opportunity. Despite a faint flavor of what became known decades later as national socialism, it fell within the American tradition.

On Saturday, June 15, 1912, T.R. arrived in Chicago for the Republican National Convention. From the stirring of the sidewalks, it was clear that he had captured popular imagination. The only question was whether the Regulars, as President Taft's political followers were called, would loosen their grip on the party machinery. William Howard Taft might be elephantine and bumbling, but his lieutenants were shrewd and power-minded. They had no intention of yielding control.

The Regulars ridiculed Roosevelt's promises of equal treatment for rich and poor, corporations and unions. They believed that the country would be led into revolution by his program, which called for a "rational" tariff (compared to the extremely high Payne-Aldrich tariff), "proper" military and national preparations, direct primaries, conservation of natural resources and women suffrage. This, said the Regulars, was Radicalism.

On Monday, June 17, Roosevelt stirred his partisans to a frenzy in the convention auditorium with an appeal ending with these words: "We stand at Armageddon and we battle for the Lord!" Arthur Pegler had doubts. The Lord was on the side of the candidate with the most delegates, he said, and the name of the candidate wasn't Roosevelt.

Tuesday noon, fifteen thousand delegates, officials, reporters and strangers jammed the Coliseum for the start of the convention. Westbrook Pegler, a gangly freckled youth not yet nineteen years old, wore a red fez on his sandy red hair for easier recognition by the International News Service stable of headliners who had gathered for the convention, including Arthur Brisbane, T. A. (Tad) Dorgan, Richard Harding Davis and Nell Brinkley. Young Pegler was supposed to make himself generally useful to these celebrities.

That very first day, when Elihu Root's election as convention chairman by a five-to-one vote foreshadowed accurately the pro-Taft strength among the delegates who were permitted by the Taft machine to take seats, Brisbane grabbed Pegler by the arm, thrust part of a running story in longhand at him and ordered: "Rush it to the wire!" In the noise and excitement, Westbrook failed to recognize the man who wrote the editorials for

William Randolph Hearst. "Rush it yourself," he squeaked in annoyance at being treated with less dignity than he thought his status warranted. Fortunately Mr. Bronx, the local INS manager, was standing nearby. He moved over to close the boy's fingers around the copy and shove him on his way.

Westbrook's contacts with other Hearst headliners had equally odd results. Arthur Pegler had warned him in advance that Richard Harding Davis was "a dude, a snob and a loner," but the famous foreign correspondent proved gracious and encouraging to the young reporter. Since he rather fancied himself as an artist, Westbrook took advantage of an intermission to bring over some of his sketches to Tad Dorgan. After the barest glance, the cartoonist handed back the sketches. "Isn't there anything else you can do?" he asked sourly.

The galleries were overwhelmingly pro-Roosevelt. Westbrook never forgot the "robust lady in a red dress and a hat the size of a manhole cover" who arose up there to shriek: "We want Teddy!" This served as the signal for a demonstration which threatened for a while to get out of control. When order was restored, the Taft steamroller resumed its slow progress on the floor.

Westbrook had been conditioned at home and in the schoolyard to praise of Teddy for "soaking the rich." Because of this, he felt as if he were "on a bed of spikes" when Regular orators at the convention condemned the former President as a demagogue. His father and other experts soon clarified the situation. This was a struggle between Regulars and Radicals, they explained. In such case, the Peglers were Reg'lers.

T. R. stalwarts began to leave the convention floor. They poured along Michigan Boulevard, with Roosevelt and his daughter Alice striding at their head. Asked how he felt over rejection by his own party, the former President bared his famous teeth. "Like a bull moose," he said, thereby providing a name for a movement. That a new party would be formed was taken for granted. Six weeks later in Chicago the Progressives held their own convention to nominate Roosevelt for President. The new party plumped for reform on the whole, but at the last minute it softened the plank against trusts to please a J.P. Morgan partner named George W. Perkins, its chief financial angel.

Woodrow Wilson, an angular Princeton University professor who had become Governor of New Jersey, was named by the Democrats for President. He ran on a New Freedom program calling for anti-trust legislation, tariff reduction and banking reform. As the campaign proceeded, Wilson managed to imply that he was not out of sympathy with large-scale economic organization—bigness by itself did not offend him, he said; it had to be *bad* bigness. Meanwhile Roosevelt was slurring over his party's deviation from old-fashioned Jeffersonian trust-busting.

Despite such hedging, which is not rare in American presidential elections, the Progressive and Democratic parties in 1912 were both left of center. Both had absorbed chunks of Grover Cleveland's liberalism and William Jennings Bryan's populism. The resulting merger—termed progressivism by such a modern historian of American reform as Professor Eric F. Goldman of Princeton University—retained such ideas as a federal income tax, the political encouragement of women and the support of trade union demands for minimum-wage and maximum-hour legislation.

For the first time in American history, two reform candidates for President were vying for national attention. They were not unduly explicit in discussing the differences between the New Freedom and the New Nationalism, but even so their public dialogue left President Taft on the sidelines. Early in the campaign he said plaintively that he had "no part to play but that of a conservative." The frustration of the Taft campaigners gradually focused on T.R. Here, they decided, was a man who wanted to undermine the foundations of the state and put the country at the mercy of the mob.

Vilification went far enough finally to sway one particular unsettled mind. On October 14, 1912, a lunatic named John Schranck shot Roosevelt just as the Progressive candidate was starting a final Midwest campaign swing in Milwaukee. The bullet entered the chest near the right nipple, penetrating only an inch because it was slowed by an eyeglass case and a roll of manuscript in an inner pocket.

After stanching the flow of blood and putting on a clean shirt in his hotel room, the indomitable Roosevelt proceeded to the auditorium. "I was shot this morning and the doctors have not yet removed the bullet from my insides," he told the hushed audience. "Whatever happens to me, I want you to know that I have had a hell of a good time on earth."

The former President was rushed to Mercy Hospital in Chicago for an operation to remove the bullet. The Regulars pursued him even there with rumors: he had not been shot at all, the whole thing was a fake to win votes, they whispered. Wilson promptly assured his own election, which had become increasingly likely because of the split in the Republican party, by announcing that he would make no more speeches out of consideration for his Progressive opponent's disability.

Arthur Pegler had charge of the *American's* coverage of the attempted assassination and the ex-President's subsequent hospital care. He persuaded the *American* to hire Westbrook, who had been dropped by INS after the convention, to report Schranck's arraignment. The over-eager Westbrook reached Milwaukee in a flurry. Finding the courtroom doors closed, he knocked and when knocking produced no result he began kicking. A jury had gone out in a murder case. Since it was expected momentarily to return with a verdict, attendants threw the doors wide open —to reveal a single frightened young reporter!

Westbrook talked fast to avoid punishment for contempt. "I just had to get in, Judge," he said. "I just had to get in! I guess I'm dumb." The court decided to be kind.

At Schranck's arraignment some of the older reporters served as unofficial defense counsel. The prisoner might be crazy, they said, but maybe he deserved a medal at that. From their point of view the Nation's Number One Radical had something coming to him and they hoped it wasn't trivial. Back in Chicago, Westbrook absorbed more anti-Roosevelt speculation from his father. He was told that the former President might have been "shot in his spectacle case" by a bullet "from a little pistol" with a resulting "trivial wound." On the other hand, he might not have been shot at all. Arthur Pegler was still looking for evidence at Mercy Hospital to support the latter theory. Bulletins handed out by the authorities were terse and unsatisfactory and hospital employees were not helpful.

Kent Hunter of the Chicago *Examiner*, Arthur Pegler's chief competitor on the Roosevelt story, prowled around Mercy Hospital one night until he located a plate which he had heard could be found at a certain spot in the drying rack of the X-ray room. Chicago journalism not being noted in those days for high-mindedness, Hunter removed the plate without permission. Next day the *Examiner* had a great front-page scoop: Theodore Roosevelt's pre-operation X-ray picture!

Though badly smudged, this proof of T.R.'s near martyrdom might have aroused additional sympathy for him in Chicago. It could hardly have changed the result, since most voters had already made up their minds. Wilson was elected by a substantial margin over Roosevelt, who recovered nicely from his operation. Taft ran a poor third with only three million votes out of thirteen million cast.

Several days after the election, the *Examiner* received some distrubing information about its celebrated X-ray photograph. "I don't think that was Roosevelt at all," declared a medical specialist who happened to be visiting a friend in the *Examiner* city room. "He is older. It wasn't too clear, of course, but I'd swear that the thing you printed in your paper was a picture of a six-month-old foetus!"

Westbrook Pegler always thought of himself as a reporter. Being one satisfied an early interior image and gave him a status transcending his ordinary limitations. As a representative of the American people (who had a right to know), a reporter need not apologize for asking questions. Usually he asked them in a half-cocky, half-dedicated way. In the tradition of the New York shipnews man who once asked Dean Inge whether he believed in the Virgin Birth, Westbrook felt himself entitled if necessary "to belly up to God himself" in search of required answers.

American reporters, according to Jacques Barzun's study of the tribe, generally were "derisive, suspicious, faintly hostile . . . the democratic ego when faced with intellect." According to Westbrook Pegler, there were two main schools. New York reporters exhibited "ethics and manners" and actually cooperated with each other in the collection of facts when working on the same story. The Chicago school in which Pegler himself was trained sanctioned the commission of "any crime short of burglary" in the pursuit of an exclusive. "We fought, tricked, and to be honest about it," he once said, "hated each other."

Much of Westbrook's competitive intensity came from his early association with the United Press, which rehired him soon after he covered the Schranck arraignment for the *American*. During the following year in Chicago he completed his basic training in newspaper work. Five days a week he chased fires, pictures and miscellaneous trouble; on weekends he held down City Hall; he also covered police stations and police courts. For a while he worked in the office on a daily feature called "Watching the Scoreboard," a round-up of the day's major league games for use in early editions of next afternoon's newspapers. This was notable chiefly for his first byline: "By Bud Pegler," using the nickname favored by his father.

In order to compete with the older and better-established Associated Press, the United Press picked up ambitious young-sters who were willing to accept low pay and miserable condi-tions in exchange for experience and a chance at glory. "We had no assurance of pay during illness, no vacations, no severance," Westbrook Pegler once recalled. "The AP usually outmanned us about three to one on a story. They were good men, but they weren't lean and hungry. We stole their pants." Regardless of the official quitting time, no UP reporter dreamed of dropping an unfinished story until he was relieved. "I never knew such an outfit of workers," Westbrook crowed. "You could hardly sweep us out of the office!" Hours were long on ordinary days and longer on Saturday. Then Westbrook usually began at seven or nine in the morning and worked until one or four P.M. After a few hours off (a doubtful benefit since no youngster was likely to find a place for a nap in that short period) he would continue right through the night to one or four on Sunday morning. When at last he got to bed, pale and tired, he looked and felt as if he had been slugged.

Saturday afternoon the weekly all-night poker game got un-der way in the City Hall pressroom. Westbrook often dropped over to watch the game even when he was not on assignment there. Since he never developed any skill at cards, it cost him money to play, but he sat in once in a while for the joy of being one of the gang.

Every fire in the city was recorded by alarms in the press-room, and when a certain combination of bells indicated a large one Westbrook would tag along with the others. As a buff, he found night fires enormously exciting. The voices of the firemen in the dark, the blows of their axes and the crash of glass remained in his memory for years.

The regular Chicago City Hall crew in those days included Alfred (Jake) Lingle, a languid smart-aleck working for the Chi-cago *Tribune* who was shot fatally in typical gangland style one afternoon years later for failing to provide promised journalistic protection for some underworld clients; and Webb Miller, an unassuming farm boy from Michigan who later became a foreign correspondent. Miller, older by two years than Westbrook, was trying desperately to atone for his lack of education. Out of his twenty-five-dollars-a-week salary from the *American,* he bought Dr. Eliot's entire five-foot shelf, read extensively in the Bible, the Koran, the precepts of Confucius, the *Zend-Avesta* of the Persian Zoroaster, the Hindu Vedas, Darwin, Huxley and Ingersoll. He took gallery seats at the opera when he could afford them and made trips to the Art Institute on Sundays to study the paintings. Chicago in those days had Jane Addams and Hull House, Harriet Monroe and her *Poetry* magazine, and many other figures of cultural and social importance. Webb Miller wanted to know something of them all. He urged Westbrook to explore these fascinating areas, but the other boy was concentrating on the job at hand.

Webb Miller and Westbrook Pegler shared one memorable experience. Dropping around to a bar before going home, they treated a printer they knew to several beers. When he failed to treat in turn, they decided they had been insulted. They trailed him as he left the bar. He went to a night market, purchased a leg of lamb and some eggplant and started for home. At the entrance to a dark alley, the reporters intercepted him with a growled: "Give us your money or we shoot!"

They had no weapons. Miller's idea was to retrieve the cost of the beers so unfairly consumed. When the printer begged, however, to be allowed to keep his eggplant and leg of lamb lest his wife complain, it seemed appropriate to forget the money and take the food. The exploit subsequently landed on the squeal sheet or unofficial complaint book at the local police station. A couple of detectives visited the bar several days later to ask questions, but there the incident ended.

The joke hold-up bolstered his confidence somewhat, but young Pegler still did not get along too well with most reporters. Arthur Pegler came to the conclusion that a few lessons in the manly art of self-defense were required. Boxing gloves were purchased and practice sessions duly called for Sunday morning at the Pegler home, but the sessions soon had to be abandoned. Setting an authorized target for Westbrook's suppressed annoyances meant far too deadly an encounter to be pleasant for anyone. Jack and Arthur Pegler found they had a choice between annihilating the youngster or being annihilated.

As Westbrook was approaching his nineteenth birthday in 1913, a thirty-year-old telegrapher named Roscoe H. Johnson, who later became president of the Commercial Telegraphers Union, was transferred to Chicago from the New York office of

United Press. Knowing nothing of Arthur Pegler's ill-fated attempt, the telegrapher also decided to help Westbrook by bringing boxing gloves to the office. During a quiet period in the lobster shift at night, he went through the motions of demonstrating his favorite one-two punch. Westbrook promptly looped a right over the other's lead and broke Johnson's nose.

"Hell, I thought you could defend yourself!" said the boy in pride and chagrin. Johnson had to pay $150 to streamline his nose, but he did not complain. "Bud's just a deadly serious kid who never learned to play," he told others in the office.

There were many streets in Chicago when Westbrook worked there as a youth. Those which introduced him to the seamier aspects of urban life stood out particularly in his mind. A reporter could learn a lot by keeping his eyes open: the endless fire sales on West Madison Street, for example, and the way Salvation Army lassies going through a Saturday night crowd on that same street turned first to a man in his cups, on the shrewd theory that he would be more generous than a sober citizen.

Saturday was a busy night on West Madison Street. For breadwinners relaxing there in a saloon from the week's turmoil, time had a way of slipping by. On the way home, some would pick up hand-painted gold-framed pictures—seascapes, landscapes, sleeping beauties and still lifes, available at prices ranging up to fifteen dollars each—as a gesture of propitiation toward a waiting wife. Westbrook used to claim that his standards of art were formed by "those marvelous high-speed painters" of West Madison Street.

One Chicago street which Westbrook would never forget was West Harrison Street. The precinct bearing its name took in the most depressed part of the city. Since it included colonies of new arrivals from Europe, some of the Negro and Chinese settlements and a large portion of the red light district where thousands of women of every nationality and color lived in houses of prostitution for want of any reasonable economic alternative, sitting through a morning session of the Harrison Street police court was an eye-opening experience.

Judge Jacob Hopkins, who presided over this court for many years, made up in vigor what he lacked in dignity. When he tired of a steady diet of stabbings, shootings and sluggings, he would shout: "Bailiff, bring me in some whores!" The judge enjoyed badinage with the girls. If one of them pleaded financial inability to pay the invariable five dollar fine, he would say with a smirk: "You know where to get it, dearie, don't you?" and give her time to earn the money. Despite his broad manners, he was a tolerant and understanding magistrate.

Except for an occasional shopkeeper appearing as a complainant, the spectators at the Harrison Street court were depressing to look at. Those washed-out faces might have strayed from some planet on the wrong side of the billboards. Presumably they were witnesses, relatives, friends and enemies of defendants, but they avoided any show of interest in the proceedings. Even lawyers drooped and turned liverish in the Harrison Street court atmosphere. What sense of urgency remained was provided by a few clean, brash and alert young men who addressed attendants, lawyers and even judges by their first names, moved briskly about the courtroom to intercept a witness or perched on the edge of the judge's desk to suggest questions which might bring out a freak news angle. They showed a careless disregard for the winos, ginsoaks and stewbums, the ladies of the evening, the hoods, hopheads and lesser delinquents who had to be there. They were the lords of the press.

Other Chicago reporters—Harold O'Flaherty, Wallace Smith and Ben Hecht among them—managed to get through to the outlaws and outlanders of Harrison Street as individuals, but Westbrook wasted no time on them. So far as he was concerned there were two layers of people in the world, the weak and the strong; he sympathized with the weak, but he lined up with the strong.

He liked to tell of the trick the cops at the Harrison Street lockup used to get a confession. They kept the prisoner on the verge of starvation for days, then started a poker game just outside his cell. Loud talk among the poker players about fancy dishes to eat on top of the prisoner's own fantasies about food would usually achieve the desired result.

The young UP district man admired "the ham-handed sergeant of the Harrison Street station" who banged around vagrants taken in the regular Saturday night round-up. He also admired the sergeant in the La Salle Street detective bureau who questioned a man picked up for rolling drunks and, when the man denied it, lifted his heavy foot abruptly and knocked him "twitching in the spillage of an overturned spittoon." This was the "old reliable discretion of police work," Pegler concluded, which really controlled crime.

Those were the days in Chicago when Clarence Darrow told prisoners in the Cook County jail that they were as honest as most of the citizens outside. Westbrook knew better. In those days, Carl Sandburg worked on the staff of the Chicago *Daily News*; Pegler could never stand what he considered to be Sandburg's highbrow pretensions. Sandburg and Ben Hecht and other young reporters were drawn to the *Daybook*, a radical labor tabloid, and for a while Westbrook read the *Daybook* because it satisfied the vague hatred of the rich which he had picked up from his father.

The editor of the *Daybook* in 1912 was Daniel MacGregor, a former reporter who had become a champion of lost causes after watching unarmed miners in Ludlow, Colorado, throw rocks against the blazing rifles of a fully equipped National Guard regiment acting in a strikebreaking capacity. MacGregor died fighting in Mexico with Villa in 1916. Years later, looking back at the crusader whom he admired briefly in his youth, Westbrook Pegler dismissed MacGregor as "just another drunken, shiftless newspaperman . . . (like) the tramp telegraphers who carried their keys or bugs wherever they went . . . (and who) could sit down and go to work wherever the necessity caught them and a job offered." It never occurred to him that Arthur Pegler had also been a boomer of sorts.

In 1913 Westbrook Pegler took a $17.50-a-week job with a Scripps-Howard newspaper in Des Moines. He never returned to Chicago to live or to his parents' home. In addition to reporting, he was supposed to do some chalk-plate art work in Des Moines, but Tad Dorgan was right; the boy had no particular talent in that field. Giving up the art work soon after arrival, he concentrated thereafter on the news-gathering end of the business. When he left Chicago, Westbrook was not yet nineteen. Though he stood almost six feet tall, he weighed only 125 pounds. He had a thin neck—his brother Jack said it "looked a yard long,"—wiry not-quite-red hair, and an aggressively apprehensive manner. He was extremely conscious that he was now entirely on his own.

To Des Moines, he brought his Horatio Alger guidelines and his police court cosmos, his entire capital, consisting of twenty-two dollars in savings, and all his worldly goods, mostly well-worn clothes, in a papier-mâché suitcase. He shared a cheap room in a rooming house with another cub and ate frugally at a one-armed joint called the Baltimore Lunch so as "to squirrel away a little money every payday . . . against bad news from the desk." He worked hard not only because he was "crazy about the newspaper business," which was true enough, but also because he was, as he later confessed, "afraid." The recurring hardships inflicted on the family by Arthur Pegler had given the boy a surpassing dread of being fired. While still in Des Moines, Westbrook brought his bank balance up to $100 and for the rest of his life he never allowed the balance to drop below that level.

Des Moines was known as a nine-o'clock town, so far as respectable amusement was concerned, though various illicit enterprises flourished after that hour. Westbrook held women in high respect and resented those who did not live up to his ideals. On the other hand, he lacked the connections and cash necessary to meet and cultivate respectable girls. Even after he obtained jobs at somewhat higher pay with the United Press in other cities, marriage was not to be considered. Since single men were more mobile and less expensive to maintain, the UP actively discouraged matrimony among its younger reporters.

Early in his Des Moines service, Westbrook wrote about a raid on a brothel. Out of an impulse of disgust, he tacked a dirty line on the bottom of the story. He expected the desk to catch it, but it slid past everybody during the noon rush and showed up at the bottom of page one. Switches were pulled in a flurry and a printer had to gouge the line out with a chisel before the presses could roll again. Westbrook received weeks of punishment details, but he was not fired. As a result of that experience, he often said, he "never wrote another line even in fun which could cause a blush to mantle the fairest maiden's cheek."

After leaving Des Moines, Westbrook worked in St. Louis for the UP with the title of manager at a salary of twenty-five dollars a week. He had a staff there consisting of an office boy for whom he was allowed six dollars a week. After struggling with a series of incompetent boys, he took over the job himself, signing vouchers with a variety of imaginary names in order to collect the extra pay without arousing comment.

In St. Louis he lived in a $2.50 hotel room which boasted a washbasin with faucets. His room-mate was a local reporter from Oskaloosa named Hick Walton who received only fifteen dollars a week because he was an entirely green hand. In this and subsequent wire-service jobs, Westbrook encountered many of the strange and threatening types for whom he had been prepared by his father's anecdotes. He experienced "the social subordination," as he put it, "which poverty imposes." Worst of all, his status earned no deference from others in the business.

While he was in St. Louis, Westbrook was instructed by his superiors to register a protest with O.K. Bovard, managing editor of the *Post-Dispatch*, over the disgraceful way the *Post-Dispatch* was pirating exclusive UP interviews by Karl H. Van Wiegand. Bovard kept him waiting an hour and a half in an outer office, listened to his message with a superior smile and dismissed him with a curt: "You may go!" The young reporter never forgot that experience. Bovard, he declared was another of those journalistic characters like William Chapin, the *Evening World* city editor in New York, of whom it could be said: "To know them is to hate them."

When Westbrook worked in Dallas, he was threatened by irate readers over minor references in his stories. He wasn't the only one; he liked to tell how Marquis James "suffered tortures of fear and finally flinched when some fellow threatened to come around to the newspaper office where he was a cub (in Oklahoma) and kill him if he didn't kill the story." James confessed this in an autobiography. "That confession," Pegler once wrote, "took more courage than he failed to show in the incident at the paper." It was the kind of thing, he added, "that deters honest people from telling the stories of their lives."

As an adult, Westbrook Pegler mentioned on several occasions that he enlisted in the Navy in 1914 after the Vera Cruz incident which brought the United States and Mexico to the verge of war. Once he said he served in the Navy in both the Atlantic and the Pacific, which might have been significant, since a later enlistment involved only service in the Atlantic. He would not satisfy the curiosity aroused by his own revelations, however. He declined repeatedly to answer questions about his first experience in uniform. At the time of the Vera Cruz incident, he was under age. To judge from the sequence of his bureau jobs, he did not stay long in the Navy. The Navy Department in Washington refused to release his file unless he gave permission, and this he would not do.

Westbrook Pegler arrived in New York, the mecca of all

Midwest journalists, on the very day in 1915 that Henry Ford sailed in his peace ship, the *Oscar II*, in an effort to mediate the war which had broken out in 1914 between Great Britain and Imperial Germany. Westbrook often made fun of Henry Ford for promising "to get the boys out of the trenches by Christmas." People sent gifts of nuts to the *Oscar II* before it sailed to express their opinion of the expedition, he noted. "If you worked for Henry Ford," he once wrote with the vulgarity he reserved for special objects of derision, "you had to let him regulate your entire life, including your bowels."

For the newly arrived, poorly paid cityside legman of the UP, New York proved expensive and aloof. However, he got the shipnews run after awhile, operating out of the barge office at the Battery, and thereby obtained exciting daily glimpses of the war through the eyes of the latest refugees from Austria, Germany, France and England.

Former President Theodore Roosevelt, who was regaining popularity by advocating United States participation in the war, arrived one day from Europe. He banged a stanchion of the vessel which had brought him into port and pictured President Wilson as a "fellow who would not raise a hand if a thug punched his wife in the nose." Recalling the tableau in later years, Westbrook Pegler wrote approvingly: "We ate it up, the papers gave it a big ride!"

To Westbrook's mind, the European war was just another glorious three-alarm fire. He was determined to get a closer look at it, but that fall, through a change in circumstances, he landed out in Denver on the *Express*, a Scripps-McCrae newspaper. He always remembered Denver as a spirited town with an excellent professional baseball team. He shifted back to the United Press in 1916, becoming bureau manager in Dallas when the manager left to cover revolutionary developments in Mexico.

All three major parties held their national conventions in June 1916. The Progressives wanted Theodore Roosevelt to run again, but he was so anxious to beat Wilson that he sacrificed the party which had coalesced around him four years earlier and threw his support to Charles Evans Hughes, the regular GOP nominee.

The Democrats renominated President Wilson, who was shifting from idealistic neutrality to preparedness as a way of keeping out of war. Westbrook Pegler had a chance to stop in

St. Louis for a look at the Democratic convention before proceeding to New York. With the help of the two most influential
officials he knew in the United Press organization—Roy Howard
and Fred Ferguson—he was on his way to Europe as a war correspondent!

6. FOREIGN CORRESPONDENT

Napoleon was once asked what kind of enemy he preferred to fight. "Allies!" he replied, out of a wealth of irritating experience. Westbrook Pegler did not intend to take a Napoleonic stance during World War I—he was only doing his job, he said —yet the French and British officials on whom he was quartered found him difficult. Some reacted with rage, others with jokes about Kaiser Wilhelm's "secret weapon." Even high-ranking Americans—diplomats, military leaders, cabinet members—felt the sting of his displeasure. He was extremely self-righteous; only in later years did he concede any mistakes on his part. "I was terrible as a foreign correspondent," he once wrote in retrospective confession. "I was in trouble all the time." He remained grateful for the chance to go abroad, but he swung around to a belief that those who did, under the existing circumstances, were fools.

Some blame should be attached to the United Press, he argued, and to its "abuse of the byline." The more staid Associated Press clung to anonymous reports by its correspondents long after the newer agency made competitive headway with personalized accounts. The United Press deliberately "sent spirited and talented kids rattling off around the globe" at substandard wages to compete with adequately paid and more experienced correspondents. A signature on stories and a shot at fame were supposed to be worth extra pay. This made sense for those who succeeded, but it took no account of the wastage among those like young Pegler who barely qualified for foreign service in the first place and who were almost doomed to failure.

Westbrook was only twenty-one when he sailed from New York on the S.S. *St. Louis* in June 1916. He took with him his extra suit and a few other modest possessions in the papier-mâché suitcase which had been his traveling companion since he left home in 1913.

He labored under a vague impression that differences in the exchange would permit "almost voluptuous living in London" until William J. Burns of the UP home office, who came aboard to see him off, warned him at the last minute to "go easy on expenses." The other passengers on the *St. Louis*, mostly buyers, promoters, entertainers and adventurers, assumed cheerfully that a foreign correspondent must be not only influential but also well paid. In the glow created by these false assumptions, the young reporter managed during a week's crossing to spend a year's savings at the bar.

Disillusionment began on arrival. Wilbur S. Forrest, whose standing in the London bureau was attested by the fact that he was permitted to have a wife, escorted Pegler to a rooming house in Bloomsbury. There he introduced his wife and baby daughter before showing the newcomer the room he was to share with Hal O'Flaherty, a native of Des Moines with Chicago newspaper experience. Because of restrictions on the use of coal, the O'Flaherty-Pegler ménage was often cold and clammy. The room offered a pitcher and bowl for washing. The house, a creaky walk-up, had bare floors, little furniture and a single tub in a makeshift room under a staircase. Since gas was expensive, a bath cost three pence extra. After taking one, an American lodger would sometimes be asked by Mrs. Jo McKenzie, the landlady, to leave the water since her little boy Joe " 'adn't 'ad 'is yet."

The UP office was located in Temple Chambers off Fleet Street in a building resembling an old stone fortress. On the night trick, to which he was immediately assigned as the lowest member on the bureau totem pole, Westbrook Pegler struggled through the dark hours with a news budget of 2,400 words which had to be handled in cablese, a system for combining words to reduce the cable tolls. His trick ran from 9:00 P.M. to 7:00 A.M. with no provision for a lunch hour. No restaurant was open during those hours anyway, but he was able to brew tea from time to time on a grate.

Despite headaches and a feeling of concern over the pollution of the air by a leaky gas heater, Westbrook took pains over a nightly feature which went by mail. Sometimes the New York bureau of United Press would not use it at all, or would feed it in as background for some newly received skeletonized news cable. When it appeared without change in print it was signed by W. J. Pegler—which had more dignity than his earlier by Bud Pegler.

The added byline out of London attracted no particular attention. Hal O'Flaherty was soon lured from the bureau by the New York *Sun* for a fabulous fifty dollars a week, plus ten dollars in expenses. Others moved on to gaudier jobs at higher pay, but not Pegler. His salary—five pounds, 12 shillings and six pence —worked out to twenty-seven fifty a week. This barely purchased subsistence: cigarettes, perhaps, and a rare glass of beer, but not cigars, liquor, taxis, fancy food, new clothes or sex.

Pegler found London inconvenient, depressing and grim. It took days to get a suit cleaned and weeks to get a watch repaired. Drably uniformed women worked in the subways and on the buses, which stopped running at midnight. Most autos had been commandeered for war work or prohibited to save gasoline, and taxis were scarce. Because of the menace of Zeppelin raids, street globes were painted black half way down, shop windows went without light at night and trams and buses ran with dimmed lights.

At the time of Pegler's arrival, the London bureau consisted of Ed Keen, the manager, Wilbur Forrest, Bob Getty, and Hal O'Flaherty. Later recruits included Arthur Mann, Lowell Mellett and Webb Miller. By 1917, the bureau had a weekly pool to see who lost the least weight. Shoppers waited in queues outside stores for rationed foods; and restaurants served soggy bread without butter and saccharine tablets instead of sugar. The effect of the food restrictions could be seen in the drawn and sunken faces of people in the street.

Romance eluded Westbrook Pegler in London. For a while he arched his neck, as he put it, at a young American vaudeville dancer about his own age whom he had met on the *St. Louis.* Since his day off (more properly, his night off) seldom came around, arranging a date was difficult. Several dates were eventually achieved, but they did not amount to much because of his lack of money for entertainment. On one occasion, the couple was starting on a stroll—"about cruising speed for a UP reporter," Pegler noted sardonically in telling the story—when Zeppelins floated overhead at three thousand feet. Noisy but futile firing from three-inch field guns, driven hurriedly into position on trucks, curtailed any possible courting that night. Westbrook had an aunt living in London near the famous tavern, The Elephant and Castle. He paid a formal visit soon after arrival and then forgot about her. Only after the war did he learn that she had been killed during a Zeppelin raid.

Though his father also came from London, Westbrook regarded "limeys" with disdain. Those whom he encountered in Bloomsbury were unforgiveably noisy. Daytime sleeping in that

69

cheap quarter would have been difficult for anybody, but it was particularly difficult for an uneasy head like young Pegler.

Every morning, it seemed, he would be awakened about the same time by the song of the same street beggar. Later a girl would cry an old chanty for sweet lavender outside the house. A milk peddler yodelled: "milk, milk," a catmeat man yelled "meat, meat," and a rose woman loudly offered roses. Time and again, the American would stumble to the window to protest and lose his sleep by defending it. Soon after he returned to bed, there would be another inevitable daytime sound—the cry of a child, perhaps, or the quarreling of adults—normal for that part of London at that time of day, but fresh proof to the harried youngster of conspiracy against his rest and peace of mind.

When he finally shifted to the day side, Westbrook tried to make good quickly in the Chicago manner. That is, he thrust inquisitive questions at every possible target. To his news sources, the questions might well have seemed "derisive, suspicious, faintly hostile."

Once a week, he and other American reporters had the privilege of calling on Ambassador Walter Hines Page at his office. The Ambassador was more pro-British than President Wilson, who owed his reelection that year to a slogan that he had kept the country out of war, but Page tried to keep his comments within the framework of American policy. He soon showed annoyance over Pegler's weekly inquisition.

The new correspondent thought he could trace the origin of the obvious strain between him and the sixty-one-year-old Ambassador. After greeting the press, Walter Hines Page had a way of dropping back into his chair and lighting his cigar to suggest informality. One day Pegler found his own chair, lit a cigarette and started puffing. The ambassador was not pleased. "Old Uncle Walter," Pegler explained to his friends, "was rude in the cultured manner and would have liked to keep us standing and do all the smoking himself." In a moment of frankness, he added that he himself was accustomed to dealing with police lieutenants and local politicians.

News agency men also visited the British Chief of Army Operations, General Frederick F.M. Maurice. His handouts seldom provided solid news. However, the military situation was becoming desperate. Roumania had collapsed and Russia was down and out. The British lines in France were being smashed by artillery fire. Westbrook sought a statement of relative air superiority over the Western Front. When he received no answer, he asked the question repeatedly for three weeks, until the General begged the UP to send around some other boy, a request which under war conditions they could not refuse.

Early in January 1917, President Wilson extended unexpected feelers for a "peace-without-victory" conference between the warring powers. Since American sentiment had been veering noticeably toward the Allies, Britain showed more disappointment over this offer than Germany. Nevertheless, no visiting Americans of importance escaped the red-carpet treatment. One day a call came to the UP office for coverage of a reception for a Harvard University medical unit, including nurses, at Buckingham Palace. Pegler was the only person available. He went to the locker where the office kept a frock coat and topper for such emergencies. After glancing in the mirror at the drape of the coat on his shoulders, he decided to stick to the blue serge suit and checked cap which had proved adequate for chasing fires and photographs in Chicago.

When the King and Queen appeared on the terrace, all but one of the reporters took off their headgear. Catching on tardily to what was expected, Westbrook yanked at his cap just as the King, trying to save the situation with politeness, murmured that uncovering would not be required at this time. Unfortunately, the remark emphasized the original mistake of the reporter and stressed the unsuitability of his cap amid the prevailing silkiness of toppers.

After receiving the American contingent in the sunken garden of the palace grounds, the King and Queen returned to the terrace. Again every reporter but one uncovered. An English journalist joggled Westbrook from behind with an umbrella, mouthing: "Uncover, you fool." Pegler turned around to glare. "Put on your hat, you fool," he replied. "HE said so!" The words were entirely too audible, and every eye focused on the blue-serge shoulders turned in incredible affront to the royal presences.

The course of history was not thereby diverted. When the Kaiser, under pressure from his war lords, broke his year-old pledge to the United States not to resume unrestricted submarine warfare, President Wilson went before a special joint session of Congress on February 3, 1917, to announce that he was severing relations with the German Empire.

The Germans were gambling on quick victory. In April, when the U.S. finally declared war, the U-boats sank 900,000 tons of shipping. By June, their bag had risen to 1,000,000 tons a month. Since the Allies had a margin of only a few million tons of shipping over the total required to carry on the war, the Central Powers seemed to be on the verge of winning. The Allies devised new tactics to beat the U-boats, including the arming of American merchantmen and the adoption of a convoy system. The first armed American liner to cross the Atlantic was Pegler's old friend the *St. Louis*, which had bolt holes for gun mounts in the stern deck from prior service as a cruiser in 1898.

Ordered down to Liverpool to greet the *St. Louis*, Westbrook discovered to his surprise that several reporters, including Jack Lawrence, with whom he had once covered shipnews in New York, were among the passengers. Lawrence grinned over the persistent efforts of his highly competitive friend to get a quick "fill-in" on the trip. Nothing exciting happened, he said, except that the stern gun of the *St. Louis* had blazed away at a submarine the day before.

Pegler rushed to a phone booth on the pier. Fortunately, a steward from the *St. Louis*, who wanted to phone his home, overheard the reporter talking to his office in London. He volunteered that the object shot at was not a submarine but a dead mule from a sunken transport. Just in time, Pegler revised his bulletin about the first American military action against the Germans, which would have made him and his agency look ridiculous. As it was, his few paragraphs about the arrival of the *St. Louis* went out immediately and led the news in American papers. The balanced, lengthy reports of Lawrence and his pals, who waited to file until they reached London, ran into censorship trouble and then were drowned in a wave of concern over a fresh German offensive in France.

Admiral William S. Sims, commander of U.S. naval forces operating in European waters, was the foremost proponent of the convoy system. To increase its effectiveness, he arranged for an American flotilla of six destroyers to base in Queenstown, the Irish port into which American traffic poured with the elements of war for Britain's defense. Pegler was sent to Queenstown just after the flotilla's arrival. The best he could obtain was one of those stilted exchanges which land inevitably in the history books.

When Admiral Lewis Bayly, the crusty old sea dog who

commanded British naval units in Queenstown, asked Commander Joseph K. Taussig when his destroyers would be fit for duty, the American replied: "We are ready now, sir!"

Putting American destroyers under Bayly's command created a delicate situation. There had already been bitter charges in the United States that our warships abroad would operate exclusively under foreign control. There was danger that Bayly would make the situation worse; he hated publicity—he had tried to keep the convoy plan secret in Britain long after it was announced in America—and he particularly disliked American reporters, since their stories about one of his early escapades had resulted in his dismissal as a young naval attaché in Washington. Admiral Sims, a wily operator who had advised American presidents from Grover Cleveland to Woodrow Wilson, therefore persuaded his old friend, Admiral John Jellicoe, first sea lord of the British Admiralty, to promote Bayly and give him a short leave. Bayly then became amenable to suggestions that his American colleague take over command of Anglo-American naval forces in Queenstown during his absence.

Despite instructions to be circumspect in his dealings with Admiral Sims, Pegler had no intention of overlooking a good story. He was determined to steal a march on his only American competitor, a good-humored and tactful AP man named Frank America. Pegler observed that American naval officers and bluejackets were regarded with jealousy because they spent more for drinks than the British. Brawls had actually broken out in Queenstown pubs over the wider swath cut by the better-paid American sailors with the local girls. He developed a short feature on the subject which passed the censor.

Sims was shocked. A story like that, he said, undermined his efforts to create Anglo-American naval unity. The United States was at war, he pointed out, and the national interest had to be considered. He got nowhere with the young UP correspondent who stuck to the point that there had been no violation of censorship.

A day or so later Flag Lieutenant Babcock, one of the Admiral's aides, told Westbrook Pegler and Frank America that an American destroyer, the *O'Brien*, had "probably" bagged the first submarine in the intensified campaign against U-boats. To keep German admirals awake at night worrying over their overdue undersea craft and to disguise the means of destruction, whether by Q-boats—as armed merchantmen were coming to be known

73

—by airplanes, submarine chasers or larger naval units, a rule barring publicity on the sinking of submarines had been promulgated. The experienced AP correspondent therefore ignored the lead but the new UP hand sent a story through without confirmation. On instructions from Ed Keen, he persuaded Commander Orelbar, the censor, to sign a carbon copy of the dispatch.

Arrested in an undignified fashion by an orderly who was not even an officer and haled before Admiral Sims on a charge of sending a "fake dispatch," Pegler shouted that he had an excellent source for his story—and censorship approval. "I have an initialed carbon right here," he said, waving his duplicate.

"Let me see it," said the Admiral.

"Yes," said the reporter, dancing nearer. "I'll let you see it, but I'm not going to let you get your hands on it!"

The Admiral's answer was a weary shrug. His formal statement that the UP had sent out "an absolutely false story" was picked up and widely circulated in the United States by the Associated Press to create an impression that the rival agency was generally unreliable and a liar.

After three days open arrest in Queenstown, Pegler was sent to London. There he remained in the technical custody of Consul Hathaway, who treated his prisoner to lectures on philology during long walks. Meanwhile, Roy Howard, the UP president, was having fits over in New York. In some danger of discharge, Pegler handed his carbon to Ed Keen, who forwarded it to Howard, who took it personally to Navy Secretary Josephus Daniels in Washington.

Secretary Daniels considered Admiral Sims to be opinionated beyond his station, and he may also have been jealous of the Admiral's influence at the White House. On the basis of the evidence, and to show who was boss of the Navy Department, he reversed Sims and ordered Pegler restored to journalistic freedom.

Before the UP correspondent could return in triumph to Queenstown, Admiral Bayly resumed his old command there. After a chat with Admiral Sims, who was leaving for his regular headquarters at the American Embassy in London, the British admiral decided to ignore the recommendation from the American cabinet officer that Pegler be reinstated. The only way to put pressure on Bayly was through the British Admiralty and the only way to appeal to the British Admiralty was through Ambassador Page and Admiral Sims. Under the circumstances, Pegler's superiors found it advisable a few weeks later to raise his salary to forty-five dollars a week and to hustle him off to the war in France.

To please the newspaper publishers and Director of War Information George Creel, President Wilson had agreed to attach a press section to the American Expeditionary Force in France. General John J. Pershing, the A.E.F. Commander, doubted the wisdom of this innovation. He could not buck his Commander-in-Chief but he could and did impose restrictions to keep the correspondents in line. No more than twenty-one persons could be accommodated conveniently at one time at the Hotel de la Providence at Neufchateau which was designated as press headquarters, so twenty-one became the limit.

Candidates for admission to this exclusive club—whose membership, including replacements, eventually reached fifty or more—were judged largely by their newspaper circulation. Each applicant was supposed to get approval from three out of four cabinet members—the Secretaries of War, Navy, and State and the Attorney General—but this rule did not apply to the news services which rotated their men.

Westbrook Pegler did have to sign the customary pledge of good behavior, which was guaranteed by a $5,000 bond. The UP produced another $5,000 in cash for the use of a Cadillac and a chauffeur behind the lines. To prevent unauthorized jaunts by the newsmen, who wore brassards on the left sleeve—green for intelligence with a super-imposed scarlet C for Correspondent-with-Cadillac-and-Chauffeur—these cars were required back in garage every day by dark, but the rule was not strictly enforced.

The first American troops landed on French soil in June 1917. Protected by convoys against serious loss of life from submarines, the A.E.F. grew enormously during the next eighteen months until it reached a total of two million men under arms. Regulations for reporting the activities of these soldiers were gradually relaxed, but they never became simple or easy to follow.

One initial difficulty was that no American in uniform, except General Pershing, could be identified by name. Heywood Broun, a large, sloppy correspondent with claustrophobia and flat feet, made an early dent in this rule by revealing in a New York *Tribune* dispatch that it was Paymaster Stanton, not General Pershing, who coined the celebrated phrase: "Lafayette, we are here!" Broun argued that the basic service rendered by the

75

press in any war was to present those who did the fighting in a sympathetic light to the worried folks back home and that this could hardly be accomplished without an occasional portrait.

Westbrook Pegler arrived at the Hotel de la Providence on July 23, 1917. Some of his colleagues had noticed a strikingly beautiful sixteen-year-old girl, Henriette Moratille, working in the kitchen and they persuaded her mother, the proprietor of the hotel, to assign her exclusively to their mess. Henriette's gentle manners and innocence intrigued all the American correspondents, but Pegler soon became her special knight errant and protector. Though his intentions were entirely platonic, they became so marked that Mme. Moratille found it necessary to warn him publicly and pointedly about the terrible uncertainties of romance in wartime.

The young UP correspondent, the baby of the mess, found many things to gripe at, ranging from the "idiotic" use of spiral puttees by American soldiers to a rule by Roy Howard, based on a patriotic appeal from the Cleveland *Press*, that he describe the soldiers as "Sammies." None of the other correspondents used "Sammies" in their stories. This irritant was dissolved by George M. Cohan's song "Over There," after which everybody wrote about the soldiers as "Yanks," but the puttees continued in use.

He knew he was "troublesome" to his colleagues and to the military authorities, but he believed that he was just doing his duty. He had to face tough competition. Neufchateau correspondents in his time included Damon Runyon, who wrote labor songs for striking Colorado miners long before he became a chronicler of Broadway sports; Floyd Gibbons, whose personal account of the sinking of the British liner *Laconia* helped to bring the United States into the war; Wythe Williams, Will Irwin, Edwin L. James and others who were already well-known.

Possible approaches to the assignment varied. Heywood Broun, whom Westbrook distrusted because he wrote without apparent effort and because he seemed to have private means—two rather similar offenses—created copy out of homely details of crapshooting, Paris leaves and language difficulties. A petulant fat man named Alexander Woollcott wandered off one morning in a battered car which did not have to return to garage that night because it was owned by the soldiers' newspaper, the *Stars and Stripes*; somehow he found Major Whittelsey's famous Lost Battalion. Most flamboyant of the every-correspondent-his-own-hero school, Floyd Gibbons caught his left eye (or said he did;

Pegler never believed it) in his palm as a bullet nicked it out of his head in a wheatfield near Chateau Thierry; ever after, he wore a conspicuous white patch over the ruined socket.

Pegler made a flight in a French artillery spotter with two propellers driven by bicycle chains from one engine, and he filed some acceptable features, but he remained generally among those who concentrated so hard on getting the news first that they often fumbled the meaning of the event or blurred the details.

Some of his colleagues reported on visits to a house which was not a home in Paris, where several rooms were lined with peach-colored mirrors and where girls of many nations were available, but Pegler heeded the warnings he received about this place and did not allow his curiosity to overpower his principles.

All the correspondents except one went over to Gondrecourt one day. Upon their return to Neufchateau, they found the UP man pounding his typewriter. By 5:00 P.M., the rumor was all over the Hotel de la Providence that young Pegler had obtained an exclusive interview with General Pershing at general headquarters in Chaumont! A meeting was called to quiz the culprit. Pegler was reluctant at first to answer questions. He looked at the ceiling thoughtfully as if in doubt as to how much of his tête-à-tête with the Commander-in-Chief he wanted to disclose. Finally he said: "I got in to see the General. I said: 'General Pershing, I'm Pegler of the United Press. Can you give me a statement on how things stand at the front?' The General looked up from his desk. 'Pegler,' he said, 'Get the hell out of my office!' "

Censorship bothered all the correspondents, but particularly Pegler. Since the United States contingents trained with the French before going into combat, the French had the final say. They refused to clear stories about soldiers getting influenza and pneumonia from living in leaky-roof sheet barns, unheated except for salamanders. The French censors considered such housing adequate for wartime. Similarly, they saw no objection to the piles of manure in the yards outside the barns; manure had a nice healthy smell, they said. They attributed most complaints to the notorious rudeness of the Yanks.

Most of the correspondents realized that there were fifteen thousand newspapermen back home eligible to replace them if they talked themselves out of a job. Pegler, at twenty-three the youngest and most insecure of the Neufchateau aristocrats, showed least caution. From the moment he reported for duty at Gondrecourt to Captain George Marshall, an aide to one of the Generals, and caught his first glimpse of a cavalry captain named George Patton for whom he contracted a "hostile admiration," he was loud in his protests over regulations.

George Seldes, who wrote for the Chicago *Tribune* during World War I, and who subsequently became a conspicuous radical, filed a report on Westbrook in a book of reminiscences in which he said that the UP man stayed at Neufchateau "only a few loud, raw and belligerent months, and the parting was a mutual satisfaction. The Army was there for war, and it did not want minor battles in its own ranks."

A series of incidents between August and December 1917 led the UP reporter to focus his resentment on Major General Dennis E. Nolan, head of intelligence, and on General Pershing himself. The first incident arose from an inspection of base ports in France. During this the A.E.F. Commander learned that working parties of German prisoners would often shout up in friendly fashion to American troops arriving in ships and that some soldiers from cities like Chicago and Milwaukee would shout back in German or toss down cigarettes and chocolate bars as gifts. At Chaumont, General Pershing dictated a sharp memorandum to Neufchateau deploring the fact that Americans did not feel enough hatred for the enemy—and blaming the press for this condition!

Pershing had touched a tender spot. Few correspondents, and virtually none of the young ones, showed any conscience or social thought in their stories. They brushed aside serious issues and great events except insofar as these contributed to enliven their dispatches.

With two or three exceptions, the correspondents did not even know enough French to make genuine contact with the natives. The kernels of truth in the General's memorandum did not prevent him from being generally denounced at Neufchateau and particularly denounced by Pegler, who considered the memorandum a personal insult in the light of censorship rules.

A.E.F. headquarters gave advance notice of an inspection of the First Division in the Gondrecourt training area. The correspondents drove over in their Cadillacs in plenty of time. General Pershing had hardly started down the line of troops when he noticed a recruit chewing gum and wearing a sprig of evergreen in the blue infantry ribbon on his campaign hat. The General stopped abruptly. "Sergeant!" he bellowed to the nearest noncommissioned officer. "Put your finger in that man's mouth and pull out that chewing gum, Sergeant. Pull that weed out of his hat!"

After the Sergeant accomplished these delicate missions, the General continued: "Take that man out of there! Make him stand at attention for ten minutes and make the rest of the company stand at attention, too. YOU, TOO, CAPTAIN!"

Several correspondents who had refused General Pershing's offer of simulated rank because they considered themselves superior to officers, agreed that the last-minute verbal slap at the captain was degrading and bad for discipline. As for the offending soldier, he had been "treated like a dog," Pegler decided, "for gawking like a movie fan at the great General Pershing." Worst of all, the censors refused to clear any references to the incident.

War Secretary Newton D. Baker paid a propaganda visit about this time to the growing American military establishment in France. Some correspondents, though not Pegler, quoted Baker —"during a visit to the front"—as saying: "This is the furthest outpost of democracy!" No doubt some Army press agent at Chaumont put the factually false, but sentimentally apt phrase in the Secretary's mouth. There were, in fact, no American troops closer to the front than Neufchateau, which was approximately thirty-five kilometers behind the line. Pegler held Pershing personally responsible for not correcting this false story—which he had missed, but which the Associated Press had used!

Eventually, the first American troops did move into the line. Neufchateau had been promised coverage, but General Nolan at G-2 decided at the last minute to try to fool the Germans by withholding the news temporarily from the American press.

Many of the correspondents, including Pegler, were lured down to Lyons to inspect field ovens where bread was being baked for the Army. Passing through Dijon on the way back, they learned from drivers of an American wagon train that the First Division had moved into the trenches while they were, in Pegler's words, "off on a wild-goose chase!"

It turned out that the Germans had been kept sufficiently informed by their spies to be able to give the Yanks a thorough shelling upon arrival in the trenches. More serious from the point of view of the United Press, the finer network of the Associated Press was able to pick up the American troop movement for a clean beat on one of the biggest stories of the war.

Unable at last to restrain himself, Pegler drew up an indictment of General Nolan who "lied to the correspondents and broke his word," and of General Pershing who "never smiled at an enlisted soldier except in pinning a medal on him for the movie cameras, when he would suddenly put out his hand and relax his iron face." He described inspection fiascoes on the Western Front with appropriate comments about Secretary Baker and General Pershing. He cited various unreported hardships suffered by the soldiers, ranging from leaky barns, porous shoes and inadequate supplies of underwear to "that idiotic British spiral puttee, which was adapted in India to repel snakes and which consumed millions of man hours in putting them on and taking them off and rolling."

Pegler arranged for Lowell Mellett to take the letter to Ed Keen, who was then in Paris, with the expectation that it would be forwarded to the all-powerful Roy Howard, who was assuming the dominant role in the young reporter's imagination which Arthur Pegler had held during his boyhood. Once Howard understood the difficulties under which American soldiers and reporters were laboring in France, he would presumably take appropriate steps. Pegler had no intention, he insisted subsequently, of evading censorship, but the fact remained that other correspondents used letters of this kind to slide censorable material into print.

George Pattulo, an amiable fellow who worked for the *Saturday Evening Post*, drove over from Chaumont one afternoon to tell Westbrook Pegler confidentially that he was about to be relieved and that his replacement, Fred Ferguson, was already chosen. Ed Keen had entrusted the letter to the mails and the censors had grabbed it. At General Pershing's request, Pegler was being discredited by Secretary Baker on the ground that he was "too young."

The UP reporter knew there was no appeal. Picking a time when most of his colleagues were out on stories, he said an almost tearful goodbye to the pure and lovely Henriette, darling of the mess, piled his gear into a car and left for Troyes and Paris. Ed Keen expressed annoyance over Secretary Baker's action but he could not contest it. Not even Roy Howard could help. Though Pegler was not fired by the United Press, it was obvious that he was finished, for this particular war at least, as a reporter in Europe.

7. THE ROMANCE IN HIS LIFE

If experience is the commodity for which a man exchanges his youth, Westbrook Pegler could no longer be considered young by the time he got back to New York. First he had a long wait in London with no prospect except an inglorious return to the United States. Then he tried a patriotic alternative which landed him in Liverpool for an interminable year of desk duty with the Navy. Both London and Liverpool gave him unlimited time to review the incidents which had brought him low. During this period he became adult by introspection—an unpleasant way to grow up.

This was the sequence: He left Neufchateau in March 1918. Fred Ferguson took his place there early in April but another UP man had to be selected in the United States, freed from existing commitments and ferried across the submarine-infested Atlantic to fill Ferguson's spot in London. Webb Miller, when he finally arrived, was shifted temporarily to Paris to cover the visit of Assistant Secretary of the Navy Franklin D. Roosevelt. Pegler therefore marked time in London until June 1918.

Roosevelt's purpose was to emphasize the growing success of the Allied anti-submarine campaign which foreshadowed eventual victory on land. In addition to being only thirty-six, handsome and smartly dressed, F.D.R. was the first high American official to reach France during the war with a fluent command of French. His manner as he leaned against the mantelpiece of the United States Embassy in Paris and chatted with the French reporters in their own language was a diplomatic, naval and linguistic triumph, Webb Miller reported upon his return to London.

Because of his service abroad as a journalist, Pegler was not registered for the draft. Instead of going to New York to register and await a call to duty which might never come, he joined the U.S. Navy in London in June. The name of Westbrook James Pegler under which he enlisted fitted his passport as well as his new "By W. J. Pegler" byline, though it deviated from the James and J. Westbrook Pegler he used at other times and places.

In view of his prior service in the Navy after the Vera Cruz incident, this counted as a second enlistment. It was for a full four years, not the duration of the war. Assigned to Liverpool, he lived in barracks there and worked in the Northwestern Hotel, shore headquarters of the receiving ship. During the twelve months he actually served, he rose imperceptibly in rank from landsman to yeoman second class. As a sailor he was never afloat.

Neither Admiral Sims, Assistant Secretary Roosevelt, Secretary Daniels nor any other important American official showed any interest, friendly or otherwise, in the correspondent's naval career. His job consisted in typing orders for the officers and in attending to their correspondence. When he was on duty, he obeyed orders. When he was off duty, according to his letters, he tried to stay drunk as much as he could. He seems to have been a glum and rather solitary drinker with no taste for collateral amusements. On occasion he went soberly at night with the shore patrol —"walking the streets of Liverpool," as he put it, "keeping bluejackets out of trouble." For all the attention he received from the busy correspondents who used to be his colleagues, he might have been dead or in jail.

Like any clerk leaving an office under a cloud, the lonely and disappointed young reporter could not help wondering where he had gone wrong. He blamed Lowell Mellett and Floyd Gibbons for the fatal dispatch of his letter of complaint to Roy Howard. The letter was to be relayed only under specified conditions and it was definitely not intended for publication. Pegler's assumption was that Howard would raise hell at the White House over General Pershing's failures in France. He told Mellett that if his allegations were deemed sufficiently serious he would take the risk of putting it up to Keen to decide whether to send the letter on to Howard. That gave the others some leeway, particularly Mellett, who was older and more experienced than Pegler. During his pre-French service in the London bureau, Pegler remembered he had been stuck unduly long on the night side because Lowell Mellett took advantage of his age and experience to avoid a regular night trick. Mellett was a "schemer," the reporter decided out of his distress and bitterness. "Doubtless he realized that I was gutting myself on my own determination," he thought, translating suspicion into fact. "He wanted to eliminate me to make one step for himself."

In retrospect Floyd Gibbons seemed even more culpable: here was a veteran who advised a kid to stake his career on an indiscreet letter! Yet the man known to the American public as the greatest correspondent in World War I had also been a personal hero to Westbrook Pegler. Nobody could "belly up" more impressively than he to an important news source. Pegler would never forget the evening when Lloyd George entered Simpson's in London. Gibbons rose immediately and swept over to the British Prime Minister, booming out what a great pleasure it was to see him—and introducing the other correspondents with whom he had been dining!

Gibbons put "guts" into his dispatches but Pegler did not rate him as a stylist with Philip Gibbs, the British correspondent, who "had a musical kind of thing with a lot of brass, like a wave on the beach." Pegler would have liked to write like Philip Gibbs. Floyd Gibbons was brave, even reckless, Pegler conceded, but he deserved no applause for contributing his eye to the war effort. In the first place, he "conned" a Marine officer into taking him to an exposed spot where they had no business at all. The officer actually refused to go until the correspondent taunted him with cowardice. The officer was punished as well as wounded, whereas Gibbons emerged a hero with a fake story about catching his eye in his hand. Subsequent reports had come to Pegler that Gibbons "never gave the Marine officer the slightest recognition afterward." His great size and loud rough voice were so persuasive, Pegler thought, that people continued to trust Gibbons even after they had been put on warning.

Gibbons's secret asset in France was his boss, Major Robert R. McCormick, publisher and part owner of the Chicago *Tribune*, who had come overseas to command a battery of First Division artillery. It was through a visit to LeValdehon, where McCormick's batteries were training, that Gibbons and Raymond Carroll of the Philadelphia *Public Ledger* got their advance tip on the October movement of the Yanks into the line which G-2 prevented Pegler and other correspondents from learning about until it was over. After Pegler left France, Gibbons himself broke censorship. He paid no penalty because he had the support of McCormick, one of the few men in France feared by General Pershing.

Pegler never forgave Gibbons, Ambassador Page, Admiral Sims, General Maurice, General Nolan and General Pershing. Walter Hines Page, almost forty years older than Pegler, had been a distinguished journalist and the editor who made the *Atlantic Monthly* the best-known magazine in America long before he entered politics, but to the reporter he was just "a pompous and fawning old fathead." Similarly the world-famous William S. Sims shrank in his estimate to "a protégé of T.R. who said little to any reporter."

Soon after he arrived in Liverpool, Pegler heard with satisfaction that General Maurice, who barred him from press conferences for asking legitimate questions, had "gotten in a jam himself and been canned." The correspondent-in-exile developed fantasies of similar disgrace for Ambassador Page and Admiral Sims which failed to come true. Again and again he recalled how he had hidden his precious carbon-stamped dupes in his long-handled drawers so nobody could discover them and how he had fished them out to show Sims across a desk but not close enough to risk a sudden grab by "that bastard . . . that old fool . . ."

Pegler was giving himself a thorough training in implacable hate. Once his views hardened toward those whom he considered his persecutors, they were not subject to change. Decades later, he was still denouncing them in identical terms. When Admiral Sims died in 1936, the columnist noted that he "went to his grave without making the slightest gesture toward rehabilitating the reputation he had been willing to destroy." Even a mental association with these wartime enemies could prove hazardous. One reason why Westbrook Pegler could never cotton to Harry S. Truman was that the President, like General Pershing, came from Missouri and looked somewhat like the A.E.F. Commander!

While Pegler remained tied to his typewriter in Liverpool, Fred Ferguson, Webb Miller, William Allen White and a dozen others went on to win journalistic renown. Ed Keen scored important news beats by sending bulletins at urgent rates to the United Press office in Buenos Aires and from there across the Andes and up the West coast of South America to New York before rivals could get theirs on the congested North Atlantic cables.

The war ended in a blaze of controversy over Roy Howard's premature armistice. Howard, who had come to Europe to show his subordinates how to beat the Associated Press, sent his dispatch about the success of armistice negotiations on November 7, 1918—four days too soon. His failure to check properly on an almost true tip produced what was called "the greatest fake" and "the most gigantic gaffe" in newspaper history. The cost to New York City alone for clearing away the debris from the false celebration amounted to eighty thousand dollars. Yet Howard remained in charge of the United Press, unscathed except for a slap on the wrist by Colonel Edward M. House, President Wilson's confidential investigator, who cleared him of malice if not poor judgment.

Those who had been playing conspicuous war roles were seeking vantage points for postwar careers. Heywood Broun began a three-day-a-week local column on literary and related matters for the New York *Tribune*. Assistant Secretary of the Navy Roosevelt made speeches around the country to draw attention to himself as a prospect for the Democratic national ticket the following year.

Floyd Gibbons had been handed the Paris bureau of the Chicago *Tribune* at the end of the war by Major McCormick, but he soon arranged his own tour of the U.S.—as a vaudeville hero. He played the Palace in New York under the personal management of Jack Pegler, who was establishing himself there as an advertising and public relations man.

The association between his older brother and the correspondent whom he blamed for much of the troubles discomfited Westbrook Pegler, but it was nothing compared to the blow delivered by Army intelligence in the spring of 1919. There had been controversy over who were legitimate correspondents with the A.E.F. and who were not, so G-2 issued a list of those accredited at any time to Neufchateau along with the dates of their service. There was one notable omission: Westbrook Pegler! He was not even on a special list of three correspondents, including Heywood Broun, who had been "suspended" for violation of censorship. It did not seem likely that General Nolan or anybody associated with him would take revenge for unpublished insults in the intercepted letter to Roy Howard, yet the fact remained that Pegler, still in limbo in Liverpool, had been treated as a non-person and that his eight months of service in France had been erased from the official records.

Some time during the night of June 11, 1920, a .45 caliber bullet, fired pointblank at the forehead of Joseph Browne Elwell, ended that individual's flamboyant double career in amour and cards. Elwell's pajama-clad body was found next morning lying on the floor in the reception room of his brownstone house in the Central Park West section of Manhattan. Since he had been the foremost authority on bridge whist in the world, as well as a notorious philanderer, the murder drew reporters from all over town.

Arriving tardily on the stoop of the Elwell house and finding the front door locked and the doorbell unresponsive, the young man from the United Press looked around for a quick fill-in on the story. The young woman from the New York *Daily News* was willing to oblige. Briskly and competently, with a trace of Southern accent in her voice, she recounted the facts at her disposal, thereby initiating a lifelong relationship between them.

Julia Harpman, known as Julie, was then twenty-four. A native of Memphis, she had worked on the *Commercial Appeal* in her home town before coming to New York early in 1920 with sixty dollars in cash, a scrapbook of clippings and letters of character from the chief of police, a judge and a clergyman. She was of medium height with long brown hair parted to the right and brushed back from a serious face. She had remarkable brown eyes, a firm nose and the sort of mouth which the women's magazines describe as generous.

She was a natural reporter; her first New York assignment had proved that. Phil Payne, the *Daily News* city editor, wanted to discover whether the vestry of the Church of the Ascension on Fifth Avenue would uphold or repudiate the Rev. Percy Stickney Grant for using the edifice as a political forum. At the church, Julie Harpman walked up the wrong flight of stairs. Encountering a tailor making altar vestments, she asked about the meeting and was told it had just been held. The tailor confided that he had been listening outside the door and that the vestry had voted in favor of Dr. Grant. Confronting some remaining vestrymen in another room, Miss Harpman confirmed the tailor's statement sufficiently for a story.

The tailor, however, had mentioned another meeting. Julie Harpman walked in on this and took a rear seat as if she belonged there. A red-headed man was haranguing the audience. In a whisper Julie asked a determined-looking woman seated near her if the speaker was the ex-Governor Sulzer who had been sent to Albany by Tammany and later impeached by Tammany. "That's Governor Sulzer, not ex-Governor!" replied the woman angrily, thereby providing the necessary identification. Miss Harpman's subsequent account of the inflammatory Sulzer speech—which included a suggestion for blowing up the Capitol in Albany—gave depth and drama to the vestry decision.

The *Daily News* was born during a conference on July 20, 1918, near a manure pile at Maruilen-Dole, France, between Major McCormick (who emerged from the war as a colonel) and his younger, socialistic cousin, Captain Joseph Medill Patterson. The first issue of the experimental paper, modeled on Lord North-cliffe's sensationally successful tabloid *Mirror* in London, did not appear until June 26, 1919. A puny and unprepossessing thing at first, Captain Patterson's New York tabloid soon began its surge toward the largest daily circulation in the world. It was called a picture newspaper because it specialized in photographs, but it was also written simply and clearly and edited carefully. It was hospitable to women reporters, who were then rare in the business. In addition to Julie Harpman, Bernadine Szold (who dressed like a gypsy and became Otto Liveright's wife), Imo-gene Stanley (a cool and beautiful blonde much admired by columnist Mark Hellinger), Irene Kuhn, Irene Thirer and Grace Robinson soon established themselves as top members of the staff.

When Julie Harpman met Westbrook Pegler on the Elwell stoop, it could be said that she outranked him journalistically since she was doing daily pieces on crime under a "By the In-vestigator" office byline, and he had no byline. The United Press had been glad to rehire him upon his arrival from London in the early summer of 1919, but it offered only forty dollars a week for general assignment work in New York, five dollars less than he had received abroad. On the theory that he was still "in dis-grace," the former correspondent avoided signing his stories. To the extent that this flight into anonymity enabled him to operate under less pressure, it was an advantage. At the ripe old age of twenty-five, Westbrook Pegler considered himself a disillusioned veteran. He had learned to mask the implicit challenge of his sandy-red hair and startled blue gaze, and he had put a little flesh on his bony six-foot frame. Whatever his internal scars, his out-ward appearance was more attractive than it had been.

Though the Elwell case was never solved, the periodic ques-tioning of suspects provided further meetings between the two young reporters. With a woman's practicality, Julie suggested that Westbrook resume his byline. She pointed out that Howard was using bylines competitively against the Associated Press to give personality to the UP report and to boost sales. Since How-ard had stood by Pegler in his trouble, she argued, Pegler owed it to Howard to go along with UP policy. Westbrook shrugged,

87

hiding his hurt under a show of indifference, but already half convinced.

The discussion continued when they covered another running story of importance, the Wall Street explosion. This mysterious blast took place on September 18, 1920, outside the J.P. Morgan and Company office next door to the New York Stock Exchange. It killed thirty persons, injured at least a hundred, caused two million dollars worth of damage, and briefly became an issue in that year's presidential campaign.

The country's two wartime giants having been removed from the political arena the previous year—Theodore Roosevelt by death and President Wilson by an incapacitating stroke in the midst of an unsuccessful campaign for ratification of the League of Nations convenant—the major parties had come up with relatively uninspiring slates in 1920. The Republican ticket of Warren G. Harding and Calvin Coolidge contended that alien and bewhiskered anarchists had planted a bomb in the heart of the financial district. Only a change to a GOP administration could check the spread of "foreignism" in the United States, they declared.

Julie Harpman developed a theory for the *News* that firemen had "flushed down the sewer manholes priceless evidence among the debris of the bomb." If so, the evidence and the debris were gone. Unable to find any proof of a subversive plot, detectives assigned to the case concluded that there had been an accidental explosion of a horse-drawn powder wagon used on nearby construction. People shrugged and lost interest. Westbrook Pegler voted Democratic that year because he admired the style of Franklin D. Roosevelt, who was running for Vice-President with Governor Cox of Ohio, but the public in general was influenced by slogans about getting back to normalcy from high prices and war hardships under the Democrats, and it overwhelmingly elected the Republican candidates.

On February 21, 1921, something happened which put Julie Harpman's relationship with Westbrook Pegler on a new plane. The taxi in which she was riding was demolished by a trolley car and she was rushed to the hospital in a critical condition. Because of a fractured vertebra and other injuries, she was out of circulation for more than a year; with lapses after recovery, it was close to eighteen months. Westbrook became a constant visitor to her bedside.

Courtship under unconventional circumstances, like a battle

in mountainous country, imposes its special disciplines. Since the reporters met either in the hospital or in Julie's furnished hall bedroom on West Fifty-sixth Street, they had to be on their best behavior. This may have been a help to Westbrook Pegler. Julie was not particularly well educated, having left school at an early age because of a family situation which she did not discuss, but she was considered a witty woman. Out on a story or in the *Daily News* city room she could put on a convincing show of hard-boiled sophistication; Pegler, despite his journalistic experiences, was sexually idealistic and socially clumsy. Under normal circumstances Julie might have proved an intimidating companion but in Westbrook's recollection they were both shy and she was artless and always sweet.

Westbrook's concept of a woman had been formed in his own family by his mother, who was forever grappling with symptoms which proved difficult to diagnose and impossible to cure. Though Mrs. Frances Pegler by now was an invalid, she bore the burden of her illness without undue complaint. Julie showed a similar gallantry of spirit. The accident which had so abruptly thrown her life out of gear, however, had created a special need for the reassurance of small attentions. These the increasingly infatuated reporter for the United Press was delighted to provide. In the sense that love speaks a secret language of buried needs and unspoken loneliness, they were falling in love.

The impact of genuine romance on Westbrook Pegler was enormous. He who had endured so many grey days in Europe suddenly visualized the world in bright colors. All his energies were engaged and the twelve-hour round of assignments which had seemed so boring became fresh and exciting again.

Count that working day lost which yielded no amusing anecdote for Julie. One day he was assigned to cover the death of Enrico Caruso. Though the great tenor was suffering from pneumonia at the Hotel Vanderbilt, the seriousness of his illness was greatly exaggerated. A hotel flunkey in striped pants chased reporters out into the cold lest they give the place a bad name—until young Pegler arrived. He led the pack back into the lobby with the laughing comment that he had been thrown out of better places, including Buckingham Palace.

Since prohibition was in effect, Westbrook did some drinking. After one Saturday night bender with Jack Lawrence, whom he had known on shipnews and in Europe, he determined on an early Sunday morning visit to the monkey house in Central Park.

He and his pal chewed up great balls of chewing gum which they passed through the bars to the marmosets, capuchins, and spiders. They then fled amidst a vast chattering and confusion as keepers came running to unstick their charges. It was decades before Lawrence or Pegler dared to revisit that monkey house.

One escapade in this period was often credited inaccurately to Westbrook Pegler. He was said to have ridden the subways during the immediate postwar years for the purpose of thrusting his cane as if by accident through out-thrust copies of *Il Progreso*, the *Staats Zeitung* or the *Jewish Daily Forward* on ground that they were "bad for circulation" of the English-language press. Perhaps the real culprit was a Pegler who was then better known, his father, who had settled in New York in 1918, after outliving usefulness on various Chicago newspapers. This kind of thing was not in Westbrook's style; anyway, he never carried a cane.

Arthur Pegler had deserted journalism to join Terry Ramsaye in moving picture work in Manhattan. It would have been all right if he had stuck with Ramsaye, who became the historian of the industry, but he branched out into what Westbrook called a "June-bug promotion scheme" which went slowly bankrupt. Jack Pegler being unable to help financially, Westbrook was obliged to stretch his salary, which had risen to sixty dollars a week, so as to cover his father, mother and sister as well as himself. He ate sparingly, rolled his own Bull Durham cigarettes and wondered if he would ever enjoy a family life of his own.

He was using a byline again, not the early Bud Pegler or the wartime W. J. Pegler but the Westbrook Pegler under which he was to build the rest of his career. Anybody with "a fine Pullman-car name like Westbrook" should take advantage of it, Floyd Gibbons had told him in Europe when they were still on friendly terms.

Gibbons had offered additional advice. "Specialize," he said, "movies, drama, sports, anything . . . A big, big journalist, representing the New York *Sun*, say, or the *World*, will carry a cane and think profoundly all over page one for seventy-five or a hundred dollars a week, but in the sports department Damon Runyon, Grantland Rice, Bill McGeehan and others are getting fabulous salaries up to three hundred a week."

Westbrook was specializing to the extent of compiling an overnight sports budget for the United News, a new morning service of the United Press entrusted by Roy Howard to the supervision of Fred Ferguson. He got along with Ferguson, he liked sportswriting, and he felt grateful for the privilege of being alive. This was 1921, the greatest year in Westbrook Pegler's life. Babe Ruth hit fifty-hour home runs that year for the Yankees, who won the pennant and then went on to win the World Series.

Making up his mind during the World Series, Westbrook sent a letter to Julie, still in hospital with a fractured spine, preparing her in arch terms for a treasure which would foreshadow a closer relationship. Eventually his present reached the hospital, gift-wrapped in a square box larger than would have been required for the trinket which Julie had in mind. Her fingers trembled so out of weakness and nervousness that she asked a nurse to open the package. There it was: a pledge of indescribable and eternal love from a sportswriter—a genuine, autographed Babe Ruth baseball.

Julie's partial paralysis yielded to treatment and she went home to continue her convalescence. With some misgivings on her part, she and Westbrook began to plan on marriage. Arthur Pegler had retrieved his family position by accepting a routine rewrite job on the New York *Tribune*. Julie had been won over to him and to Jack Pegler, and Westbrook rarely saw anybody in her family. The fact that one of her parents was Jewish and one of his Catholic presented no problem, since Julie was prepared for conversion to Catholicism on religious as well as practical grounds.

What bothered Julie Harpman was the threat of domesticity. She was determined to continue her newspaper career. Domestic chores must not be allowed to get in the way, she insisted. Westbrook was willing to accept the idea that they would "remain individuals" within the matrimonial bond. They were therefore married on August 29, 1922, after she reported back to work at the *Daily News*. The date of the ceremony was fixed so as to squeeze a honeymoon into his only free time between the Davis Cup matches and the World Series that year.

The Reverend Thomas G. Philbin officiated at the Church of the Blessed Sacrament on the upper West Side in a ceremony attended only by a few close friends.

The couple took a wedding trip to Norfolk and Richmond, Virginia, before moving into an apartment on Walton Avenue in the Bronx where they were to live for the next two years. "I never had a sitting room," Pegler once wrote with the muted sound of trumpets reserved for references to Julie, "until I was married and blundered into a beautiful new world of elegance and grace."

Katharine Brush, one of Julie Pegler's most intimate friends, wrote a romance in the 1920s about a sportswriter who wants to distinguish himself professionally. *Young Man of Manhattan*, as it was called, had considerable popular impact. It appeared as a *College Humor* serial before publication as a book, and it was later made into a movie by Paramount featuring Claudette Colbert and Ginger Rogers. Norman Foster, then Claudette Colbert's husband, played the title role of the Young Man.

The plot of the novel and the movie was banal enough.

The Young Man has trouble deciding whether to become famous by developing a new approach to sportswriting or by writing high-class fiction. He is handicapped by a fondness for drink and a paralyzing conviction that his wife, a moving picture columnist for a New York daily, possesses the greater literary gift. Sometimes his drinking spells are triggered by his sense of inferiority. "It was a little cruel," muses the hero on one occasion, "that she could write so well, better than he, much better."

Despite his ambitions, which are generally unsuspected by his happy-go-lucky colleagues, the Young Man suffers from a laziness common to the trade. Sportswriters are all alike, the author points out editorially at one point in her narrative. "There was something about the life they led, the playboy schedule they followed, that made chronic procrastinators out of all but a few. They were glib men and each believed his glibness was ability, his trick a talent. This was to be demonstrated, but not today. Ball game today. Fight tomorrow. What's the hurry? Mañana."

To please his talented wife, the Young Man tries to be different. While covering the Yankee baseball training camp at St. Petersburg, Florida, he experiments with personal characterization and small individual dramas along lines suggested by her. Instead of writing about Babe Ruth hitting five home runs in practice during a single hour, he focuses on the odd behavior of the fans afterward: the girl who begs the Babe to write his autograph in ink on the white collar of her dress, the boy who weeps hysterically over a handshake, the little old lady in a red shawl who insists on a snapshot of herself with the great ballplayer to be mailed to her son in Colorado.

Assigned to the Red Grange troupe of professional football players organized by C. C. Pyle of bunion-derby fame, the Young Man ignores the game in favor of a derisive account of the Broadway chorines hired as cheerleaders—to such good account that the outraged girls threaten physical retaliation. This kind of thing, done in a fresh iconoclastic style contrasting strongly with the respectful prose of oldtimers like Grantland Rice, gradually attracts attention to the Young Man. Unfortunately, his wife leaves him. She may be in Hollywood but he can't be sure because he hasn't heard from her. He isn't even sure that she will read his stuff. At this moment of crisis, the absent movie critic, who is really in New York, loses her eyesight drinking some methyl alcohol at a party—a not uncommon occurrence during prohibition.

Told about the disaster by telephone in the midst of a mild bacchanal with ballplayers and show girls, the anguished and repentant Young Man hurries to his wife's bedside, but she will not receive him.

In a frenzy of wish fulfillment, while his wife is slowly regaining her vision, the Young Man knocks off his long-postponed novel about the disintegration of an alcoholic former All-American football player who has become a rubber in a Turkish bath. This achievement convinces the sportswriter's wife that he loves her after all. It restores his self-respect.

Deciding to give marriage precedence over career, the sportswriter's wife assures her husband that he has a special literary gift, greater than her own, which she will help him develop—"a mine untapped in his mind, a deep rich vein of phrase, skillful style and technique." The Young Man is happy to hear this and the reunited reporters are left on a properly triumphant note to love happily thereafter. . . .

Katharine Brush knew the sports field well. As a roving reporter for Roy Moore's chain of Ohio newspapers before she began writing fiction, she had covered everything from World Series baseball games to championship heavyweight boxing matches. She had achieved sufficient intimacy with ranking sportswriters to persuade them as a sort of game to submit snappy final paragraphs—some of them too snappy to be printed —for her own dispatches. In the month immediately prior to starting to write *Young Man of Manhattan*, she had lived with the Peglers in their apartment-with-a-view on Davis Islands,

Tampa, within easy reach by hired car of the Yankee camp at St. Petersburg and the other baseball training camps which Westbrook was covering.

Katharine Brush and Westbrook Pegler were supposed to be working on a novelette-length piece of sports fiction for a magazine during this period. He had agreed to create the part of the hero, a punch-drunk prizefighter called "Punchy," while she developed the character and conversation of the prizefighter's girl. Nothing developed from this collaboration, because Westbrook had no energy left over from his day-to-day sports copy production.

After the appearance of *Young Man of Manhattan*, several critics assumed that the hero was Westbrook Pegler. He did not fit the part, if only because he was insufficiently happy-go-lucky. Like all fictional characters, the Young Man was presumably a composite of various persons in real life known to the author, but James Renwick Harrison, Richards Vidmer or Bill Corum resembled the hero more closely than the sobersided Pegler.

Toward the end of her life, Katharine Brush expressed regrets over the way her most successful book had turned out. *Young Man of Manhattan* had been "an honest, true-to-life story," she said, "spoiled by a string of trumped-up plot devices toward the last." What she seemed to be saying was that the basic conflict in her book concerned the incompatible journalistic ambitions of a man and his wife and that the overlooked central character was not the hero but the heroine, her close friend, Julie Pegler, who resolved that conflict. Westbrook had soon revolted against the agreement that he and Julie were to remain individuals within the matrimonial bond. He needed more woman hours out of her, he said frankly and furiously on one occasion. Without her, he was only half a person, journalistically, socially and every other way, he said. Since it never occurred to Westbrook that compromise was possible on his part, the fate of the marriage was left up to Julie.

8. SPORTSMAN

To Westbrook Pegler the 1920s were always "the era of wonderful nonsense." His fondness for the phrase indicated that he enjoyed himself, and that he considered the spectacles on his beat—sporting events and occasional social, economic and political happenings which could be given a sports treatment—to be meaningless as well as entertaining.

Like most syndicated sportswriters of the day, Pegler followed the professional baseball teams south to their training camps every winter. He covered championship bouts and other major sports events wherever they were held, but his headquarters and happy hunting grounds for copy were in the Times Square-Broadway area of New York. Here converged the gamblers, the big spenders, the promoters, Wall Street speculators, entertainers, dubious celebrities, mobsters and others riding the waves of postwar inflationary prosperity. These were the precursors of café society, though their cafés then were speakeasies.

Everything, including the stock market, seemed to be going up in the 1920s. Buildings were getting taller, cars longer, subways more crowded. Office boys became partners in Samuel Insull's utility empire, and charwomen bought shares in mythical oil wells as a stay for their old age. Judgeships ranged upward in price from twenty-five thousand dollars. A New York City magistrate named Macrery fell behind in payments for his robe and was beaten to death. A Supreme Court Justice named Crater who disappeared amid similar speculation may have landed in one of the crematories set up by the underworld for its private use.

It was a period of cynicism as well as of success; of all-night drinking and dancing and fast driving in autos and airplanes; of dollar cigars and midnight jewel robberies; of speakeasies owned by prohibition agents and burlesque houses owned by the District Attorney; of Texas Guinan greeting customers as suckers; of doctors, rich from abortions, flaunting their mistresses in night clubs; of shysters affluent from heart-balm suits; of political crooks, subservient judges and mobsters worth millions.

Tabloid journalism accentuated the trend toward careless

95

living. The enormous success of the *Daily News* in New York spawned two lurid imitators, William Randolph Hearst's *Mirror* and Bernarr Macfadden's *Graphic*. The three picture papers pushed each other and their older competitors to extremes in sensation. Their front pages and entire news sections were overloaded with sex, sentimentality and violence. Whole pages toward the rear were invaded by comic strip characters like Little Orphan Annie, Dick Tracy, Moon Mullins and Harold Teen, who seemed more real to many readers than the show people who were given impersonal dosages of intimacy in Broadway columns written according to a formula developed by a former hoofer named Walter Winchell.

The tabloids created a world of their own: of Charleston contests at the Polo Grounds and beauty contests at Atlantic City; of the Countess Cathcart, kept from the promised land because of moral turpitude while John S. Sumner turned up moral turpitude by the ton at home for the Society for the Suppression of Vice; of human beings frying in the electric chair and feminine hysteria at the bier of Rudolph Valentino; of showgirl Joyce Hawley dunking nude in a tub of champagne at a producer's party; of Daddy Browning, the eccentric elderly real estate millionaire, his child-bride, Peaches Heenan, and their pet duck quack-quacking at the public daily in composograph photos.

From such reading matter, a stranger might have concluded that the New York standard of community concern was a pair of Siamese twins making public demand for an impossible severance so as to enjoy sex privately. Actual conditions were not quite that shabby. A majority of honest, industrious, relatively responsible citizens managed to subsist in New York and other big cities throughout the era of wonderful nonsense. Some were limited in education and imagination, others were willing and able to discuss James Branch Cabell and Sinclair, Lewis, John Dewey and Sigmund Freud, or weigh pre-New Deal reformism against the radical doctrines blowing out of Bolshevik Russia.

Many thoughtful persons visited speakeasies in those days. Prohibition made it difficult for them to criticize the sporting crowd on other grounds. When John Roach Straton called New York "a feverish, unbrotherly, Sabbath-desecrating, God-defying, woman-despising, lawbreaking monster without ideals or restraint"—a fair enough appraisal of the hotter parts of town—most idealistic and restrained citizens avoided comment lest they be labeled bluenoses. They applauded columnist Heywood

Broun's comment that if the city were destroyed like Sodom, Dr. Straton would surely be turned into a pillar of salt, like Lot's wife, for looking over his shoulder to see if his name were spelled right in the destruction extras.

Westbrook Pegler had some puritanical impulses in the field of sex, but these ran counter to his feeling about prohibition and his journalistic training. When Dr. Straton imported the Rev. J. Frank Norris, an evangelist known as the Texas Tornado, to enliven his local campaign against immorality and bootlegging, the United News selected Pegler as ghost.

After a briefing at the fundamentalist pastor's Calvary Baptist Church, the Tornado and his ghost visited some of the better known Gotham sin-spots. The pair wound up at the Little Club, which was famed for a strip-poker act staged by Al Woods and for another act called "Ladies' Night in a Turkish Bath." Right then and there the Tornado wanted to blow up a storm, but to the disgust of Al Woods, who figured publicity might help business, he was quieted down by his ghost and led out into the street. Pegler, of course, had an exclusive use for Norris' indignation. To his newspaper colleagues the reporter confided derisively that a Tornado was "just a vacuum surrounded by wind."

After Norris returned home to Texas, his ghost remarked that they had both done their best, but "we failed and New York slid into the pit." Several years later, Norris turned vehemently against the Catholics in his home town of Fort Worth. When an unarmed official of the Knights of Columbus came over one Sunday evening to complain, the Tornado shot him dead. With help from the Grand Dragon of the local Ku Klux Klan and other influential Texans, the Holy Circular Storm was acquitted of murder on grounds of self-defense. In view of this, Pegler was asked if he regretted his earlier association with the Texas Tornado. He was not a hypocrite. "No regrets," he snapped.

Additional conditioning in detachment was provided by Pegler's assignments as a ghost for sports headliners ranging from Jess Willard to Babe Ruth. Though he was a man of outlandish size who reigned for a while as heavyweight boxing champion, Willard did not count for much in combat and the fight racket itself smelled of the underworld. The Babe was an unequaled exhibitor, whose strength and accuracy with a baseball were of a piece with the madness for crazy pleasure, unheard of speed and aimless bigness convulsing the nation, but he also proved on close acquaintance to be unbelievably mean, foulmouthed and violent.

Worst of all, Ruth gave his amanuensis no real help. When Pegler finally threatened to get him fired unless he produced some genuine impressions about his own achievements, the Babe sent the following wire to New York from Detroit, where he was playing: "Poled two out of the park today. High fast pitches. Send check immediately."

Having been trained to some extent in cynicism by his father, Westbrook adjusted fairly well to the 1920s. Arthur Pegler himself found the era entirely to his liking. Already in his sixties, he left the *Tribune* to bounce like a bad elderly cherub from one tabloid to another. At the *Daily News* he specialized in overt fakes. One characteristic story concerned an unknown who had been found dead in a rooming house. According to Arthur Pegler, he was Professor Nicola Coviello, a famous European composer of opera who made the mistake of going to Coney Island. There he had his first exposure to American jazz, and the sound killed him on the spot. Since the professor was purportedly on his way from Australia to Saskatchewan, local musical authorities were deterred from any complaint that they had never heard of this celebrity.

After switching to the *Daily Mirror*, Arthur Pegler did society notes under a juicy byline of his own invention—"By Ravenswood Huntsbottom." Occasionally he substituted for the society editor himself under a more prosaic byline which married two well known streets for convenience: "By Barclay Beekman." In this capacity, he liked to portray nouveau riche dowagers—nameless to avoid libel—juggling peas on a knife at a swank dinner or arriving at a ball, in his own immortal phrase, "like a clipper ship with a pedigree flying from her spanker boom."

Pegler père's greatest exploit in this period concerned a world trip which he did not take. Mark Hellinger, a Broadway specialist noted for his biography of Joyce Hawley, the chorine who bathed in champagne, was assigned originally to this adventure. Hellinger started off well but he became diverted from his purpose in Vienna. Since the articles had been sold in advance to a number of newspapers, Arthur Pegler was drafted as ghost when Hellinger dropped out of sight. With the help of James Whittaker, a gifted rewrite man, and a great stack of travel books, he galloped imaginatively through the Balkans, across the Punjab of India and over the mountains of Tibet.

Hellinger did not get in contact again with the *Mirror* office until his ghost was riding in a rickshaw along the Great Wall of China. Then he phoned: he had quietly returned to Manhattan and was holed up in a midtown hotel. A strong-arm squad was dispatched to keep Hellinger incommunicado until he could arrive officially from abroad. With fresh energy, Arthur Pegler zoomed like Superman across Manchuria, Japan and the lonely reaches of the Pacific. When he finally reached the office he had never left, the entire Hearst hierarchy exhaled relief. He had made Magellan and Nelly Bly look like pikers, but nobody claimed any records in his behalf. It was typical of the era of wonderful nonsense that several purchasers of the Hellinger series wrote in subsequently to express the fervent thanks of readers who felt that the trip had widened their intellectual horizons.

Westbrook Pegler's original approach to sports was romantic. His sympathies went out to prize-fighters who were brave and honest, to ballplayers who were exploited by their owners and to all not-quite-successful athletes who were under-appreciated by the public. He was thrilled, for example, by the Gene Tunney-Harry Greb fight for the light heavyweight championship of the world at Madison Square Garden in 1922. Grebb smashed Tunney's nose with a butt during the first round. The injury made Tunney's eyes almost pop out of his head, but he was still on his feet at the end of the bout. Such gameness gave the young reporter "a bashful longing to touch this kid's arm or carry his bucket." Noticing Tunney groping blindly around the ring after the fight, deserted even by his manager, Pegler forgot his own story to guide the defeated battler home.

By the time Tunney became heavyweight champion of the world four years later, Pegler was saying in print all the rude things generally said by sportswriters about Tunney plus insults beyond their scruples or imagination. How could such a changeover be explained? Partly it was due to the atmosphere of the sports world at that time, and partly to Pegler's own gradually developed techniques of exposure and attack. Though he began with the romantic intention of "deglamorizing sports in rebuke to grubby box-office mercenaries," he ended by cutting down almost everybody but himself.

He took inordinate pains with his copy. Telegraphers assigned to move his football stories complained that he kept them shivering in the deserted stadium long after the game was over and everybody else had left. Colleagues kidded that he wore a hat to save his hair from being rubbed off entirely by his knuckles during creative fits (in point of fact, he rarely wore a hat).

He studied shorthand for a while, giving it up only when other sportswriters convinced him that it "scared the hen off the nest." In those days he did not really need shorthand, since sportswriters were not hesitant about improving a quote or making one up out of sheer ozone. Later in his career, when he dealt increasingly with persons who were not rendered speechless at the sight of a notebook and pencil and who insisted on being quoted accurately, he could have made good use of shorthand.

Any sportswriter who kept an ear open to the tomfoolery among the athletes found an easily mined source of humor. Pegler won chuckles by suggesting that George Earnshaw, a dignified ballplayer, was an aristocrat who "bled blue" or by referring to Comiskey as the "noblest Roman of them all" because he had a Roman nose. Once the sportswriter built a whole essay around the fact that Bing Miller had been "called out of his name." It seems that Manager Hawley of the St. Louis Browns always called the ballplayer "Booker T. Miller" because of his dark complexion.

The sports approach to racial matters then was breezy. Negroes were barred from organized baseball as a matter of course, and nobody protested much when Gene Tunney announced in advance of his first bout with Dempsey that if he won he would not accept any challenge from a Negro contender. On the other hand, some Jewish sports fans always recalled with nostalgia Pegler's columns on Leaping Lena Levinsky, an energetic woman who mismanaged the fistic fortunes of her brother, King Levinsky. Ethnic sophisticates of a later era would have worried over references to King Levinsky as a former fish-monger with a "by no means negligible nose," but the very callousness with which the fighter and his sister were portrayed implied acceptance of Jews on terms of rough equality with everybody else.

There was no shortage in the 1920s of eccentric sports characters to be celebrated with tongue in cheek: Tex Rickard, the moneyed bandit who invented the million-dollar gate; C. C. Pyle of bunion-derby fame; Little Boy Blue, Albie Booth, the coal miner's son who played football for Yale; Art (The Great) Shires, the ballplayer who fancied himself a standout at every other sport including boxing; Uncle Wilbert Robinson, the fat, absent-

100

minded manager of the Brooklyn Robins who once forgot all about a close ball game while he sprawled out on the grass watching a partial eclipse of the sun through a piece of smoked glass; even Aimee Semple McPherson, the amorous evangelist who earned inclusion among the freak swimmers of all time by disappearing in the ocean off the coast of California and emerging considerably later from the middle of the Arizona desert.

Out of his prolonged wrestling with words, Westbrook could draw greater resentment against these stock figures than any of his colleagues. Having once staked out a victim, he hated to be pulled off. When a subscribing Midwest editor phoned a long distance protest over the verbal hiding he had given Knute Rockne, the famous coach, for posing as a sportswriter with a byline, Pegler agreed politely that he had probably been too severe and would be more kind in the future. In his next story the sportswriter described the coach's rugged homeliness, his spoon-shaped nose and over-all resemblance to a slap-happy pugilist. Words flowed out of Rockne's mouth, the dispatch said, "like champagne out of a battered oilcan!" After this tribute, what did the ungrateful coach do but bar the young sportswriter from the Notre Dame campus for life!

In describing fights, Pegler often sounded as if he had a personal grievance against one or both of the contestants. He would start off: "Jack Sharkey, the prizefighter who took up failure as a vocation in life and made a brilliant success of it, is fighting his old friend, Tommy Loughran, in Philadelphia tonight. There is a contest in which it ought to be possible to stir up the wildest possible disinterest."

Or he would write: "Paul Berlenbach, assisted by John Barleycorn, Johnnie Walker, Old Tom and several kindred high-proof spirits, stopped Battling Siki of Senegal tonight . . . Considering Siki's life among the grobberies of Paris, Havana, New York riverfront and the Mississippi levee at Memphis for the last three years, it seems fair to assume that the battler was whipped by stronger foes than Berlenbach before he ever advanced to the center of the ring." Philosophizing was not his strong point. When Siki died, Pegler produced a sports obituary to the effect that the African pugilist had become "a victim to a too savage civilization." Siki was just an alcoholic.

Heywood Broun and Ring Lardner, who pioneered in the "aw nuts" school of sportswriting—as opposed to the classic Grantland Rice-W. O. McGeehan "gee-whiz" school—always

101

retained a compensatory feeling of respect and appreciation for sports and for the young athletes taking part. This began to drop out of Pegler's copy. His tone remained truculent whether he was declaring that Blue Larkspur, a race horse, would be more usefully employed in drawing a grocery wagon or hinting that Art (The Great) Shires had used brass knuckles on his bride as well as on his manager.

Pegler did extend debunking into fresh areas. He disqualified Walt Whitman as a nineteenth century sportswriter on the ground that the only preserved fragment of the work of this "darling fellow" for the old Brooklyn *Eagle* was: "Mr. Johnson struck the ball well in the seventh inning."

He derided the classic "Casey at the Bat" as doggerel and for a while—until he saw Dizzy Dean pitch—he tried to prove that curving a baseball was impossible. Sometimes he treated athletic animals in human terms. Thus he wrote that O'Hara the Horse could only run a quarter of a mile at a time. Entered in the Kentucky Derby, which was longer than that, O'Hara had to rest after every quarter of a mile, so that some doubt was aroused as to whether he would ever finish. Finally his jockey took things into his own hands and there through the dusk the unbelieving stablemen saw the jockey riding home—with O'Hara up!

Everything he wrote was readable, and by 1925 Westbrook Pegler's salary had increased to $125 a week. That year the Chicago *Tribune* News Syndicate hired him away at a breath-taking $250 a week, with the title of Eastern sports editor. All sorts of people were discovering the new sports sensation. Edna St. Vincent Millay, who read the Racing Form regularly and who was often visited at her place in the Berkshires by her bookmaker, Frank Erickson, was out in Hutchinson, Kansas, for a lecture on poetry when she glanced at the local newspaper. Hurrying to the telephone, she informed the local editor that he had a genius on his sports staff. "That man ought to be in New York," she declared. "I'd be happy to introduce him to some people I know there." Rather drily, the Kansan replied that the fellow referred to—Westbrook Pegler—was already being syndicated out of New York.

Another admirer was Louis Maragon, a semi-illiterate, accommodating tout originally from Kansas City who hung around the baseball training camps in Florida during the winter. Maragon would wait patiently an hour or more on the sidewalk while the sportswriter worked in a restaurant revising an already painstakingly phrased story.

When Pegler appeared, his self-elected tipster would run copy to Western Union, carry bags to the station or do anything else that was required, with no thought of reward save the privilege of association and perhaps the chance of exchanging a few sentences of cynical inside comment. Since Maragon was amazingly well informed and Pegler was audacious in references to the raffish side of sports, they made a good team.

The sports atmosphere in those days was pretty rough. One evening in 1924, Gene Tunney's manager, William Gibson, became embroiled in an argument with Gene Fowler, the writer, at Billy LaHiff's Tavern in New York. Gibson's first punch, with the aid of a diamong ring on a middle finger, raked away most of Fowler's right eyebrow. Westbrook Pegler, who was among the spectators, could not understand Fowler's wild laughter during the brief bout. He was informed that Fowler always laughed like that when he fought—and always lost.

The syndicated sportswriters often traveled in a group. When they reached Philadelphia, they were entertained by Max (Boo Boo) Hoff, a sallow little man wearing a bullet-proof vest. From his profits as Chicago's chief bootlegger, Hoff had organized a business-and-sports empire which included the promotion of fights and the ownership of night clubs. One of his lavish dinners for reporters, athletes and chorus girls was used by Katharine Brush for a central incident in her *Young Man of Manhattan*. These affairs were not quite orgies (to the disappointment perhaps of the girls, Pegler once noted) but he and others took full advantage of the unlimited liquor supplied by a character known as Sam the Gassman.

Pegler was present at a private gathering during the 1925 Pittsburgh-Washington World Series in Pittsburgh when Joe Jacobs, manager of Max Schmeling, flourished a pistol at Eddie Brannick, the road secretary of the New York Giants. Sam the Gassman delicately but firmly removed the pistol from Jacobs nervous hand. When Pegler also expostulated with Jacobs for this breach of the peace, he got his thumb bitten. The wound was painful, but not critical.

After Tunney won the title from Jack Dempsey in 1926, Pegler was tipped off by one of Boo Boo Hoff's boys that the bootlegger had a slice of the champion through an arrangement with

William Gibson. Tunney always resented this story, though it was legitimate news, since Boo Boo Hoff soon brought suit for 20 per cent of all Tunney's earnings. The champion outpointed Hoff in court as handily as he had outpointed Dempsey in the ring.

Sports activities were never quite free in those days from the hovering backstage presence of the mob. While covering baseball training camps down South, the reporters often received invitations to visit Al Capone's home-in-exile on a Miami island. On one such occasion, a stenographer from Tex Rickard's office felt herself sitting on something hard and pulling back some canvas uncovered a machine gun. The discovery almost spoiled her visit. At a New York speakeasy called the Stork Club, Pegler once overheard the proprietor, Sherman Billingsley, ask Frank Costello, the gambler, to lift a picket line outside the club. Costello obliged by phoning Arthur (Dutch Schultz) Flegenheimer, who made the necessary arrangements.

Broadway columnists in this era—including Walter Winchell, Mark Hellinger, Sidney Skolsky and Ed Sullivan—were reported to have bodyguards against possible mob intimidation, but not the sportswriters, who were presumed to be on terms of cameraderie with the underworld.

Westbrook Pegler was known as an honest sportswriter who refused to accept "oil" or "ice" from promoters who wanted extra consideration. That did not make him immune to the point of view of the dominant segment of the sports audience in the 1920s. In his columns he began to argue that the quality of the show rather than the relative honesty of the participants was what counted. Thus he attacked the baseball moguls who had urged severe punishment for the bribed players in the fixed World Series between the Chicago White Sox and the Cincinnati Reds. Baseball, once his favorite game, had become "a faded folkway," he wrote; the real national game was craps!

Pegler defined an amateur as an athlete who refused to accept a check—he wanted cash instead. Amateur sports even in colleges should be handled on an open-salary basis, he believed. He recommended that betting be legalized along with drinking.

The doping of a race horse was nothing to get excited about, Westbrook Pegler argued, since this added an unpredictable element to the race which might rebound to the benefit of the ordinary bettor, who usually lost. He came out finally in favor of fixed fights. "A bold hilarious phony," he declared, not only provided an excellent show but also gave shrewd spectators a chance

104

to experience moral indignation. In one of those eye-opening summations which sometimes made a Pegler column a confessional, he wrote: "There are some of us who dwell in spiritual lowlands so close to sea level that the phony fighter is the only one we can look down upon."

Against a background of athletes who were crooked, vain, daffy and futile but not quite believable as human beings, Westbrook Pegler's personality played an increasing role in his columns. He claimed to be doing quite a bit of drinking and brawling on his own account.

While drunk on one occasion, Pegler reported, he sold the Cardinals a left-handed pitcher who could make a ball stop in mid-air just before it reached the batter. His column on this subject ended abruptly: "Hey, what can they do to me for this?" On other occasions he reported that his caustic comments on the mute and the muscular of the sports world were arousing indignation here and there. George Trafton, center on the Red Grange troupe of professional football players whom C.C. Pyle sent barnstorming across the country, did not like being described as the South Bend Tornado, along with a footnote that a tornado was merely a vacuum surrounded by wind. Ty Cobb, who had been known to surge up into the stands after a heckler, also objected to some Peglerian epithets. One athlete who actually did something about it was Cozy Dolan, the baseball coach. After Pegler accused him of "snitching" on a team-mate who had become unduly chummy with gamblers, the two exchanged blows in a Chicago speakeasy.

"The bartender stopped us as a favor to the other customers," Pegler explained. "Next night, somebody drove by the speak and tossed a pineapple through the window. Blew the front right out of the place! People always said it was because the fight was so lousy."

Another brawl involving Pegler occurred in a saloon near Chicago's City Hall. Somebody stopped it by turning out the lights. The columnist promptly accused the city of inhospitality in not keeping the lights on. He never suggested that this or any of his other fights was fixed.

Julie Harpmen's career entered a new phase with an assignment to cover the checkered affairs of Hollywood's enticing but naughty luminaries. "The INSIDE DOPE on Movie Stars," as it was called, was displayed prominently in a double truck of the *Sunday News.* Her pieces described how William S. Hart, the tight-lipped, thin-hipped stalwart of the Westerns, had been called a cream puff by Winifred Westover during their honeymoon; how a friend of Rudolph Valentino and Charlie Chaplin, the Latin and Limehouse lovers, concealed a family skeleton in her closet; and how Lew Cody, the he-vamp, was really a butter-fly man. This kind of tabloid pap was probably no more vulgar and cynical than the tripe produced by many sportswriters. At least Julie did it well; she was soon offered the job on a permanent basis.

The offer posed a problem. Westbrook's new prominence as a nationally syndicated sports columnist required frequent trips out of town. If Westbrook or Julie had to leave New York for an extended period, the other tried to arrange a simultaneous trip or vacation, but this matching up of schedules proved increasingly difficult. If Julie accepted the Hollywood job, it would involve frequent trips to the West Coast. What effect would these have on a marriage which was already under strain? Julie handled Westbrook's mail and his wardrobe as well as the family finances. She was his indispensable companion, social buffer, critic and adviser, he said, and it was probably true that his reputation among his colleagues as a "fun guy" rested to some extent on her tactful participation.

Julie Harpman made up her mind; she did not like the movies, she said, and she detested Hollywood stars. Regardless of any proposed raise or prestige, she did not want the new job on any terms. Her refusal was clear and final.

A new suggestion arose. Having signed an exclusive agreement with Gertrude Ederle, the Chicago *Tribune* News Syndicate hoped to borrow Julie Harpman to ghostwrite the swimmer's daily impressions during a new attempt to conquer the English Channel. The *Daily News* was offered a fat slice of the syndication in exchange for Julie's services, so the offer came with backing from her own boss. Acceptance meant an extended absence from New York and her husband, however, which was what she was trying to avoid. "Take Westbrook along," suggested the CTNS manager, when he understood the situation. "He needs a vacation anyway." That settled it. Julie accepted.

Gertrude Ederle was the daughter of a Bronx butcher, a husky young woman in her early twenties, gentle and already somewhat deaf from excessive immersion in water. She had set more amateur swimming records than any other woman in the world before turning professional. In her poorly financed effort

106

to cross the Channel the previous year, she had refused the touch which meant disqualification even after it became apparent that she could not gain the English shore. Half-conscious, crying and moaning, she had to be forced out of the water. With more adequate financing through the news syndicate, Trudie (as she was known to millions of sports fans) felt confident of success this time.

The official party which sailed on the *Berengaria* from New York on June 2 consisted of the swimmer and her father and sister; Julie Harpman, listed as "companion and chaperone"; Westbrook Pegler, listed as the husband of Miss Harpman; and Arthur Sorenson of Pacific & Atlantic Photos which had exclusive picture rights.

On the trip across the Atlantic, Julie groped toward an understanding of the swimmer. A big girl, already weighing 149 pounds, Trudie expected to scale somewhere between 155 and 160 by the time of her big swim in August. "I eat five meals a day and am always hungry," she confided. "I need all the encouragement that can be given me. If I dance in the evening or pick a ukelele for pleasure, I don't think it should be reported as a scandal, as happened last year. You swim the Channel for the fun and glory of it. I don't want to be nagged. I want to talk about clothes and shows and the Charleston and things in the paper. I can't stand the Channel for breakfast, dinner and supper. Outside of training hours, I want to forget."

The Bronx girl's naïveté colored the ghosted dispatches. "Most of the passengers drank champagne last night," she said, "but I stuck to lemon soda. I have never in my life drunk alcoholics (sic) except once, as a child, when my uncle offered me a penny to drink a glass of beer." She rejected suggestions that she try a boyish bob. "I have been noted for my mannish shoulders and carriage and naturally I want to keep my hair over my ears and remain as feminine-appearing as possible."

Gertrude Ederle's competitive quality became apparent after she reached her training camp at Cap Gris Nez on the French side of the Channel, where other swimmers of assorted nationalities were also rounding into shape. Late in June, she tried a tune-up swim of seven and a half miles from Gris-Nez to Wimereux. The silk edges of her bathing suit chafed her sunburned skin and her goggles failed to keep out the water, but her crawl stroke continued without interruption.

Finally a squall sprang up from the British side of the Chan-

107

nel and Miss Ederle quit, saying: "I suppose you are as disgusted with me as I am with myself. I intended staying four hours in the water and I stayed only three and a half."

This was the biggest sports story he ever witnessed, but Westbrook Pegler appeared in none of Miss Ederle's ghosted pieces, Julie Harpman's own dispatches or Art Sorenson's photos. Until time ran out on his complimentary vacation, he remained in the background. After a brief final visit to Paris with his wife, he left quietly for the United States.

"She is burned as brown as a walnut," wrote Julie of Trudie on August 5, the day before the swim, "and though she weighs 156 pounds there is no sign of fat anywhere and her muscles are smooth and soft as swimmer's muscles must be. She sleeps long and as peacefully as a baby." Nevertheless, Trudie was keyed up. "Things which would cause hysterics in another woman leave her unnerved, yet the slightest irritation at times drives her almost into a frenzy."

Not as a ghost but as an observer of a woman with whose struggle she had come to associate herself deeply, Julie wrote four columns of copy on Gertrude Ederle's swim. Her flawless story —how did it miss a Pulitzer prize?—appeared verbatim in hundreds of newspapers throughout the U.S. and abroad to the greater glory and profit of the Chicago *Tribune* News Syndicate and the New York *Daily News.*

"At six o'clock, when she had been in the Channel eleven hours, the sea was a frightful thing, with the wildest of unfavorable winds blowing now. Burgess (the trainer) suggested to Pop Ederle and Margaret (Gertrude's sister) that it would be well to take Trudie out and abandon the attempt but Margaret objected citing no complaint from Trudie as yet. With great waves dashing against the tug *Alsace,* Burgess insisted that she should come out but Trudie was still unaware of his advice and she smiled to her friends on the boat . . .

"At 7:11, Burgess said to me: 'She must come out. I will not take the responsibility of waiting for a sign from her.' Someone yelled, 'Gertie, you must come out!' Trudie looked up in amazement and said, 'What for?' while those aboard the tug cheered . . ."

Two hours later, Gertrude Ederle waded ashore at Dover. No woman had previously swum the Channel and the best male time for the crossing was a full two hours slower than her record of 14 hours and 31 minutes. She was a world heroine, even if

108

she did not act like one. Instead of hurrying back to the United States to choose between offers of indorsements and appearances and exhibitions, she paid a leisurely visit to relatives in Germany. Even so, when she reached New York on August 24, the ticker tape parade up Broadway and the subsequent reception by Mayor Walker at City Hall were surpassed in size and enthusiasm only by the turnout the following year for Colonel Lindbergh.

Julie had a grievance. When Westbrook met her at the Battery, they went off to lunch to settle it, without bothering over the parade or the reception. During his visit to Cap Gris Nez, they had divided the English Channel into squares, with a number for each square, so she could pinpoint in her dispatches Ederle's precise progress. Unfortunately, Westbrook had been away from the office on a sports assignment when the swim took place and his substitute had mishandled the code. Long before lunch was over, he was able to show that he had no part in the mixup and no alternative but to cover the fight in Boston. His apologies were accepted in a mood of reciprocal fondness.

Coverage of the swim gave Julie a vicarious experience with feminine success, and it sufficed. She had already arranged to move from the city to a more stable suburban setting in a rented Larchmont house near the homes of friends working on the *Daily News*. The next step toward resolving the matrimonial issue between them was for Julie to resign from the staff of the *Daily News*. This occurred the following spring. Thereafter, except for one or two special assignments in journalism and a diminishing flirtation with fiction, she put writing behind her in favor of a wifely career with Westbrook Pegler.

9. HEAD OF THE FAMILY

One weekend in 1932, when legitimate sports events were scarce, the Chicago *Tribune* News Syndicate made the mistake of letting Westbrook Pegler get a good look at Washington. His impressions created such a furor that he was soon snapped up by a rival syndicate. That was the legend, and to some extent it was true. E. S. Beck, managing editor of the *Tribune*, did take the sportswriter to the 1932 Gridiron Club dinner in Washington. From then until he went to work for Scripps-Howard in December 1933, Pegler did focus more than usual on national problems. However, he had been turning out occasional non-sports features, series and exposés over the years. His reputation as a slugger in the minor leagues was established. The question was whether he could field ideas well enough for the major leagues.

Enemies always said that Westbrook Pegler thought with his glands. This was unfair; emotion colored his work to an unusual extent, but his mind was capable of wide-ranging association of ideas within certain prescribed limits. His guidelines to thinking resembled the wooden partitions which herd cattle to predestined ends in the stockyards. One of them, dating back to boyhood experiences in Excelsior, was a phobia about prohibition. Anything connected with the enforcement of the laws against drinking infuriated him to the point of making him sound like a social rebel. On the other hand, he classed as a strong supporter of law and order in general, as a conscious patriot, a regular in politics and an orthodox believer in religion. In any serious discussion outside the sports field, his problem was to reconcile conflicts between his channels of thought.

Perhaps the most important non-sports story which he covered during the 1920s was the Scopes trial in 1925. Because William Jennings Bryan, a former Secretary of State who in his dotage had become a salesman of Florida swampland and the leading national advocate of prohibition, appeared as counsel for the State of Tennessee in its attempt to enforce a silly law against the teaching of evolution, Pegler joined Henry L. Mencken and most of the other correspondents in ridiculing the fundamentalists of Dayton, but even then he wasn't comfortable about his own attitude, and his dispatches, as he confessed, "laid an egg." It took only a few years for him to realize that he should have stood for law and religion with the self-respecting small town and rural folk of Tennessee against the irreverent and intellectual big-city slickers.

Like clockwork every four years throughout the 1920s, Westbrook Pegler covered the national conventions of the Democratic and Republican parties. Since all Americans are known to be political experts from the cradle, no question of competence could be raised in this area. Pegler followed certain convenient assumptions of his father. A national political convention, he wrote, was a senseless affair at which a mob cavorted in public while insiders—the vested interests—made decisions behind the scenes. Male delegates would sell their votes "preferably for money but for a two-dollar shirt, if necessary," and female delegates were ill-favored bird-brains.

The columnist's reportage of the 1928 conventions was not earth-shaking. At the Republican affair in Kansas City, he concluded that J. P. Morgan and the Wall Street crowd—the insiders —were conniving to deny the front-running, publicly supported Herbert Hoover the presidential nomination lest, if elected, he "pass some laws which would injure their business."

He had previously assumed, Pegler wrote with a wink at his audience, that "the only national legislative bodies were the two houses of Congress and the Anti-Saloon League." At the Democratic doings in Houston a couple of weeks later, he expressed doubt that Governor Alfred E. Smith of New York could beat Hoover unless his party cracked down on "its ecclesiastical snake-charmers" in the South, by which, he explained, he meant the prohibition-minded Billy Sundays as well as the anti-Catholic Texas Tornadoes. Though Hoover's handshake "felt like a fistful of mashed potatoes," the columnist leaned toward the supposedly anti-Wall Street Republican. By coincidence, so did his employing syndicate and most newspaper publishers. Hoover rewarded them all by carrying forty states, to become the nation's first Quaker President.

Particularly in later years, Pegler placed great stress on his independence, but like any newspaperman he tended to absorb by osmosis the beliefs of his boss. For a sportswriter working for Colonel McCormick, any candidate except Herbert Hoover in 1928 would have been out of the question. Conditions changed as the Hoover administration ran into economic and other difficulties. Reflecting the national mood of irritation at the White House, Pegler complained that he could not obtain a personal interview with the President when he wanted it. An American business man visiting Cuba got in easily to see Machado, he noted in one of his regular sports columns, and a tourist in Andorra could sit right down with Madame President "as soon as the goats were shooed out of the front parlor," yet Hoover had taken on the ceremonial trappings of monarchy and become almost inaccessible. One of Colonel McCormick's pet ideas for years was that American Presidents were really kings.

Sportswriter Pegler slipped into one of the President's rare White House press conferences, but that did not satisfy him, either. Questions had to be written out in advance, he discovered, and few were answered. Regular White House correspondents joked that the President responded only to questions which he had written out himself. Pegler was inclined to believe this; Hoover was particularly evasive, he noticed, about anything which might displease the Anti-Saloon League or the Methodist Board of Temperance and Morals. "He wouldn't commit himself to the time of day from a hatful of watches," wrote the sportswriter, adding that he had never seen such a timid and indecisive man at a press conference.

Pegler did not need to be physically in Washington to write a serious column. His rage over prohibition and his antipathy for the rich could be expressed in any locale. He was upset when President Hoover sanctioned the prosecution of Al Capone for evasion of federal income taxes on the ground that the national leader of the liquor syndicate had proved immune to ordinary prosecution. After all, Pegler pointed out, Capone had done more than any other individual to expose the sham of the Eighteenth Amendment. The Chicago bootlegger, he argued, was a social benefactor compared to some sponsors of prohibition and some bluenoses supporting it.

Clarence Darrow—the Chicago lawyer who had defended John T. Scopes, the idealistic high school biology teacher of Dayton, Tennessee—began a series of debates on prohibition with Clarence True Wilson of the Methodist Board of Temperance and Morals. Pegler had a bone to pick with Darrow, but he could not very well side with Dr. Wilson. When Darrow went so far in an interview as to express personal respect for Dr. Wilson, the columnist compared the debates with the famous wrestling matches between the Rev. Billy Sunday and the Devil.

The Devil always lost but he always showed up undamaged and full of fire for the next session. Naturally reports spread that these contests were fixed. So far as he was concerned, Pegler concluded in a tone changing abruptly from the jocular to the truculent, such courtesy to an enemy was "a degrading thing, denoting moral decay." His own slogan, he said, was no social mercy for bluenoses.

The columnist acted out his beliefs. He drank conspicuously. During a train ride across Indiana, which had a noxious "frisk-and-sniff" enforcement act, he would go to the observation car to toss out emptied gin bottles containing insulting messages for the local Anti-Saloon League officials. "I'm not one of those milky, tolerant observers who can be relied upon to say that Pontius Pilate was good to his mother," he explained. "Tolerance to my mind has been greatly overrated . . . I take as much pleasure in detesting the good brothers and sisters of the League as they have in hating me."

During the spring of 1929, he wrote an exposé of the way prohibition was "suspended" along Florida's gold coast during the winter months. He named various wide-open joints and described the gambling and other activities which went on there. His problem was not in gaining admittance to these places, but in spending his $500 advance. For almost a week he had obstinately good luck at roulette. Since he could not drink enough to absorb the profits, the time came when he faced journalistic disgrace in having to return an advance. Fortunately, his luck changed at the last minute.

The sportswriter's adventures in illicit enjoyment aroused national interest. In Florida itself there were raids and arrests. The state legislature denounced him for bringing Florida into contempt. From a safe refuge up North, the columnist retorted that the legislature had no ear for music. "The boys thought your correspondent was blowing a whistle but that was no whistle— that was a saxophone."

A kind of pseudo-proletarian gruffness came naturally to Pegler. In the course of his articles on unrestricted upper-class drinking in Florida, for example, he noted that as soon as the rich visitors left for the North "the law will be snatching ragged swamp niggers and sallow crackers by the slack of their overalls and tossing them into the state road camps for owning, possessing or transporting pints. The unfortunates will live on grits and fried sowbelly and toil in the jungle, beset by mosquitoes as big as

113

buzzards and goaded by the lowest form of political appointee that crawls upon this earth, the convict gang boss, whose quirt is a thirty-ounce pickhandle."

After the collapse of stock market values in the fall of 1929, Pegler's distaste for the rich, particularly the idle rich, became an increasingly useful journalistic commodity. Returning to Florida early in 1930, he began to specialize in gibes at society women. Those who came to watch Philip (Fainting Phil) Scott of England train for his heavyweight bout with Jack Sharkey had no conversation, the columnist declared. They either complained about their servants or bragged about their yachts. Julie, down on a visit, had to straighten out one of them on the yachting situation. Her own yachts, said Mrs. Pegler, the "Flying Erie," the "Leaping Lackawanna," and the "John F. Hylan," were kept in the lower harbor in New York. Her love for yachting, she said, was inherited from "grandpaw in Caldwell, Idaho." The society matron wanted to know whether grandpaw sailed in the big regattas. "He used to hold private regattas, nobody else allowed," countered Julie. "In Idaho?" pressed the matron. "Oh yes," said Julie. "Grandpaw had a private ocean out there. He was so exclusive!"

Love involves a willingness to fight for the object of one's affection. If Julie were actually involved in some unpleasant social situation with one of the overbearing winter-colony dowagers, her husband more than made up for it. When Fainting Phil Scott —who according to Pegler was the most boring fighter in the world, next to Gene Tunney—became the house guest of a millionaire in Palm Beach before his fracas with Jack Sharkey, the columnist showed his displeasure by naming a Chicago society woman who lost her panties in public at the Everglades Club dance in honor of the visiting British pugilist. He also revealed that the society women who sneaked off to a small Palm Beach fight club got a larger thrill than they anticipated when a preliminary boy, upon being introduced, "threw back his bathrobe with a flourish and fainted dead away at discovering that he had plumb forgot his tights."

To male millionaires who wanted to reform prize-fighting, Pegler suggested gruffly that they start with the brokerage business. "When a man gets into the ring he knows he has only one man to fight, but when a customer gets into a brokerage office he is one man against a whole crowd, without any referee to see that he gets a square deal." As a boxing reporter, he discovered,

he could mingle on equal terms with any winter-colony pluto-
crat, but he wasn't sure he wanted to mingle.

Nobody in society down there ever accomplished anything
worth while, he wrote sharply, whereas some of his colleagues
"had the ingenuity and drive to write fairly respectable plays and
books." He still believed that his own future involved writing
high-class sports fiction—as soon as he could find the time for it.

National income dropped from $87 billion in 1929 to $40
billion in 1933. Unemployment rose from 4,000,000 in 1930 to
8,000,000 in 1931 to 12,000,000 in 1932. Only one in four among the
jobless obtained relief, and that was generally restricted to
food benefits. The only moral way out of the depression, said
President Hoover, was self-help, but nobody knew what he meant.
Poor people were too entangled in their miseries to be rebellious,
but there were alarming lapses of nerve among the rich and the
powerful. The business community fretted over the possibility
that a broad relief program would "spell the end of the republic."
Senator Reed of Missouri suggested that America might need a
Mussolini to put its house in order. The Republican fiscal experts
who had accelerated speculative tendencies during the 1920s
by reducing taxes were now making the reverse mistake: they
were increasing taxes in time of depression. Naturally the public
complained. Colonel McCormick started a journalistic campaign
to get everybody to pay full taxes—but he estimated his own personal property that year at twenty-five thousand dollars and paid
only fifteen hundred dollars to the collector of internal revenue.
Other millionaires shipped their funds abroad to escape taxes.

As one deflationary spiral followed another in the early 1930s
some stores had taken advantage of unemployment to hire clerks
for as little as five and ten dollars a week. Barbara Hutton, the
dime store heiress, who was not associated with the management
of the stores from which her enormous income was derived, began to be singled out as the prototype of the idle rich girl.

There was no particular risk in belaboring Miss Hutton, since
so respectable a person as Captain Patterson, the former Socialist, used to write editorials for the *Daily News* on the "idle
rich" starting: "What a filthy tribe of vultures they are!" Pegler
took special enjoyment in pouncing on symbolic evil: here was an
indoor sport at which he was prepared to go farther than any
rival. During one of his treatments of the "scions and scionesses
of wealth," he described "Miss Hutton, Tommy Manville, Billy

115

Leeds, the current Marshall Field and about a hundred upper and lower-case Astors, Vanderbilts and Goulds and their in-laws and off-shoots" as missionaries and propagandists for higher income and inheritance taxes. Such taxes, he wrote, were the only way to end the payment of tribute to the founders of great American fortunes. "Economics be damned," he exploded in summation. "The people are not economists. All they know is what they feel and they are feeling sore enough to repudiate these perpetual debts."

Considering his personal situation, encouraging higher taxes came under the head of unselfishness. Westbrook's income hit $25,000 in 1929. He took no depression pay-cut; in fact, his salary continued to increase. He joked about it—all he needed, he said, was a protective tariff to shield himself and other well-paid domestic sportswriters from cheap foreign labor. In the fall of 1929, he and Julie left Larchmont for their new, specially designed, nine-room Bavarian-type stone house and its separate Bavarian-type stone writing shed on a twenty-five acre estate in Pound Ridge, New York. This estate had a private lake, a couple of acres of lawn and a great deal of scrubwood and hilly rock. It was the most comfortable and beautiful place they ever owned.

Hoovervilles for the homeless were growing up meanwhile out of junk material in vacant lots on the outskirts of all the big cities. In his columns, Pegler made frequent use of his quarrels with shiftless and crooked rural workmen who had helped on his luxurious new home, with no apparent concern over how this might sound to those who were less fortunate. Though he had risen in the world, he did not then or ever feel that he belonged in the top drawer.

People generally blamed President Hoover for the depression. It was apparent by the time of the 1932 national conventions that he could not be reelected. Colonel McCormick broke with him over prohibition, and William Randolph Hearst helped to nominate the Democratic candidate, Governor Roosevelt of New York. Roosevelt campaigned in a mild manner and won without trouble, carrying forty-two out of forty-eight states.

Westbrook Pegler encountered Josephus Daniels for the first time at the inaugural ceremonies in 1933. He thanked the former Secretary of the Navy for his support against Admiral Sims during the war, and Daniels reminisced a little. President Wilson once told him that somebody-or-other was the worst god-damn fool who ever represented the United States abroad, but Daniels dis-

116

sented, saying he would "like to agree" but that he was "firmly committed to Admiral Sims." This pleasant refurbishment of an old hatred ranked in the columnist's mind with President Roosevelt's moving inaugural message that the only thing to fear was fear itself.

In the early New Deal period, Pegler was as fully committed to F.D.R. as he had once been to Gene Tunney. His conversion was completed by attendance at one of the new President's first press conferences in the White House.

Writing about it in an unusual vein, the declared non-hero-worshipper from the field of sports noted how the regular correspondents "barge in with a scuffle and whoop, and there he sits at his desk with a cigarette holder, apparently one of the three-for-a-nickle kind, cocked in his mouth and his head canted to the left to give clearance for the smoke as it drifts past his eyes . . . sits there and turns his smile from one wing of the line-up to the other as questions fly out of the gathering and answers them as easily as a traffic cop telling a stranger the way to Walnut Street. I heard him stall only once and that on a question which was pretty badly put . . . I am afraid I couldn't be trusted around Mr. Roosevelt. For the first time in my life in this business, I might find myself squabbling for a chance to carry the champion's water-bucket."

Julie felt apprehensive when she first heard that Monte Bourjaily, general manager of the United Features Syndicate, believed that he could promote Westbrook as a serious commentator. She wondered whether her husband would be under greater strain in that kind of job. Would he be away from home more often? The depression had lessened public interest in sports, anybody could see that; the era of wonderful nonsense might never return. Even so, Westbrook was contemplating leaving a kind of writing which he had mastered in favor of much more complicated work. There was a tradition of relaxation in sportswriting, a built-in social security of sorts which by now he scarcely noticed but which, she thought, he might miss. She was still weighing her doubts when she suffered a coronary thrombosis in June 1933.

Julie's condition was critical at first, and her improvement was slow despite every possible medical attention. Westbrook's anxiety affected his sleep and his work. In August he tried unusual therapy. He ordered the largest pair of silver fox furs he

117

could locate by telephone and had them sent to Pound Ridge by messenger. As a wedding anniversary present (their eleventh), he draped these around his wife's shoulders. For weeks thereafter he insisted that she sit up in bed wearing them. Whether or not this had any effect, Julie was up and around the house again by Thanksgiving.

In December the delivery trucks of the New York *World-Telegram* rolled through town announcing the advent of a new columnist with "the drollery of Ring Lardner, the iconoclasm of Henry Mencken, the homely insight of Will Rogers," and sincerity to boot. They were referring to Westbrook Pegler. His new arrangement called for $30,000 a year plus one-half of all syndicate sales above $60,000. If syndicate sales should hit $150,000—surely not impossible—he would be earning as much as a President of the United States. How could a man reared on Horatio Alger road signs to success resist such an offer at a time when the best rewrite man got $100 a week? It involved risk, but everything involved risk. As he pointed out to Julie, if he side-stepped an opportunity like that he might very well get clunked on the head with a foul ball the first time he went to the Polo Grounds to watch a game.

Pegler was committed to writing six eight-hundred-word columns a week for distribution by United Features, the Scripps-Howard syndicate. His new employers were his old boss Roy Howard, who had used the United Press as a springboard to control of the Scripps-Howard chain of eighteen newspapers, and Colonel Frank Knox, former Hearst general manager who had taken over the Chicago *Daily News*.

Each of these entrepreneurs had a special need of Pegler. Colonel Knox wanted new readers in his circulation war with Colonel McCormick. Howard, who became Pegler's real superior since the columnist would base in New York and receive most of his salary from the *World-Telegram*, sought journalistic balance—plus insurance against Heywood Broun.

Roy Wilson Howard, then fifty, was a pompadoured, mustachioed little man who liked to exhibit a green hatband which had been made specially for him from the neck feathers of a rare Hawaiian bird at a cost of $150. Despite his foppishness, nobody could question his competence as an operator in the newspaper field. His partner, the huge, red-bearded E. S. Scripps, had built up the chain on shoestring budgets and crusades for the underdog, but he had never tackled New York. After Scripps died in 1927, Howard purchased the rundown *Telegram* in New York for less than two million dollars. The following spring he gave his acquisition status by hiring Broun as a columnist. Though he had been dropped by the *World* after a series of controversies, Broun was about the best known columnist in the country, if you excluded such old-timers as O. O. McIntyre and Arthur Brisbane. Howard whetted public interest by printing a daily box with the column specifying that Broun's views were "presented without regard to their agreement or disagreement with the editorial attitude of this paper." Howard purchased the *World* for another three million dollars in 1931 and merged it with the *Telegram*, and the combined publication soon made great progress.

By supporting Fiorello H. LaGuardia for Mayor in 1933 when all the other papers ignored the bumptious little reformer, Howard showed capacity as a kingmaker. He still courted social recognition, and he was grateful when Broun, a shambling giant with entrée anywhere in town, agreed to take him night-clubbing.

The publisher and the columnist made an odd-looking pair —"Howard and his tame bear," somebody called them—but they got along well enough until Broun started to advocate a union for reporters. "The fact that newspaper editors and owners are genial folk should hardly stand in the way of the organization of a newspaper writers' union," Broun wrote boldly in his August 7, 1933 column. "Beginning at nine o'clock on the morning of October 1, I am going to do the best I can to help in getting one up. I think I could die happy on the opening day of the general strike if I had the privilege of watching Walter Lippmann heave a brick through a *Tribune* window at a non-union operative who had been called in to write the current Today and Tomorrow column on the gold standard."

Realizing that Broun was serious enough despite his light tone, Roy Howard called a meeting of *World Telegram* employees to warn them against "an idealist who never finishes what he starts." The newspaper's net profit the previous year, declared the publisher, was less than Broun's $40,000 salary. Ordinary reporters and rewrite men did not accept Howard's figures. They were as excited as other wage-earners over the encouragement given to unionism by the New Deal and they had a feeling that they were as badly exploited, in relation to their intellectual and educational attainments, as any laundry worker. Their enthusiasm for the union idea could not be restrained. A national convention to organize a Newspaper Guild—so-called to avoid any white-collar uneasiness over the word union—was held in Washington the same month that Pegler joined the *World-Telegram*.

Broun's "It Seems to Me" had been occupying two columns of space at the top of the left side of the *World-Telegram's* famous split-page—really the front page of the second section—and he had been the only columnist on that page.

Then Pegler's "Fair Enough" arrived. Pegler received a column and a half of space at the extreme right hand side of the page while Broun's space on the other side was simultaneously trimmed to a column and a half. This reduced Broun from solo and featured performer to parity with a newcomer whose views were suspect. Roy Howard always disclaimed any intention to put a rightist on the right to balance a leftist on the left, but that was the public version, and Broun's following was upset before anything happened.

Roy Howard had instructed Pegler to "write the way you have been writing—only more so." He wanted a "lowbrow, rowdy, red-blooded" discussion of "the story of the day" which would provide some contrast to Broun's "bleeding-heart approach." If Westbrook was perplexed by these instructions, Julie was not. On the day when they began discussing possibilities for his first column, the big story concerned the lynching and mutilation, by a mob in San Jose, California, of two men who had been arrested on a charge of kidnapping a Santa Clara University student.

Governor Rolfe of California praised the lynching as "a fine lesson for the nation." Julie had no particular politics, she used to say, but she had absorbed a normal quota of Southern bourbon prejudices during her girlhood in Memphis. She agreed with Governor Rolfe and she said so at the breakfast table to Westbrook, who took anything she said as seriously as a remark by Roy Howard or Arthur Pegler himself.

Broun swung into action promptly to rebuke Rolfe.

In the beginning [he wrote], it seemed to me as if this thing were so monstrously and obviously evil that it would be enough to say calmly and simply: "Here is one more sadistic orgy carried on by a psychopathic mob under the patronage of a moronic Governor of a backward state." Governor, I don't believe you can get away with it! There must be somewhere some power which just won't stand for it.

When Pegler submitted his contrary, pro-Rolfe version, Howard praised its "manly, forthright quality" but suggested holding it up a day or two since it seemed rather controversial for a debut.

The substitute first column appeared December 11, 1933. While it had some odd overtones, it seemed to be modesty itself. As a sportswriter, Pegler confessed, he had often filled space by inventing yarns about celebrities. "Back where I come from," he wrote, "if you wait a couple of years after Babe Ruth didn't kill any kidnappers with a ball bat, there is your story and you can go to bed." Not being too well acquainted with the Governor-do-your-duty bunch, the gold-standard boys and the whither-are-we-drifting alarmists, there would undoubtedly be days when he would pine for Uncle Wilbert Robinson and Primo Carnera. In short, he admitted, the new job scared him; he wished he were back where he came from.

Prohibition had been repealed the previous week, when Utah became the thirty-sixth state ratifying the twenty-first amendment, and Pegler missed his old punching bag. He conceded on December 12: "My hates have always occupied my mind much more actively and have given greater spiritual satisfactions than my friendships . . . The wish to favor a friend is not as active as the instinct to annoy some person or institution I detest."

Finally on the third day the delayed and slightly revised lynching column appeared. "As one member of the rabble," it began, "I will admit that I said 'Fine, that is swell,' when the papers came up that day telling of the lynching of the two men who killed the young man in California, and that I haven't changed my mind yet for all the storm of right-mindedness which has blown up since."

He had checked with some wives of representative men, Pegler reported (meaning that he had checked with his own wife at breakfast), and they had agreed with him privately, though not for publication. "Having no public position myself," he wrote, as if he were invisible, "I can be consistent."

Every newspaper city editor, continued the columnist, periodically established public opinion by phoning a standing list of persons for their views on specific issues. The list usually included the head of the bar association, a university president, a couple of judges, some crime committee members and "several prominent ladies who go in for right-mindedness and good works in a grim way." Since the rabble, of which he was "a member in good standing," was not consulted, checking with such a group on lynching would produce a routine response that everybody was entitled to equal protection under the law.

121

One advantage of a lynching, the column ground on, was that persons lynched were deprived of a chance to escape punishment through a politically arranged pardon or some legal technicality raised by a shyster. What if such persons were definitely proved later to be innocent? Well, their cases would be balanced, Pegler wrote callously, by "the innocent persons who were murdered."

Nothing in his sportswriting career had prepared Pegler for the spate of abuse which greeted this column. Apparently he did not realize that lynching—even more than segregation—was a prime instrument in the social subjugation of the Negro in the United States. As such it was abhorrent to every liberal. The fact that the two men lynched in California were white did not matter; to the liberals, a lynching was a lynching.

Excuses might be made for Westbrook and Julie Pegler on the ground that they were unsophisticated, but no such disclaimer could be put forward for Roy Howard. He knew what he was doing. He had the greater responsibility since he cleared the column; but he escaped public censure. Remembering the E. S. Scripps liberal tradition, readers directed their complaints at Pegler, the newcomer who seemed to be upsetting the paper's routine. Broun fanned the fires of protest with another angry protest. "Is this to be the measure of justice in California?" he wrote. "Men with blood and burnt flesh on their hands to be set free . . . Tom Mooney in jail . . . freedom for the guilty, punishment for the innocent!"

Pegler was dumbfounded. The roof had fallen in on him, he complained, before he got his chair warmed. What he really had in mind, he explained when he found time to realign his thoughts, was "the failure of law enforcement to protect victims of crime all over the U.S., a failure which finally called upon the federal government almost to place Chicago in receivership." The growth of wealthy gangs during prohibition, particularly the Capone gang in Chicago, had created unparalleled political corruption and lawlessness which were only beginning to subside. In Pegler's view, the open clubbing of mobsters was preferable to invoking income tax regulations against them. However, the column did not *say* this; it noted merely that the law could not be relied upon to punish the guilty. Furthermore, Pegler was an instinctive vigilante. As a boy, he had delighted in the Saturday night cuffing around of drunks and vagrants by the ham-handed sergeant of the Harrison Street station in Chicago, and in later years he went so far as to urge the formation of a national association of vigilantes.

"What about Heywood Broun?" Pegler asked friends anxiously. "Why did Broun greet me with a club from around the door as I entered the *World-Telegram* building?" Eventually, at Broun's suggestion, Pegler and Broun talked things over. Pegler explained that he intended not to justify any particular lynching but to call attention to public hypocrisy and the danger of inadequate law enforcement. Broun concluded that he had been fooled by Pegler's lowbrow style. Accusing himself of being unkind to a green hand, he was apologetic, friendly and charming. Pegler in his turn expressed relief that they understood each other.

"I don't think Broun acted with any hatred," Pegler decided. "Anyway, its part of the game. If you can't take it, don't dish it." Broun had invited him to some affair out in the country where they both lived, and he intended to accept the invitation in the spirit in which it was tendered. Even so the impression lingered in Pegler's mind that he had been struck a foul blow which would have to be avenged sooner or later.

The death of a parent is often a time for taking stock. When Frances Nicholson Pegler died of a heart attack at her home in New York on March 26, 1934, it focused emotions which had been lying under the surface of family life for years. As far back as Westbrook could remember, his mother had been ailing. Because the origin of her complaints was obscure, Arthur Pegler often waved them away as imaginary or blamed them on self-pity or a desire for attention.

As a boy, Westbrook generally shared his father's viewpoint. He began to have doubts as he grew older. He wondered if his father were not staying away from home too much and neglecting his wife for other interests. He said as much on one occasion in the 1920s, and for a while he and his father were not on speaking terms.

Frances Pegler, the youngest child and the one closest to her mother, always suspected the men in the family of callousness. When the discovery was made in 1932 that Mrs. Pegler actually had a cardiac condition, the men were thunderstruck. In a mode of almost triumphant self-righteousness, Frances gave up her idea of a banking career to stay at home as a companion and nurse during her mother's final two years of life.

Newspaper accounts of Mrs. Pegler's death featured the fact

123

that her son Westbrook was a "well known"—one paper even said "famous"—columnist. Lesser mention went to Arthur Pegler, still active at seventy-one as a rewrite man on the *Mirror*; to Westbrook's older brother Jack, a successful advertising man with the Lord & Thomas agency; and to Frances, who prepared the obituary and answered inquiries. Her mother taught all three children the fundamentals of writing before they were old enough to attend school and had "engaged in incidental writing of her own," Frances informed the Associated Press.

Frances was almost thirty and unmarried. When the funeral was over, she announced her intention of seeking a job, perhaps as a real estate saleswoman, and of living by herself in the city. She had no intention of seeing much of her brothers, who had their establishments in the suburbs, or of her father, who was also prepared to be self-sufficient in town.

Arthur Pegler's central position in the family could not survive his wife's death. Though he never understood why Westbrook "got paid so much for that stuff he wrote" in view of the small rewards for his own more spectacular contributions to the profession, the old man would strut proudly around the *Daily Mirror* city room on days when his son found some new chin to punch in public. "Chip off the old block, chip off the old block," the cranky, deafish veteran of the Chicago newspaper wars would rumble. He still wore his stiff derby and cane and at the end of a long day at the office he always padlocked his old-fashioned monster of a typewriter lest some cub try to use it illicitly during his absence. Apparently he never knew that he owed his continuing employment to Westbrook.

Emile Gauvreau, the *Mirror's* managing editor, had received a confidential memo one day from Arthur Brisbane, the Hearst editorialist, noting that Arthur was "the father of Westbrook Pegler, who writes with the kick of a mule." The memo continued: "Every time that boy lands on Mrs. Hearst's prize-fighting philanthropies my day is wasted. There's no use trying to talk to anybody about stopping him. His column is a dose of prussic acid. Treat his father right and maybe his son will become human."

Treating Arthur Pegler right was not always easy. In receiving a story from a young reporter over the phone, the septuagenarian would cover up his deafness with shouts and profanity. When a bottle passed around the city room, he got positively ugly after a couple of drinks though he never reached the stage of incapacity for work. His chief interest was crime stories, but his job also required roughing out editorials on political issues from time to time.

After getting a broad slant from Gauvreau, he would confer ill-naturedly with Frank Farley, the paper's political expert, over how things should be phrased to avoid annoying the "high priest" —meaning Gauvreau. Since he wound up by taking Farley's advice, the editorials usually passed muster. On the whole, the veteran earned his salary. He was still a legend in the business, and William Randolph Hearst made a point of being pleasant to him when they met.

Arthur Pegler, however, had one hurrah left, and he was assisted in delivering it by Floyd Gibbons. The famous war correspondent and vaudevillian wanted an interview for his Famous Features Syndicate and Arthur was glad to oblige. Since they were well-matched in imagination and credulity, the resulting collaboration was historic. Every familiar exaggeration and a few new ones were recorded as Gibbons traced the career of his subject, from the time he "got out of Oxford" and began a journalistic career with the London *Telegraph* by personally tracking down a murderer named Percy Leroy Mapleton for killing a millionaire named Gould in a railroad tunnel, and then making sure that Percy "climbed the gallows."

"Still, things weren't exciting enough in staid old London, so Peg hopped a boat and the U.S. got another doggoned good newspaperman. The great George Augusta Sala wrote letters about Peg to American editors. Ballard Smith of the New York *World* grabbed him, but the London reporter didn't come all the way over here just to settle down in another big city."

Arthur Pegler liked Le Mars, Iowa, it seemed, because of a saloon there named the "House of Lords," but he was soon stirring things up in Minneapolis. Having carried his hero so far, Floyd Gibbons devoted the remaining half of his space to the Indian skirmish involving Chief Old Bug the Bootlegger. In presenting this fiction, Arthur sometimes said that no other paper carried an account of the war because the other reporters were all scalped and dead. This time he added a new wrinkle: some of his scooped competitors might have survived, he said; he merely tacked a final paragraph on his own story implying that they were dead because "they were dead as far as getting the story to their papers was concerned."

In his breezy style, Floyd Gibbons concluded: "Couldn't

125

drag Art Pegler away from the newspaper business. They tried to make him a movie scenario writer. But the smell of printer's ink was too strong and back he came . . . That's my candidate for chief of our tribe . . . apostle of our creed . . . dean of our craft. Folks, you've met SOME newspaperman."

10. COUNTRY SQUIRE

The roads were rough and the village store sold patent medicines, licorice whips and overalls. As more city folk moved in, the roads improved and the store learned to stock imported ale, charged water and Camembert. Despite periodic quarrels between the natives and the new arrivals over zoning, Pound Ridge remained restful and relatively isolated. Deer nibbled the grass along the rim of Westbrook Pegler's very private pond, around which the willows wept. The pond was well stocked with bass for purposes of captive fishing. If turtles ate too many fingerlings, the squire strode out with a double-barreled shotgun to blast them. He took delight in fighting the Japanese beetles with rocks.

The only close neighbors were the Benders—Robert J. Bender, a friend and former associate at the United Press, Mrs. Bender and their daughter Beverly. When they first moved to Pound Ridge, the Benders gave weekend parties. Since they had no indoor toilet, they and their guests used two outhouses on a hillside over toward Pegler's place. During one large and noisy party, the guests starting making pilgrimages around dawn. According to H. Allen Smith, who got the story first-hand, the creator of "Fair Enough" awoke and decided to take a hand in the fun. There he sat on the porch of his Bavarian castle, putting careful holes through the outhouses with a .22 caliber rifle. He sustained his fire until the interlopers took to the woods. Then he went back to bed.

Invasion of privacy played a role in Westbrook's growing feud with Walter Winchell. His expressed contempt for the Broadway columnist's admitted habit of employing bodyguards and carrying loaded automatics for protection led Winchell to retaliate by announcing over the radio one Sunday evening that a kidnap scare had driven the Peglers into hiding in a New York hotel.

Listening to the broadcast in his Pound Ridge home, Westbrook almost burst as Winchell added in solicitous tones that he hoped to hear soon from Peg that the report was exaggerated or untrue. Winchell could have picked up a studio phone and disproved the story by a thirty-five cent phone call, Pegler pointed out furiously to Julie. Then his phone began ringing. To one of several neighbors who thought there must be a kidnap threat if Winchell reported one, the author of "Fair Enough" shouted: "My only bodyguard was my baby nurse!" and hung up.

In an ensuing column, Pegler referred to Winchell's radio stint as "a weekly phenomenon of fantastic gall verging on possession" and added that not even Hitler "showed greater effrontery than this nightclub and underworld chronicler of pregnancies, intimacies and erroneous and spiteful reports." He went on to such good effect that Winchell devoted scores of columns to rebuttal. Having drawn blood, however, the squire of Pound Ridge ignored Winchell. To friends he explained that the Broadwayite was undersized as a literary antagonist.

With nature at the door, the squire considered it appropriate to read Fabre on ants. He bought a magnifying glass to study the talented midgets. One day he was sitting in the weeds, using his scientific equipment, when a farm boy wandered by. The youngster watched Pegler and the ants impassively before turning away with a smothered "For God's sake!" The columnist had other difficulties with the wild life of the region. Rabbits did not bother him; he grew carrots specially for them to eat, dismissing the superstition that rabbits prefer lettuce to all other food. He bought a female sheep to keep down the grass, only to discover that this particular sheep was a dog-killer and would attack humans, too, if balked of its natural prey. The sheep finally had to be sold to quiet the nerves of the family dog.

Even when lounging on the lawn, strolling through the woods or slapping at insects, Pegler was never far away in his mind from a column. As soon as he captured an idea, he would retire to the study on the second floor of his writing shed, which had murals on the walls and a portable typewriter on a long desk. There he would settle down for an homeric struggle with the muse, sliping in a sheet of paper, lighting up a cigarette, banging out a couple of lines, then tearing the paper from the roller with a groan of dissatisfaction and starting over again. Soon the floor would be littered with cigarette butts and crumbled balls of paper.

When Pegler got to tramping up and down, kicking the waste basket and swearing violently in his search for the proper figure-skating phrase, he could be heard distinctly in the main house several hundred feet away, but nobody paid any attention.

The columnist was as insistent on neatness as he was neurotic about other people's noise, and he felt obliged to retype any page containing the slightest error. After four to six hours of agony, the job would be done and he would jump into his station wagon to drive in an impulsive fashion to the telegraph office in nearby New Canaan, Connecticut, where he also picked up his mail. From New Canaan, the column went to the *World-Telegram* office in New York, and Pegler would drive back to Pound Ridge to spend the evening worrying over a couple of drinks about changes which might have been made in the column.

Though the strain of switching to serious writing had given him a duodenal ulcer, Westbrook still smoked two packs of cigarettes a day. Such lack of self-control seemed shocking to Gene Tunney, with whom he had become reconciled because Julie liked Gene's wife Polly. If Pegler could not seem to give up nicotine any more than alcohol, he had an excuse: he was facing nerve-wracking difficulties as a commentator. In the first couple of years at the task he did score some limited successes with sports analogies. Since the depression had brought with it a sense of impending change, he would point out that a political cause waned and waxed like the fortunes of the Phillies. For a long while this ball club got nowhere for lack of cash or a trading margin in players, but then it stumbled over a few good youngsters and developed some others at a time when the leading clubs were getting older and making mistakes; and lo and behold, there were the down-trodden Phillies at the top of the National League!

During a visit to Washington, the columnist would come up with the idea that lobbyists were like racetrack touts. Legislators must be pretty stupid to pay any attention to them, he would write lamely, since smart bettors at the track had stopped patronizing touts long ago.

Similarly, he would discover that the national debt had risen under the impetus of New Deal spending to a record thirty-five billion. Pegler recalled oil-rich Texas teamsters rolling dice for piles of hundred-dollar bills on the floor of their hotel suite in Cincinnati during the fixed 1919 World Series with the White Sox. A few years later, those same teamsters were back in Texas, no longer rich, "pushing a lot of hardtails around in the mud." The rather elephantine moral was that a country "shooting a billion or no dice" must soon go broke.

The former sportswriter discovered that people whom he criticised reacted more violently than in the past. Democratic National Chairman James A. Farley would still grin at the columnist, calling him Westbrook and inquiring solicitously after Julie's health the day after a revelation that a niche had been found in the New Deal hierarchy for Wild Will Lyons, a raffish veteran of the New York fight racket. However, Farley had become accustomed to abuse as New York State boxing commissioner, and his attitude was that criticism did not matter if they spelled your name right. New Deal officialdom proved less placid. Secretary of the Interior Harold L. Ickes made a face at Pegler at a Gridiron Club affair and walked away with gestures of disgust. Others complained to Roy Howard, who kept friends in every camp.

What Pegler needed was a big new issue. He could hail the economic contribution being made by the rash of cocktail lounges opening up all over the country or do a retrospective piece on the way President Hoover used to "whine and hedge" over repeal, but the prohibition issue itself had definitely lost its zing. Even his old antipathy toward the rich proved less reliable. The Philadelphia *Bulletin,* a reluctant subscriber to "Fair Enough," promptly cancelled in protest over a jeering discussion of the late Mrs. E. W. Stotesbury, a dowager of overpowering local consequence.

The issue for which he was searching turned out to be antifascism. How he stumbled on indignation against the European dictators he hardly knew. It was in the air. Newspapers and magazines were full of it. The subject was certainly discussed at Nick's Upstairs Bar, the favorite after-work meeting place for *World-Telegram* employees. Heywood Broun's Newspaper Guild was the favorite topic, of course, and many a man and woman enrolled as a member there, but everything came up sooner or later.

Anti-fascism was also a favorite theme of Quentin Reynolds, the rollicking foreign correspondent who had rented a summer place for several seasons on Mill Road in Pound Ridge not far from the year-round establishment of the Peglers. Acquaintance between the two men dated back to the days when Reynolds covered the Southern baseball camps for the *World-Telegram.* Reynolds could even be considered a Pegler protégé. Pegler was getting his hair cut one day at the Hotel Roosevelt barbershop in New York when Walter Davenport of *Collier's* strolled in and mentioned a sports vacancy on his magazine. Pegler wasn't interested, but he suggested Reynolds; and Reynolds got the job, which permitted him gradually to move into the foreign field. It might well have been Reynolds who gave Pegler the idea of a European trip.

Adolf Hitler had been Chancellor of Germany since early 1933, but he was obliged to share power with President von Hindenburg until the latter's death on August 2, 1934. Then the German people approved the consolidation of Chancellor and President into the single office of Leader, giving Hitler a dictatorship by constitutional means over an emotionally surcharged country whose avowed purpose was the extermination of Communists and their agents. By 1935, the Soviet Union was shopping around frantically for friends in the Western countries. Communist party officials in the United States and their fellow-travelers focused on opinion-makers in the press. They were delighted to discover that Westbrook Pegler was among those receptive to anti-fascist propaganda.

Many non-Communist Americans—Democrats, Republicans, Socialists, liberals, independents—loathed Hitler. They objected to his regimentation, racism and imperialism as strongly as the Communists, but they were not always as ostentatious about it. One technique of the party-line workers was called "prestige-involvement." When an influential writer jumped tentatively on a CP bandwagon, a carefully arranged barrage of praise sought to keep him there. Pegler received the full treatment as soon as he began berating dictators and potential dictators. In return for the indirect lynching of their international enemies, the Communists were willing to forget if not forgive the columnist's defense of lynching in his debut as Roy Howard's staff philosopher.

Robert Forsythe, editor of the *New Masses*, invited the columnist in 1935 to write an article for a special issue of his Communist publication.

Pegler replied: "Dear Mr. Forsythe: Excuse great haste, plse. I gotta get to Europe and there's so much to do that I can't attempt to join you at this time. Hope there'll be a return date." The excuse was genuine enough. Not since his disastrous experiences as a correspondent in World War I had Pegler been abroad. Now he was planning to cover the scheduled winter-sports Olympic games at Garmisch-Partenkirchen, Germany. He saw this as

131

an opportunity to wipe out earlier disgrace and, at the same time, to get a closer look at the great world which lay uneasily beyond the sports scene.

Those were united front days. George Dimitroff, Comintern head, was chiding the C.P.U.S.A. for tardiness in befriending Socialists, liberals and anti-fascists of various kinds. It was therefore not surprising that Mike Gold, a *Daily Worker* columnist, should hail Pegler on October 24, 1935 as "an outstanding figure in the world of sports" for urging that the winter games be boycotted as a gesture against Nazism. When Chairman Avery Brundage of the American Olympic Committee dismissed such protests as "a Communist plot," Pegler replied that Brundage was a child, so charmingly amateurish in his love of sports that he would join in singing the Internationale if he thought that would improve the quality of athletics in Russia.

Pegler's coverage of the games at Garmisch-Partenkirchen was generally praised, and it drew special encomiums from the Communist press. A full column of excerpts from his attacks on Nazi censorship and propaganda and the use of Storm Troopers at a supposedly peaceful international affair was carried in a February 23, 1936 dispatch to the *Daily Worker*. The only other correspondent mentioned—and briefly mentioned at that—was Paul Gallico, who had succeeded Pegler as Eastern sports editor for the Chicago *Tribune*.

Pegler had expected to cover the summer Olympics in Germany, but the Nazis were disturbed by their recordings of the stories he had phoned from the press house in Garmisch. Hitler told Fred Oechsner, Berlin manager of the United Press, that the young American could not come unless he submitted copy to Goebbels for censorship. When Pegler said he would rather stay away than accept censorship, Goebbels attacked him in a speech, thereby making him more of a hero than ever at home.

Immediately after the winter Olympics, Hitler moved troops into the demilitarized Rhineland while France stood by helplessly for want of firm support from Britain. Mussolini was preparing to invade Ethiopia. With American concern over dictators reaching a new peak, Pegler's syndicate was delighted to let him expand his itinerary to include Italy, Czechoslovakia, Spain, France and England. He obtained a Russian visa too, but a last-minute request by a Soviet travel agency for forty dollars to cover telephone calls to Moscow for final clearance annoyed him to such an extent that he cancelled that portion of the trip.

The American public wanted to read about Hitler, so Pegler obliged as he moved through Europe. He had been "slow to take the spark" of admiration for the German dictator when he saw him at Garmisch-Partenkirchen, he explained, because he had previously seen such persons as Edison, Ford, Shaw, Einstein, Clemenceau and Eugene V. Debs. The Germans, he declared, "broke their words about the Olympic games, they pay no bills, they claim everything and concede nothing, they send agents into more or less friendly countries to murder and agitate."

"Official conspirators" of the Nazis were undoubtedly already at work in Hoboken and other German-American communities in the United States, the columnist warned. "The ferocity of Hitler's Ku Klux" could not be exaggerated, he wrote. Then, in an entirely different tone, from Prague in Czechoslovakia, came one of his most moving columns.

The German child who is a Jew [he wrote] is compelled to listen to the most unspeakable vilification of his parents, and the child's first attempts at spelling out public notices on the billboards will inform him that he is not a human being, like other children, but a beast whose parents were not human beings, either, but loathsome animals.

Thinking back, perhaps, to Excelsior, where his own boyhood had been spoiled by a few narrow-minded zealots, he described in detail the sanctioned harassment of the Jewish boys and girls. He concluded:

It is absolutely certain that their childhood, the few hours of innocence which are given to all of us and which civilized people try to invest with beauty and joy, has been destroyed by a man with a mustache, adopted from the makeup of a famous comedian, who has been seriously nominated by some of his followers not for king, not merely for ruler, but for God the Redeemer of the German race. It would be a mistake to call him a baby-killer. You can't torture a dead child.

Turning his thoughts homeward, Pegler warned against the potential American dictators—Huey Long, the Louisiana kingfish who "already had a terrorist organization" like that of Hitler, and Father Coughlin, the Michigan priest who was advancing a combined anti-Wall Street and racist program. Because of his cloth, Coughlin had been treated in a gingerly fashion by most American anti-fascists, but from Europe he was summarily dismissed by Pegler as "a clerical demagogue" and "a mad monk."

In Italy, the debunking tourist was amused by Mussolini's big chin and his cult of super-masculinity.

A military attaché from one of the powers which were trying to restrain Mussolini from his adventure in Africa became so annoyed at the overdone scowling of the dictator's underlings on one occasion that he flapped a hand at them and called "Yoo-hoo," Pegler narrated. The Italians dubbed British Foreign Secretary Anthony Eden "Pretty Boy," he continued, on the mistaken assumption that "because Mr. Eden is so lovely he is a little short of ability and gumption." This particular column concluded with a moral: "Never take a man for a sissy because he wears a mustache like a day-old Pekinese pup and carries his handkerchief in his sleeve. He might be Anthony Eden."

The secret police in Italy did frighten him, Pegler confessed, because they reminded him of American gangsters. Their customary procedure, he wrote, was "to call at night in a body on a victim of a political error, twist his arms and legs until the bones crack, then pour down his neck a quart of castor oil which may be mixed with kerosene. It is inartistic to use kerosene, however, for enough castor oil taken all at once is almost certain to rupture the human plumbing and to bring about death from natural causes within a few days. There is always plenty of castor oil."

Passing through England on the way home, the commentator argued that the English and the Americans were natural allies against the European dictators. In a final devastating fling at the Nazis, he noted that Horst Wessel, the hero of their national marching song, had "lived on the earnings of a stable of street-walkers."

Before he left the United States, Westbrook Pegler had been floundering. He kept splashing about, of course, but there had been a rising suspicion in the trade that he couldn't swim or even touch bottom.

Whatever the degree of his professional danger, the success of his European columns carried him safely ashore. Subscribing editors reported that his foreign dispatches had aroused more interest than any of his domestic stuff. Production of his first book of collected columns a year or so later confirmed this; it consisted largely of his European impressions.

The column about the Jewish children lingered particularly in people's minds. Eddie Cantor, the actor, told Pegler at lunch how he had enlarged it at his own expense and distributed it extensively among his friends. Rabbi Stephen S. Wise of the

American Jewish Congress hailed Pegler as a hero. Dorothy Thompson, an expert on European affairs who got her start as a columnist for the New York *Herald Tribune* while Pegler was on his European swing, remembered the column two years later when she was appealing by radio for money to hire a lawyer for Herschel Grynszpan, a Polish Jewish youth who had assassinated the secretary of the Nazi embassy in Paris. She wanted Pegler to read the column over the air. He refused, but sent a contribution and gave permission for Robert Montgomery, the actor, to read the article in his place. Montgomery performed so eloquently that many listeners wept. Contributions in excess of thirty thousand dollars were received within a week.

Under the impression that Pegler was a valuable possible recruit, the Communist publications were particularly fulsome in their praise when he returned from Europe. Blaine Owen, who had been doing lengthy interviews for the Sunday *Worker* with such celebrities as Jack Dempsey and Heywood Broun, produced one with Pegler on June 18, 1936, in which the columnist was quoted as saying that the Communist party convention scheduled for June 26 would be "a more important event than ever before."

Fascist tendencies are popping up everywhere [the remarks attributed to Pegler continued] and I don't want to pull any punches on that stuff. I'm against Fascism in any garb they put it, Nazi-ism, probably its most malignant form, and despotism in any shape. You can take that any way you want, 'cause that includes the despotism of your Raskobs, your du Ponts, Hearst or who-have-you. I'm not a Communist and I'm not for Communism but this idea of forming a Farmer-Labor party to put through real social legislation and progressive policies in government is okay. Call it any name you want to—People's Party, American Party, Progressive Party or Farmer-Labor—but go ahead and form one! The stuff I saw under the Nazis in Germany and under Mussolini scared me! That stuff can't be allowed to get in here, and I'm with anyone on that. Yet you can see how they're trying to smuggle it in. Read the Hearst papers. You'll see a story here praising Hitler and an article there saying nice things about Mussolini. Hearst is sneaking that stuff in one way or another, but not for me.

Pegler took no notice of the interview. He may never have seen it in print. When it was called to his attention later, he declared that if he had been interviewed by Blaine Owen, a fairly well-known Communist journalist who died eventually of tuberculosis in Arizona, he did not realize at the time that Owen was

135

working for the *Worker*. Nevertheless, the quoted remarks sounded like the columnist in an informal mood. Soon afterward Pegler interviewed Earl Browder and William Z. Foster at Communist headquarters in New York. The *New Masses* cited Pegler as "an honest, courageous and observant journalist," reporting that he had sent greetings to the Communist national convention of 1936.

Westbrook Pegler swung closer to Communism during this period than he apparently realized. Almost twenty years later, he was asked publicly for his reaction to a statement that communism is "the reaction to poverty, oppression and the exploitation of the masses by the few, and represents the drive of the masses for a strong central authority to curb their enemy." He muttered angrily that it was "pro-Communist propaganda, very familiar in the Communist line . . . utter nonsense . . . false." The definition had come from his own column of January 6, 1937.

At various times Westbrook Pegler referred to himself as a trade unionist, but he rarely thought or acted like one. During his service on the *World-Telegram*, his primary loyalty was reserved for Roy Howard, his publisher and friend. This did not prevent him from playing a role of sorts in the early Newspaper Guild. He held a membership card, paid dues and attended at least two meetings of the *World-Telegram* unit. "I didn't join, Heywood Broun put me in," he explained. On another occasion he said: "I didn't consider that I joined because I never voted. I abstained from voting for very definite reasons in the very few meetings I attended." He made no speeches at meetings, he did no writing for the union, he did not organize, agitate or picket. It could be said that he lingered near the door of the house of labor for a while without stepping inside.

The Newspaper Guild was uncertain at first whether it wanted to be a professional newswriters' association which would fuss over standards and a monopoly place in the community, like the bar and medical associations, or a union focusing on wages, hours and economic conditions. Heywood Broun, with the authority of a founding father, offered at one time to abandon the trade union concept if the publishers would show good faith by making a few concrete improvements. The gesture may have been less naïve than it sounded. At any rate, the publishers ig-

136

nored it; they saw no reason to give the Guild any recognition, however indirect.

So far as he understood what was going on, Pegler sympathized with the professional faction in the Guild but he played no role in the struggle. The question was debated hotly at sessions of the Representative Assembly, the legislative body of the New York local, which was larger and more influential than all the other locals put together. Those delegates favoring a trade union, including a few active and knowledgeable Communists, met in secret caucus before each RA meeting to discuss tactics against the professional faction. As victory of the trade union group over the others was signalized in a series of early strikes, a few influential leaders of the professional faction, like Walter Lippmann, dropped out, but the union as a whole gained muscle.

A busload of pickets from New York, heading for the Newark *Ledger* plant during the 1935 strike there, was electrified by an announcement that Westbrook Pegler, the columnist, had contributed fifty dollars, the largest contribution to date. This represented instinctive generosity on Pegler's part rather than any commitment to the class struggle.

During this same strike, Heywood Broun took Harry Raymond of the *Daily Worker* off the picket line in New Jersey and brought him to New York as a humorous Exhibit A of the "red menace in the labor movement." A Rand School committee sponsoring a forum-broadcast at the Mecca Temple looked grim and disapproving as Broun declared he had already been accused of communism and that he would now be charged with "boring from within," since he had just come through the tunnel from Newark. Broun went on to laud the contribution of Communists and other left-wingers in the Guild. "If you belong to a union without any reds in it," he advised, "for God's sake go out and recruit a few!"

As international president of the Guild, Broun presided at meetings with a water tumbler of gin on the table in front of him. Sometimes he wore one brown and one black sock. He looked, somebody said, like an unmade bed, yet he was as serious about his causes as he was careless about his person. The Guild constitution specified no discrimination against members on political grounds, and he considered such discrimination divisive. (Like most liberals of his day, he accepted the Communist party as a bona fide political movement, not as an agent of a

137

foreign conspiracy as it became known later.) In one column, Broun wrote that no American could be really informed without reading the *New York Times* and the *Daily Worker* every morning. He joined many Communist fronts. The Socialist Party, which he had served in an uncertain fashion, finally expelled him for addressing a Communist rally for the Scottsboro boys.

Behind Broun in the ever expanding Guild, the Communists were making converts among rank-and-filers who showed special ability in organization, agitation or actual strike work.

Ferdinand Lundberg, author of *Imperial Hearst* and *America's Sixty Families*, became concerned. Since he had been serving as secretary of the trade union caucus in New York, where Communist strength was focused, he knew exactly what was going on. He sought out Carl Randau, a gifted *World-Telegram* rewrite man who had recently been elected president of the New York local. Over a cup of coffee in a cafeteria, Lundberg told Randau all about the Communist maneuvers, one of which had been to advance Randau, purely on merit, to leadership. Randau listened carefully and left without comment. Within a few days, he was being seen regularly in the company of the Communists who were exercising power behind the scenes. The next Communist step was to abolish the trade union caucus; thereafter Communist party faction meetings would suffice to guide the RA.

Like everybody else, Pegler heard rumors that the Communists were becoming influential in the Guild. He respected those few employees who were willing to report secretly to Roy Howard on union matters. The publisher followed developments with an agonized intensity. Hearing on one occasion that a Guild leader had spoken harshly of him, he summoned a sub-editor from Yonkers to his own New York residence at midnight and in the presence of guests including Helen Worden, he asked: "Joe, tell me, am I a son-of-a-bitch?" Joe told him no and went back to Yonkers.

Pegler often discussed the Guild with Howard either at the office or during weekend trips on the publisher's 110-foot yacht, the "Jamaray," which had once been owned by Charles F. Kettering. The columnist sympathized with the publisher's inability to fire some of the more annoying unionists.

Because of unfair labor practice laws, Howard had to move cautiously, though on occasion he managed to eliminate an unwanted employee by abolishing his job. In fairness it should be said that the relationship between Pegler and Howard extended beyond the issue of unionism. They had known each other a long time and had a similar background. Each scorned the fine distinctions and elaborations of the professorial mind. Howard delighted in the Artemus Ward school of humor and discerned something endearing about a frank expression of ignorance. He and Pegler even shared a puritanical streak at variance with their professional experiences. Since Howard had no flair for writing, Pegler in a very real sense had become his voice—"He was to Howard what Jenny Lind was to Barnum," a *New Yorker* profile once put it. Yet there were things which Roy Howard did not want written for him, and one of these was how he felt about the Guild at a time when negotiations were reaching a critical point. He asked Pegler to hold his fire for a while and the columnist had to agree.

By this time Heywood Broun no longer faced Pegler across the top of the *World-Telegram* split-page. On the ground that the newer commentator was developing his own following, Roy Howard had pushed Broun down, and moved Pegler over on top of him. To many readers of Broun, the change seemed like a symbolic blow. Howard's next split-page acquisition was General Hugh Johnson, who had become disgruntled with the New Deal after handling its ill-conceived National Recovery Administration. A Howard memo to Scripps-Howard editors stressed that the general's "increasing importance" could be deduced from "his relative position on the page" between Pegler and Broun. Since Broun had been pushed down another notch, it could be deduced that his importance was declining further.

Syndicating Broun in the hinterland was said to be proving more difficult as a result of his radical ideas and associations. In any case, he was treated with even less courtesy after Howard added Mrs. Eleanor Roosevelt as a columnist, letting her know that he hoped she would avoid politics as much as possible in her diary-like column called "My Day." The "smorgasbord arrangement" of four columns, one on top of another, never seemed to cut into Pegler's top space, but it frequently required trimming of Broun at the bottom. To *World-Telegram* employees, and to Guild members generally, the message was unmistakable: Broun was being penalized and Pegler rewarded for their respective attitudes toward the union.

In the spring of 1937 the *World-Telegram* unit took its long-awaited strike vote. The meeting raged for hours. Pegler attended, though he considered himself an independent contractor

139

—he did have an individual contract—who could not be bound by Guild action. Heywood Broun, who had a similar contract, was challenged during the meeting to say what he would do if the Guild walked out. Waving a piece of paper which might have been his contract, Broun shouted that if the pickets marched along West Street in the morning, he would be out there at their head, contract or no contract.

Pegler sat in silence. A spokesman for the printers' union promised to respect any Guild picket line and see to it that "no scabs, rats and fakes" got into the plant. Pegler considered this a personal threat of violence, but he made no comment. James Street, a pint-sized shipnews reporter who was already writing novels on the side, roared that the twenty-five members, supposedly friendly to management, whose back dues had been paid up the day before the meeting, should not be allowed to vote.

Others challenged Street, but not Pegler. Eventually Street's motion was defeated and the strike vote itself lost by a lesser margin than the number of last-minute dues-payers.

Feeling ran high after the meeting. Despite his passive position, Pegler was lumped among the company unionists and management stooges. On the theory that he had been kissing Howard's boots, some hotheads talked of asking him to wipe the blacking off his face; they didn't do it. Two militants claimed to have elbowed him into a urinal in the washroom; it didn't happen. But the apocryphal story attested to the tension in the city room.

Westbrook Pegler had held manual jobs in the stockyards and elsewhere before he had fuzz on his face, and he felt he had more right to the title of worker than those who remained "study-bums" in universities at their parents' expense long after they were grown. He had known Roy Howard since 1910. Did the union have any right to choose his friends for him? Supposing he were a boss-lover, as charged, he reserved the right to contend that the boss was "a better man than the whole pack of curs in the union which was trying to destroy him."

A split in the American Federation of Labor had produced John L. Lewis' Congress of Industrial Organizations. Without any grinding of gears, the newspaper union shifted in the summer of 1937 from AFL to CIO affiliation. The CIO espoused vertical rather than craft unionism. For the Newspaper Guild this meant enrolling all the unorganized workers in the plants

140

from advertising solicitors and circulation men to porters and elevator operators.

When he saw these strangers at a meeting or listened to a militant non-journalistic adviser from headquarters, Pegler grumbled that the Guild had fallen into the hands of foreigners. He talked of resigning. Broun explained that anybody who withdrew his designation of the union as his collective bargaining agent thereby excluded himself from employment at any plant which subsequently adopted a preferential or closed shop in agreement with the Guild. That very day Pegler sent in his resignation.

According to Guild officials, the resignation arrived at Guild headquarters in an envelope with a pencilled notation: "For Mrs. Roosevelt, President." The President's wife was a member though never an officer of the union. She became eligible for membership, like Pegler, through writing a column. When she first announced her intention of joining the Guild, she was visited secretly by two anti-Communist leaders on the *Telegram*, George Britt and Fred Woltman. They wanted her to know what she was getting into. After listening intently, she said: "Well, if the Communists are in control, as you say, then it is up to the rest of us to attend meetings and vote them out of control." She joined the union, attended meetings and in the end things developed more or less as she expected.

11. THE SHORT ESSAY

Tax reform lay at the heart of the New Deal. Back in 1932, the top rate on individual incomes had been only 25 per cent. Within three years, as the administration sought to pay for expensive new programs and to reduce the extremes in poverty and wealth created by the depression, the highest surtax rate rose to 75 per cent. In the summer of 1935, President Roosevelt asked for various new taxes falling heavily on corporations. A day or so before a modified version of his program was enacted by Congress, he received a letter from Roy Howard declaring that men who had once given him sincere support were becoming "not merely hostile but frightened" at the thought that he was "looking for revenge on business rather than revenue." Howard's idea was that the national income tax base should be broadened to bring in less wealthy layers of the population.

F.D.R.'s insistence on tax reforms began to cut deeply into his journalistic support. Colonel McCormick's Chicago *Tribune* and the Hearst papers coast to coast groaned that the President was "soaking the rich." When the phrase failed noticeably to stir the masses, William Randolph Hearst modified it to "soaking the thrifty." Even this did not unduly disturb those who had never been able to put much aside, so a solemn conclave of fifty-thousand-dollars-a-year Hearst executives coined a new slogan: "Don't Soak Success!"

Because of the tax issue, and because of the President's use of such phrases as "economic royalists" for his enemies, the 1936 presidential campaign was extraordinarily venomous. Conservative Democrats, led by Alfred E. Smith and John W. Davis and backed financially by Jouett Shouse and the du Ponts, formed the Liberty League to oppose Roosevelt. Canards about the President's health were enlarged to include doubts about his sanity. Publisher Hearst wrote editorials that the Communists were voting for F.D.R. on orders from Moscow. Henry L. Mencken said the incumbent could be beaten by a Chinaman. A *Literary Digest* poll predicted the election of Governor Alfred E. Landon of Kansas, the Republican candidate. Even so, and with eighty-five per cent of the press against him, the President carried every state but Maine and Vermont.

Westbrook Pegler took a relatively minor role in the 1936 campaign, but after it was over he revealed that he had voted for Roosevelt. "I was more against his enemies," he explained, "than I was for him. He had tangled with Huey Long, a really bad man, and Father Coughlin." What Pegler overlooked was that Long and Coughlin were beating the drums for tax reform louder and with more flourishes than the President. In fact, Charles Beard, the historian, always suspected that the Revenue Act of 1937, which Roosevelt brought forward in accordance with his campaign promises, was designed primarily "as a stick to beat off the storm troops of Senator Long and Father Coughlin."

Pegler plunged into the tax thicket in the spring of 1937. A Congressional investigating committee had been asking a number of wealthy men, including Roy Howard and other Scripps-Howard officials, about the personal holding companies they utilized to reduce their taxes.

Howard's particular scheme, wholly within the law, had saved him eighty thousand dollars in taxes on a taxable income of five hundred thousand dollars in 1936. For several months before the committee issued its report, Pegler hammered away at the government's high-handed and inquisitorial tax methods. This was embarrassing to Roy Howard, since it made him look as if he were trying to avoid exposure. More than once, the publisher must have been tempted to ask the columnist to stop, but he did not interfere with the freedom of the press.

By this time Pegler had tax grievances of his own. He was now earning in excess of fifty thousand dollars a year. Just as he got in the chips, he grumbled, that man in the White House came along to grab most of his hard-earned cash. Heywood Broun wisecracked that his colleague had been "bitten by a tax," but Pegler was in no mood for levity. From 1934 on, every one of his returns had to be rechecked because of his large and necessarily unorthodox expenses. He began to suspect persecution.

The federal tax was then not nearly as broad as it subsequently became. It affected only three to four million persons in the entire country. Having landed among this privileged few, the writer worried over those who escaped federal taxation. When the Supreme Court ruled in 1937 that state officials need pay no income tax on their official salaries, Pegler tried to prove that President Roosevelt, as a former New York Governor, was a tax-dodger on the same moral level as "these Wall Street artists who convert prefabricated loopholes in revenue acts into triumphant arches through which millionaires march untaxed."

Pegler kept campaigning on this subject until the law in New York State was changed. As a result, his first major journalistic award came in 1937 from the National Headliners Club for exposing income tax evasion, which was not precisely what he started out to do but which was, after all, in line with Roy Howard's thinking. When he added anti-unionism to his anti-tax crusade, it was apparent that Westbrook Pegler had finally turned against the New Deal.

His first catlike pass at the Newspaper Guild came during the summer of 1937. The organization he wrote about—to which he gave a funny name which was not the Guild, but which could be recognized sufficiently to justify reprinting the article in *Editor & Publisher*—had been "taken over by the Moscow crowd because most of us didn't bother to vote," he declared. Members of his organization were upset when a national convention voted to switch from the AFL to the CIO, to adopt the clenched fist as a new high-sign among members and to come out for oysters over clams, he continued. Pegler preferred clams, he said. "I would join that Fascist Johnstown Citizens thing in a minute," he added surprisingly, "except that you never can tell what an organization will do after you are in. They might come out for tapioca."

In view of the existing national labor situation, the Johnstown Citizens Committee reference was inflammatory. The committee was sponsoring a back-to-work movement in Johnstown, Pennsylvania. Armed deputies had fired into a crowd of strikers, women and children there, killing some and wounding more than fifty, as the indirect answer of the Bethlehem Steel Corporation to attempted unionization of its plant. Since the Johnstown Citizens Committee was transparently inspired by the company, its very existence rubbed salt in an inflamed wound.

Having finished for the time being with the Guild, Pegler began to look around for other anti-union material. Julie as usual came to the rescue. George L. Berry, president for forty-one years of the International Printing Pressmen and Assistants Union, had popped up in a high New Deal post. Mrs. Pegler recalled some highly discreditable things which had been brought out about

Berry at a trial down in Tennessee which she had covered twenty years earlier. Westbrook duly utilized the tip to produce one of his bone-crunching exposés. When Berry wrote to complain that the columnist had ruined him, Pegler replied stiffly that Berry's character was "executed by a court" long ago.

Mail began to come in from various rank-and-file unionists, and Julie would pass along the more promising letters to her husband. Most complaints involved old-fashioned business unions which had slipped into the grasp of racketeers. (Though often radical, the new CIO unions were likely to be clean in an economic sense.) Ultimately Pegler began to focus on a racketeering side of unionism which up to then had largely escaped scrutiny but which was quite foreign to his own experiences in the Guild.

There was a Memorial Day massacre in 1937 outside the Republic Steel plant in South Chicago. When it was over, Pegler reported gloatingly, "Twelve rioters were dead, about seventy lay broken and bloody, but all the police passed muster." According to the columnist, the police were suppressing "a local insurrection," but newsreels taken at the time showed that the marching workers were peaceful until the police attacked. All the men killed were shot in the back, and a Senatorial investigating committee reported that "the consequences of the Memorial Day encounter were clearly avoidable by the police."

From the Johnstown and South Chicago steel incidents, Pegler drew one primary conclusion. "I predict," he wrote approvingly in his column, "that there will be more blood shed for and against a free man's Constitutional right to stay out of a union and retain his right to earn a living than over all the other issues put together." This was the sum of his personal experiences in the Newspaper Guild—a manifesto for the oppressed employer and the open shop.

A tall, serious man with a furrow in his freckled brow walked into the Westport, Connecticut studio of Justim Sturm one warm day in August 1938, and asked if he could get some lessons in sculpture. He had entered a competition for a monumental figure in San Francisco, he explained, and if he won he would receive free transportation there. Sturm figured he was dealing with an eccentric country gentleman of some kind, but it turned out that his visitor was Westbrook Pegler, forty-four, an amateur cartoonist who also produced a newspaper column. Pegler had taken offense at a gigantic statue of St. Francis by

145

Benjamin Buffano which was scheduled to go on San Francisco's Christmas Tree Hill. To judge by newspaper photographs, he said, Buffano's opus "looked like a drainpipe." It would certainly "affright the whole populace save for a God-sent fog." The columnist had posted a hundred dollars that he could produce a better statue than this "stone-cutter's nightmare," and Buffano had covered his money.

You could expect this kind of thing from members of the ex-urban intellectual fellowship whose play space extended across the New York-Connecticut border from Pound Ridge well into Fairfield County, where Westport was located. They were forever doing something with their left hands of which their right hands were ignorant. They included Gene Tunney, the Shakespearean authority; Bernard Gimbel, the department store sportsman; Justice of the Peace George T. Bye, who was Eleanor Roosevelt's literary agent; John Erskine, Deems Taylor, Ursula Parrott, Quentin Reynolds and a dozen others including, of course, Heywood Broun, master of the revels.

One fall Broun would be running for Congress on the Socialist ticket and the next spring he would be producing a cooperative musical comedy for unemployed actors, called *Shoot the Works*, with himself as the star. Sometimes it seemed as if his diurnal essays were just sparks cast off by the feverish consumption of his life. During poker games with Franklin P. Adams, Alexander Woollcott and other cronies of the Thanatopsis Literary and Inside Straight Club at the Hotel Algonquin in New York, he would ask to be excused for a couple of hands and come back with a finished column. Pegler saw this trick performed once during a poker game at Broun's own Sabine Farm north of Stamford, Connecticut, and it gave him a shock. Here was a man who played the typewriter like a professor in a honky-tonk, and yet what came out was limpid literature! To Pegler, who bled for every phrase, this was the unforgivable excellence.

Pegler followed the Broun routine with his attempt at sculpture, but it didn't work out quite as he anticipated.

True, he obtained plenty of publicity; the back-scratching tradition among his colleagues attended to that. First it was reported that he had spurned the starting blocks, hammer and chisel sent him by Buffano. He was going to model in mud, he declared; of course he didn't. Somewhat later it was revealed that he had experimented with an anchor, a compass and a shock of wheat which could be recognized as a shock of wheat by any

Pound Ridge wheat grower after three drinks. Next he produced an epic elf toting a gingerbread homunculus in one hand and a sheaf of carrots in the other while a mesmerized mouse looked on. The odd appearance of this creation was explained by the fact that two grapes and a pineapple disappeared from the cornucopia during the casting.

After the artistic doubletalk, a caricature in granite finally appeared, called Miss Special Delivery. This rather bare and brawny wench carried a letter in one hand and a pigeon in the other. The part-time artist then rested from his labor; his heart had never really been in it. The supposed competition with Buffano was quietly settled by contributing the stakes to charity.

Broun held four or five big stud poker games a season on the central table in the living room of his farmhouse. Westbrook Pegler and his brother Jack attended occasionally over a period of several years. Westbrook was no good at games; he would lose thirty to forty dollars each time in a good-natured, fatalistic manner. Other players included Frederick Tisdale Jr., the New Milford newspaper editor, and Mrs. Tisdale; Colvin Brown, the advertising man; and such regulars as Bye and Reynolds. Connie Madison, a sensible chorus girl from the *Shoot the Works* company who had become the second Mrs. Broun in 1935, might also play, and Woody Broun, Heywood's son by his first marriage, would sit in if he were home from college.

The intellectuals went in for weekend exercise in a conspicuous manner. Broun had a rocky midget golf course on which visitors competed for a championship cup presented originally to him by the *Shoot the Works* chorus. Sometimes the cup was won a dozen times on a Sunday afternoon, with the host retaining possession each time after the winner drained it of champagne. The heavy drinking and the bohemian behavior of some of the younger guests on these occasions displeased Pegler. More to his liking was the comic-opera softball team organized under Broun's auspices.

Gene Tunney captained the Nutmegs, as the ballplayers were called, Jack Pegler held down third base and Broun ambled around the outfield. Other players included Stoopnagle, the comedian; Hendrik Willem van Loon, the historian; Vincent Richards, the tennis player; Harold Ross, Bernard Gimbel and Quentin Reynolds. Westbrook caught, after a fashion, and a photographer snapped him intent on athletic duty, eyes closed, head half turned away, fingers straight out in front.

At least twice, with baffling results, the Nutmegs played Lowell Thomas's Nine Old Men in Pawling, New York. Once they played the Pound Ridge Fire Department on its home grounds in a meadow about a mile from Pegler's picture-book chateau. After the game, both teams and their rooters poured like an avalanche onto the columnist's chosen acres. Bars and grocery stores for miles around were requisitioned to satisfy the local and visiting firemen. Pegler remained an amiable host despite one raucous guest who proceeded to name the private pond Lake Malice and to shout "Rancors Aweigh" at sight of the columnist's rowboat.

In the spring of 1938, eight members of the intellectual aristocracy of the countryside founded a weekly newspaper called the Connecticut *Nutmeg*. Jack Pegler and Colvin Brown began to rustle advertising. John Erskine, Frank Sullivan, Stanley High and Ursula Parrott were among those accepting assignments. After shying away from sports topics, Gene Tunney produced an article defending Chamberlain's position at Munich. A suggestion that he be lynched from the nearest apple tree was tabled by the editorial board, but his article never saw light.

Westbrook Pegler had declined to invest any money in the enterprise or to serve on its editorial board, but he promised a contribution. Delivery of it was considerably delayed. As the moving spirit in the magazine, Broun found more and more of the work landing on his shoulders. Meeting Leonard Lyons, the Broadway columnist, in a night club one evening, Broun grumbled that the *Nutmeg* had finally received "something out of Peg's trunk"—meaning an old, rejected manuscript. It was true enough; not being as facile a writer as some of his colleagues, Pegler had dug up an unpublished piece, but he winced just the same when Broun's comment reached him. Minor irritations frequently arose between the two men, particularly over the Roosevelts and the Guild.

Mulling over the 1937 strike vote at the *World-Telegram*, Pegler asked Broun at the office what he would have done, in a professional sense, after a strike. Broun replied that the Guild, if it won, would have insisted on restoration of his contract as a condition of settlement, the way Actors' Equity won amnesty for members with broken contracts after its strike. Pegler shook his head. He was still visualizing his own plight, in case of a strike, if he had remained loyal to the contract. Wasn't the actual effect of Broun's militancy to throw people out of jobs, put picket lines around and shout "scab" at them when they were not scabs? Under such circumstances, how could Broun pose as a humane, warm-hearted man? Was he insincere?

While not yet ready to print such suspicions, Pegler did increase his columnar sniping at Broun. After one scathing reference to "old Bleeding Heart," he encountered Broun in a night club. Since he rarely visited night clubs, he did not feel quite at home. Rather nervously he commented: wasn't it nice that they could remain friends despite differences of opinion at the office? "What I write by day," growled Broun, "I live by night!" But he didn't mean it; the rivals were soon chatting amicably over drinks.

During this period, Westbrook Pegler did not take himself too seriously. He found time to play a lot of golf with Patrick (Packy) Dyer, an Irish-Catholic pro-Roosevelt Democratic politician, at the Ridgewood Golf Club. At a dinner party, he specialized in jokes about his baseball days. People found him bright, witty, funny. They admired him but they were not in awe of him. If he embarked on an anti-New Deal tack which was likely to provoke controversy, Frederick Tisdale Jr., his closest friend, would say firmly, "Come on, Peg, you don't believe that," or Julie would drawl, "Now Bud . . ." to keep him in orbit.

Though admiration for the Roosevelts was almost an article of faith in the Broun circle, the columnist's Washington contacts were uniformly scornful of the White House family. They included Walter Trohan of the Chicago *Tribune,* John O'Donnell of the New York *Daily News* and Lyle Wilson of the United Press, each of whom was more than willing to provide leads for critical stories about the various alphabetical agencies and officials of the New Deal.

Considering the malicious whispering among the followers of the Colonel McCormick-Captain Patterson-Hearst journalistic axis in Washington, it was remarkable that Pegler retained his New Deal badge as long as he did. When President Roosevelt experimented with a beard, Walter Trohan promptly raised a crop of mutton-chop whiskers in what he declared was self-defense. When the President decided to resume shaving, Trohan claimed a personal victory over the New Deal. Trohan also spread a story that he, O'Donnell, Wilson and Pegler, in that order, were on a presidential blacklist for ignoring an invitation to lunch at the White House with the President's wife and mother.

The women in this circle had a worse bite than the men.

149

According to a Pegler column, Constance Wilson typed up a private news release for the other wives about Mrs. Eleanor Roosevelt's all-female soirées at the White House. "To hell with her kiss-the-pillow parties," it began. The very next day, she reported, Lyle's tax returns came under official scrutiny. She was prepared to name other critics of the administration who had been kicked below the belt in their income tax.

Westbrook Pegler had mixed feelings about President Roosevelt for a long while. The hero-worship engendered by that first White House press conference soon evaporated. After a later press conference, the author of "Fair Enough" expressed annoyance at the "sycophancy" of the regular correspondents. A personal interview with the President did not allay his doubts. "Now look, West," said F.D.R. at one point, gesturing with his cigarette-holder. That tore it; nobody referred to Pegler as "West" and he hated being called out of his name. "What was that, Frank?" he replied, glowering. General Johnson, who had arranged the interview, laughed uproariously when he heard from Pegler how the two men parted in mutual enmity. Yet there was something about the President that the columnist could not easily dismiss. One day in the mid-thirties, he had a dining car conversation with John W. Vandercook's mother on a train bound for Poughkeepsie. "Will you see the President?" she asked. "I hope not," he answered. "Why not?" "Because he bemuses me."

As a member of the ex-urban softball set, Pegler became socially acquainted with Mrs. Eleanor Roosevelt. He met her three times, not counting one occasion when they were joint guests at a syndicate party to announce the debut of "My Day," which attracted eighty-eight immediate subscribers.

First there was a picnic in honor of Mrs. Roosevelt at Broun's Sabine Farm. Pegler said hello to Franklin P. Adams, the former *World* columnist enjoying a revival on the New York *Post*, Deems Taylor, Quentin Reynolds and others. Then he found the bar, and thereafter clung to it in preference to listening to a discussion of the issues of the day by the First Lady of the Land. They exchanged polite words upon parting, and when he threw one of his bingo columns at her several days later, Mrs. Roosevelt was surprised. "I guess he didn't like me," she told friends.

Next she invited him, among others, to a picnic at Hyde Park. This time Pegler ignored the other guests. Borrowing a

150

typewriter from his hostess in imitation of Broun's quick-writing gesture, he labored in a room apart. Julie explained to Mrs. Roosevelt that her husband had to be angry to write well. The result of that visit was another vigorous anti-Mrs. Roosevelt column. "I guess he doesn't like picnics," she said, deciding to invite him to a White House gathering.

Once again, Pegler accepted. Once again, he reacted to a pleasant social occasion with unpleasant columnar remarks. As a cultivated woman with a slow but inexorably logical mind, Mrs. Roosevelt concluded that the columnist must dislike the things for which she stood in his mind. She also reached some conclusions about Pegler. "I frequently read him," she confessed in "My Day," "because it entertains me to see how things may be twisted, according to your own bias and your lack of knowledge and understanding. If you believed him, you would be depressed about human nature, not only in the individuals whom he mentions but in the feeling you get of general cynicism about people."

Having no children of their own, Westbrook and Julie lavished extra affection on the handsome offspring of Jack Pegler and Mrs. Pegler, the former Mabel Kelly, a musical comedy actress who had appeared in the old Winter Garden shows in New York. The boys were named Arthur James Pegler, II and Westbrook Pegler, II which were soon transformed into "Buddy Poo" and "Wessy Poo" because of a childish inability to pronounce "II." Since the Jack Peglers lived nearby in Pound Ridge, the columnist dropped over frequently, willing and anxious to gratify any reasonable wish from a softball catch to a visit to the circus on the part of the boys who bore his own boyhood and adult names.

The main purpose of the trip to New York one particular Christmas was to exchange conversation with department store Santa Clauses, but Westbrook was inspired to take the boys first to the Amsterdam Theatre on Forty-second street for what turned out to be an historic showing of the first half-dozen spools of a new American art form. The columnist's reaction, promptly reproduced in "Fair Enough," was that Snow White was "the happiest thing that has happened in this world since the armistice." The boys were less excited about Disney than the adult, who would have liked to have seen everything all over again. Some of the more highbrow members of the Broun circle sniffed at this "infantilism" but the columnist stuck to his guns. When Pinocchio, about whom he was equally enthusiastic, arrived two years later, Pegler asserted that his columnar verdict on Snow White was the only one he had never been tempted to revise in the light of later knowledge.

In appreciation for all this free advertising, Disney sent Westbrook Pegler four special Donald Duck shirts, one of which the columnist usually managed to be wearing when guests arrived at his Pound Ridge chateau. When he injured his spine during one of the Heywood Broun softball games and was threatened for a while with a fusion operation, Disney cheered him by dispatching a production crew to Pound Ridge along with six or seven films of feature length—his entire production for the coming year.

Such a treasure had to be shared. The columnist phoned a New Canaan undertaker for folding chairs and sent out invitations for a special showing. A huge screen was rigged across the massive chimney in Pegler's living room, which had a fourteen-foot-high ceiling. More than sixty neighbors and friends crowded into the room to watch the performance and consume sandwiches and other refreshments. Gene Tunney, representing the largely absent Broun circle, was as excited as the host and insisted on seeing some portions of the carnival over again.

Julie had a theory that Westbrook worked too hard and stayed too close to the hearth. She did not object when he began to breed Scotties in a deliberately amateurish way—they could always give the puppies to friends. When he expressed an idle wish for a baseball diamond of his own, she had one constructed on the estate as a birthday gift while he was away on a trip. She did not wish him to feel tied down by her own invalidism. When they went to a country social function, he had a habit of wandering over to touch her hand. If it felt cool, he would quietly say goodbye and take her home, since a cool hand to him indicated a dangerous strain on her heart. If she were having a good time, she might protest the order to depart, but in the end he had his way.

During a Broun-circle poker game at Pegler's place one evening, a guest knocked over a screen by accident and disclosed oxygen tanks which were kept in readiness in case Julie's heart condition should take a turn for the worse. Westbrook shrugged and went on with the game without comment. Though she did not play herself, Julie liked her husband to play. In the presence of friends, she would sometimes rail at him as a stay-at-home.

"Why don't you go out on the town Saturday, Peg?" she would inquire. "Live a little!"

"Stop it, Julie," Pegler would say, his heavy brows bent in a scowl. He would just as soon have a drink or two at home and turn in, he said. Yet he probably did more talking about drinking than drinking; it was part of his fun-guy pose from sportswriting days. He often wrote about the black horrors of his hangovers. Once he produced a column consisting of a single sentence repeated fifty times: "I will never again mix champagne, whiskey and gin." In the late thirties, a New York distilling company issued some publicity to the effect that hangovers from blended whiskies were less severe than bonded whiskies. Two or three days later, they received a note from Pegler on his New Canaan, Connecticut, stationery reading: "My interest in a prophylaxis or cure for hangover is not academic and information on your marvelous discovery would be gratefully received." An employee of the company passed the letter to a member of the Broun crowd which enjoyed a laugh at the columnist's expense. Curiously enough, the columnist did not like to see Julie drink. He contended that she did too much drinking when he was away. She may have done more than usual in periods of loneliness, but she was far from being a toper.

Westbrook revealed a similar reform zeal toward his father, who had retired from newspaper work after the 1936 presidential election. Arthur Pegler was almost broke since he had never saved money and since his Hearst severance amounted to only thirty dollars a week for six months. He and his second wife, Julia Kenny, a woman from Minneapolis who had been a friend of the family for years, were living in a shabby little house in Madison, Connecticut, only ten miles from Pound Ridge. Though he blamed the second Mrs. Pegler for allowing Arthur to retire, Westbrook drove over frequently to see them. Because it was his duty, he usually paid their bills.

The veteran was supposed to be writing an autobiography entitled *Twenty Thousand Headlines*, but he made little progress since the various imaginative versions of his career were so much more colorful than the actuality. He also cut cordwood and puttered about the garden. Upon arrival, Westbrook's first act would be to scan the high places like tops of bookcases and mantelpieces where Arthur Pegler was wont to cache innocuous-looking glasses of water, which was actually gin. Westbrook would seize each glass indignantly and pour it down the sink. The old

153

man had done lots of drinking in his time, of course, but he was never seen drunk. He may have staged the exhibits for Westbrook's special benefit, and Westbrook, in riding herd on his father and wife, may have been trying indirectly to keep down his own alcoholic consumption.

In one way, Westbrook Pegler showed complete tact with his father. Outside the family, only a few oldtimers like Roy Howard still remembered the columnist as Buddy and addressed him by that name. Newer friends and acquaintances had taken to calling him "Peg," the abbreviation once reserved for Arthur Pegler. In his father's presence, however, Westbrook always looked toward Arthur Pegler if anybody used the name "Peg." The old man continued to call him "Buddy" and Westbrook still addressed his father respectfully as "Governor."

By instinct and experiment, Westbrook Pegler arrived at conclusions reached a half century earlier by Robert Louis Stevenson in the preface to a volume of "short studies."

It is from one side only [wrote Stevenson] that he [the writer of brief essays] has time to represent his subject. The side will be the most striking to himself or the one most obscured by controversy.

Stevenson urged the darkening of shadows and the raising of highlights for verbal contrast, a requirement which Pegler also appreciated, though it would not be reasonable to suppose that he had read Stevenson, since he did not as a rule bother with literary essays.

Nobody could be quicker than Pegler in seizing upon a striking personal approach for one of his short studies. Friends liked to tell about the little old lady who was summoned to the platform at the 1936 Republican national convention in Cleveland. As she struggled forward, she became so confused by the photographers' bulbs flashing in her face that she tripped. A cameraman trying to snap her as she fell in a heap on the floor was brushed aside by a kind-hearted reporter. The bedlam startled Pegler; spurning current political developments, he typed a scorching indictment of "lens-lice" for his next column.

At the Democratic convention in Philadelphia that same year, Pegler was in the get-together room of the Scripps-Howard contingent on the eighth or ninth floor of the Ritz-Carlton Hotel, when a parade passed by outside. Running to the window as if in pain, he called: "Hey, cut out that goddam noise down there!" Sure enough, his next column raged against the pandemonium which had to be endured in selecting presidential candidates.

Robert Louis Stevenson believed that an essayist must be authoritative and must maintain a consistent point of view. Pegler abided by no such simple rules. He shifted his artillery from column to column and often within the same column. In a controversy, he would sometimes attack both sides and content himself with asking embarrassing questions. Once in a while he would totally abandon the columnar pose of omniscience.

"Of all the fantastic fog-shapes that have risen off the swamp of confusion since the big war," he wrote in one frequently quoted article, "the most futile, and, at the same time, the most pretentious is the deep-thinking, hair-trigger columnist or commentator who knows all the answers offhand and can settle great affairs with absolute finality three days or even six days a week.

"As nearly as I can figure it, this trade began as a sort of journalistic vaudeville intended to entertain the customers and exert a little circulation pull of a slightly higher tone than that of the comics. Actually, even now at our grimmest, we aren't one, two, six with a real good strip in which some man is plotting to put out a little girl's eyes or throw a little boy into a blast furnace."

Unworried by the consistency which is supposed to be the hobgoblin of little minds, Pegler kept his readers guessing from day to day. Following expressions of concern over Communists in the Newspaper Guild, he would turn indignantly against the Dies Committee, a forerunner of the House Un-American Activities Committee which was trying rather clumsily to ferret out Communists. The columnist threatened to start his own Dies Committee which would designate Westbrook Pegler as Fellow-Traveler Number One!

One day he would appraise Tom Mooney, the union labor leader imprisoned for life in California on perjured evidence, as "an old labor slugger" whose plight appealed chiefly to "thinkers who think Stalin is all right." Some days later he would call the Communist-hunting William Randolph Hearst a "never-to-be-adequately-damned demagogue and historic scoundrel" and the "nation's Number One Fascist."

Once in a while, in startling contrast with his new anti-tax and anti-union modes, Pegler would revisit his old antipathy for

155

the rich. This sensible but radical-sounding statement appeared early in 1937:

There are too many $35,000 fur coats in the audiences of the New York theatres, too many women whose jewels glitter and clank and mock the misery of the people like the trappings on old Franz Josef's horses.

No man, least of all who has never worked, nor his father before him, deserves enough income to pay one of his divorced [wives] $1,000,000 a year and the rich should have better sense if not more human conscience than to squander from $50,000 to $100,000 on a debut party for a child.

Among Guildsmen, Pegler was sometimes referred to as Roy Howard's "kept columnist." Eventually even that pigeonhole failed to hold him. Rumors spread that the publisher was refusing to print a column by him supporting the Spanish loyalists on religious grounds. On May 11, 1938, the *New Republic* bootlegged the suppressed piece to the public.

I cannot see [Pegler had written] why the working class Catholics are expected to be indignant against the government side in Spain. I think their indignation should be directed against those members of the Spanish faith who neglected a duty that was placed upon them. I ask whether it is now intended to drive the Spanish masses back to the Church at the point of Franco's bayonets, some of them in the hands of Mohammedans, some in the hands of pagan Nazis, without so much as a gesture from the Church to punish or rebuke its guilty and negligent servants.

If I were a Spaniard who had seen Franco's missionary work among the children, I might see him in hell but never in church!

And he followed *that* up with a column accusing Americans of hand-wringing hypocrisy because they bewailed the iniquities of foreign dictators while ignoring the plight of domestic Negroes!

Pegler was creating a kind of *coup de pistolet* column. Its primary purpose seemed to be to startle readers, to imprint on their minds a single idea which might stay with them, even haunt them, whether or not that idea had any relevance to other ideas expressed on other days. His updating of Robert Louis Stevenson's formula for short subjects attracted increasing attention, though not everybody liked it. Ernie Pyle, who had been writing a low-keyed travel column for the Scripps-Howard newspapers, was asked early in 1938 whether he wished general syndication as the successor to O. O. McIntyre. "I don't give a damn one way or the other," replied Pyle. "It seems you have to be a demagogue and whale the air like Pegler to get anywhere, and I can't do that." Ernie was in a minority. Most readers found Pegler exciting. He could be counted a success. His syndicate sales were rising.

12. OVER THE TOP

Under continued pressure from critics of his tax-and-spend policies, President Roosevelt gave Treasury Secretary Morgenthau permission to balance the budget. The result was a massive collapse of stock market values on March 8, 1938. Higher unemployment and an increase in business failures soon convinced the President of his mistake; in mid-April, he took to the radio to ask Congress to appropriate three billion dollars for relief, public works and housing. By this time considerable damage had been done to the economy. There was one small silver lining: Richard Whitney's firm on the New York Stock Exchange was forced to suspend. Since Whitney was the leader of Wall Street's Old Guard, subsequent revelations of his criminal dealings removed the last barrier to reorganization of the nation's security markets.

The recession caught J. David Stern, a Philadelphian who had been operating the New York *Post* for several years on borrowed money, in a precarious position. He had been the first publisher in New York to extend recognition to the Newspaper Guild. Presuming on his status as a pro-labor employer, he told a meeting of his editorial employees that he would sell the paper unless they immediately accepted a pay cut, to be repaid out of revenues—when there were revenues. The resourceful publisher took other steps to bolster his position. According to one sensational but unverifiable story, Stern went to the White House to inform President Roosevelt that the only New Deal paper in New York would founder unless it got help. Roosevelt talked to CIO President John L. Lewis, Lewis called Heywood Broun, president of the Newspaper Guild, and Broun spoke to a Communist functionary in the New York local who then rammed the pay cut down the throats of the reluctant Guild members at the *Post*.

This was not the first time that there had been economic betrayal in the name of politics by Communist underlings in the Guild, but for some reason it proved decisive.

Almost overnight a secret anti-Stalinist caucus developed in the New York local. The Socialist party and the Association of

158

Catholic Trade Unionists contributed more individuals to the caucus than any other groups, but anybody was eligible, from Trotskyite to Republican, who had a solid record of rank-and-file union activity and who was certifiably non-Stalinist.

Westbrook Pegler knew nothing of the caucus. Even if he had remained in the Guild, he would not have been eligible for membership. New members were taken in only after thorough investigation and discussion. The case of Whittaker Chambers illustrated the severity of the screening process. This roly-poly writer was interviewed as a prospect at the suggestion of Lawrence Delaney, the caucus representative at *Time* magazine. Chambers seemed to know a great deal about the inner workings of the Communist apparatus, but he talked wildly. He kept a pistol under his pillow at night for fear of assassination, he said, and people at the office were watching him and stealing his research in efforts to get him fired. Though he was rejected by the caucus as a member, Chambers remained in contact with Delaney and made frequent cash contributions to the group.

By 1939, the caucus had grown sufficiently to venture into the open. Its chairman (a New York *Post* reporter named Pilat) ran that year for President of the local against Carl Randau. This was the first contested city election since the Guild was founded in 1933. Randau won easily but the rebels made converts during the campaign. For purposes of education and agitation, they began to issue a monthly leaflet called the *Guild Progressive*.

Several of the leaflets fell into Pegler's hands. The columnist immediately opened a fresh offensive against the Guild on the ground that the Progressives had proved what he had been saying all along. The caucus met in emergency session. It had been trying to separate various layers of fellow-travelers from a small inner core of Communists. This involved parliamentary maneuvers to expose hidden party members and simultaneous missionary work among strategically placed non-Communists. It was a delicate process, like peeling an onion. It simply would not work in the atmosphere induced by a prominent outsider shouting Red.

The crucial question at the emergency meeting was how to tell Pegler this. How would he react if he were informed to his face that his approval of the caucus was hurting its standing in the union? What assurance was there that a session with Pegler might not be blurted out by him—or leak out in some fashion? The only safe policy, it was decided, was that of no-contact. For trade unionists, the man was simply untouchable.

Later Pegler intervened again in Guild affairs, this time with almost catastrophic effect. The New York anti-Stalinist caucus had established an "out-of-town committee" under Edward Hunter, a former foreign correspondent. Its function was to organize a national anti-Communist coalition in the Guild. Hunter's obvious ally was the Philadelphia local, second in size only to the New York local. Max Ways, Art Riordan and other Philadelphia stalwarts disliked Communists thoroughly but they were fussy about being called Red-baiters, a term then more dreaded by some liberals than being called Reds. With an eye on an impending national convention, the Philadelphia local sent a statement of policy to the *Guild Reporter*, national organ of the union, raising the standard of revolt in trade-union terms.

Pegler had no way of knowing that representatives of the New York insurgents and the Ways-Riordan group in Philadelphia were secretly in contact. After reading the *Guild Reporter*, he became a howling dervish. While continuing to lavish his disastrous praise on the New York Progressives, individually and as a group, he described the ostensible Philadelphia revolt as a trick, a "Trojan foal" movement designed "to confuse the American opposition and capture the political strength of the Old Red Men."

Max Ways' political sympathies were not clearly stated in the Philadelphia manifesto, Pegler pointed out. It was therefore fair to conclude, he concluded erroneously, that the difference in leadership between the New York and Philadelphia locals was negligible. If the Philadelphia crowd won, it would be Tweedledum succeeding Tweedledee. "Moscow still rules the American Newspaper Guild!" he trumpeted.

Pegler's uninformed opinion rolled back and forth across the country like Victor Hugo's rollicking cannon aboard ship. Many good unionists still read "Fair Enough." Enough of them were disturbed by the suspicions it raised to disrupt the anti-Communist coalition at the Guild's national convention in Memphis, July 8-12, 1940. Some of the delegates always contended that Pegler delayed the takeover in the Guild by a full year.

Heywood Broun and Westbrook Pegler had no chance to catch their breath. Each was now taking a fresh look at his political past. It was a paradox unrecognized by either that in their final desperate months of maneuver they got closer rather than farther apart in their attitudes.

Roy Howard had instructed Broun not to wage what he called "a hatchet war" across the split-page. That did not prevent Pegler from growling periodically in his column that the Reds were running the Newspaper Guild, whose unpaid international president, as everybody knew, was Heywood Broun. Picking up an old remark attributed to Broun that many persons considered communism "the greatest experiment ever made for human betterment," Pegler would write that anybody who said a thing like that should not mind being called a Communist. He would add that it was strange that the greatest experiment for human betterment should find it necessary to go all the way to Washington to assert that he was not an enrolled Commie.

Broun was in an uncertain mood. He suggested half-heartedly to James B. Carey, national secretary of the CIO, that they sit down sometime with Pegler and try to convert him to unionism. Carey said it wasn't possible.

At the urging of his wife Connie, who was a Catholic, and out of his own growing need for security, Broun joined the Catholic Church on May 24, 1939. From that moment the Communists considered him an enemy. Their moves had to be carefully planned, because of his strategic position and his capacity for leadership, but it was not too many weeks later that they floated a trial balloon among non-Communist leaders in the Guild that a change in the presidency might be desirable.

To exploit for circulation purposes the widely discussed feud between the columnists, *Life* had persuaded Pegler and Broun to write articles about each other. The result was so sulphurous that *Life* became doubtful, according to Leonard Lyons. *Collier's* bought the articles from *Life*, it was reported, and was about to publish them when Pegler withdrew his contribution. Broun reworked some of his ideas into an article for the *New Republic* which Pegler interpreted as a declaration of war. Thereafter the two men did not speak when they met in town or country.

Mutual friends tried to heal the breach. George T. Bye brought one of Pegler's anti-fascist effusions to Broun and persuaded the latter that he should present a laurel leaf—an actual laurel leaf—to his colleague. Broun started dutifully toward Pound Ridge, but on the way he saw a reference to himself in the paper as Old Bleeding Heart Broun. Changing his destination, he went to Bye's home and told the literary agent just what he could do with his laurel leaf.

Broun had finally assumed complete control over the *Connecticut Nutmeg*, renaming it *Broun's Nutmeg*. In the June 10 1939 issue, he wrote frankly about himself and his colleague.

If a man went around forever crying out: 'Observe how my heart beats for humanity,' he would undoubtedly be set down as a fool or a hypocrite. And he could be both. But how about a fellow who encases himself in triple brass in the pretense that he has no heart at all? His would be the deeper folly. It may be a good idea for a columnist to keep his shirt on, but that is no reason why he should insulate himself like a telephone wire.

The tragedy of J. Westbrook Pegler consists of the fact that by nature he is not the man he pretends to be. His native sympathies are wide and deep. When he is aroused about some ancient wrong he can be more eloquent than any man I know. The most understanding and sensitive column I can remember was written by Pegler in Germany about the peculiar persecution visited upon Jewish children. And recently he broke through a long string of his regular high-bracket moans to cry out passionately against the fearful housing visited upon one-third of the nation. And yet upon all too frequent occasions he writes as if he has taken over the role of light heavyweight champion of the underdog and game warden for the preserves of the over-privileged. Some day somebody should take the hide off Peg, because the stuff inside is so much better than the varnished surface which blinks in the sunlight of popular approval.

How has it come about that so much of the best of Peg is mislaid? I blame it on his technique and his talent for fictional creation. Peg has created a character called Westbrook Pegler and, except when he forgets himself, tries to live up to the role. The fictional fellow is hardboiled, querulous and materialistic. But the man who assumes this part is actually shy, sensitive and sentimental . . .

Frankenstein fashioned a rough guy who destroyed him. Peg's monster didn't have to go to that slight trouble. When the last clay tonsil was modeled by this syndicated sculptor, he said in high artistic pride, 'Why, this is me to the life,' and proceeded to cut his own throat under the theory that in a troubled world one Westbrook Pegler might be sufficient.

Pegler shrugged it off; he seemed more sure of himself than ever. When the affairs of Moses L. Annenberg of Philadelphia came under official scrutiny that summer, the proprietor of "Fair Enough" delivered his most caustic income-tax sermon to date.

He called Annenberg low, cunning and criminal. He charged that Annenberg's national racing news monopoly was in league with the underworld and that Annenberg himself had been corrupting the government which gave him his chance at wealth. But Annenberg was also publisher of the Philadelphia *Inquirer*. At that very moment, the *Inquirer's* delivery trucks were rolling through town with huge red signs: "Read Pegler. Exclusively in the *Inquirer*. Pegler Doesn't Pull His Punches."

That fall, the Second World War was begun. The Soviet-Nazi pact which initiated hostilities further reduced Broun's ebbing respect for the Communists. He faced an overpowering, paralyzing obligation: to tell the Guild rank-and-file of the ignoble role he had played, and what must be done now. He realized that an internal struggle might destroy the union, which he had come increasingly to regard as his monument. Slack and exhausted from decades of living beyond his energy, he felt unequal to the task. With his Scripps-Howard contract due to expire soon after his fifty-first birthday on December 7, he decided to postpone any Guild step until his professional future was settled one way or another. He had a feeling that Roy Howard hated him and would block any new contract.

Knowing nothing of Broun's travail, Pegler returned to the attack on October 19. J. B. Matthews, a former fellow traveler, had bobbed up as chief investigator for the Dies Committee. With another target in mind, Pegler argued that Matthews should not be treated with dignity "merely because he squealed." He added:

All those who recently quit the party or denied the sympathies they formerly showed, especially in labor unions, are the same today as they were before the petty differences estranged them. The Soviet government has done nothing in the past two months or the past ten years any more savage and treacherous than it had already done when these individuals on that record nevertheless regarded it as the greatest experiment ever made for human betterment.

Then Pegler had an inspiration: he called up Harold Yudain, managing editor of *Broun's Nutmeg*, to ask if it were a union shop. It was a small shop, replied Yudain, but efforts were being made to get him a union card. He was being paid above the Guild scale, he pointed out. Pegler insisted on a yes-or-no answer. When he got it, he wrote a column ridiculing the president of a newspaper union who ran a non-union paper.

Late in November, Roy Howard informed Broun that he had been unable to persuade his board of directors to offer a new contract. Broun felt humiliated and crushed. Where could he go? He cast about, but only one small offer developed.

J. David Stern had sold his New York paper after his proposal for a second pay cut had been resoundingly rejected by his employees. The new publishers of the *Post*, Dorothy Schiff and George Backer, admired Broun, but as the operators of a single newspaper they could offer only a fraction of the pay he received from syndication. Even so, the columnist accepted their bid, with the hope of arranging new syndication later.

As Broun was composing a farewell column for the *World-Telegram*, Pegler hit him hard on two consecutive days. Among other things, he wrote that Broun was in sympathy with Soviet press censorship.

Such being the case [Pegler continued] the declaration of purpose in the first article of the Guild constitution in favor of honest journalism and high ethics need be mentioned only as an example of droll cynicism.

I discuss Broun impersonally as a union official committed by certain declarations which have been supported by his official conduct. I have seen recent superficial expressions of disappointment in Moscow, but never an outright recantation, and even if I saw one I would have to treat it the same as I treat changes of front by Stalin, Hitler and Earl Browder.

According to Dale Kramer's biography, "Heywood Broun," Broun was in bed with a bottle of liquor and a heavy cold when he read this. He was feeling sorry for himself. "Pegler calls me a liar!" he groaned. "Why does he do that? Pegler knows I'm not a liar." Harold Yudain remarked: "With you moving to another paper, most people would have put it: 'Good luck, Heywood.'"

According to Kramer, "Broun uncapped the bottle. 'I've been honest, Harold.' He took a drink. 'No one ever tried to take that away from me. Not before Peg. I've been wrong. I've eaten words and whole columns. But I never wrote anything I didn't believe when I wrote it."

Ernest L. Meyer, a *Post* Guildsman and columnist, wrote on June 12 that Broun and Pegler did not see eye-to-eye because Pegler wasn't tall enough. Others rallied around the Guild leader in a similar excited fashion, but there was nothing they could do. Broun was seriously sick.

164

Despite increasing weakness, Broun prepared an opening column for the *Post*, which appeared December 15. Contrary to the new Communist line of international isolation, it proposed that President Roosevelt, who had been working steadily to prepare the United States for a possible clash with Germany and Italy, be drafted for a third term. It was the last column he ever wrote. On December 18, 1939, Heywood Broun died of pneumonia.

Since Westbrook Pegler still thought of himself as a friend of Broun, he attended the funeral at St. Patrick's Cathedral. He was appalled by the rudeness of the reception he got from friends of Broun at the cemetery. Several weeks later, he came to a memorial service for Broun at Manhattan Center. Resentment erupted more violently than ever. James Kirby, Scripps-Howard reporter in Cleveland, wrote that "Pegler saw nothing inconsistent in attending the funeral of the late Heywood Broun within a few days of his most disgraceful diatribe against that great American while Broun lay on his deathbed." Quentin Reynolds added: "I think Broun, who is dead, will live a lot longer than the little men who try to defeat ideas by hating their fellow men."

Whispers spread in the Guild associating Pegler's attacks with Broun's death. This was ridiculous. The apparent collapse of his life work in the Guild conceivably did contribute to his death. With his own paternal role at stake, the columnist had been fretting that the union itself might not survive. Pegler was far outside this internal center of anguish.

The Communist Party may also have contributed to Broun's death. Stalinist leaders in the Guild had been trying for months to isolate him from contact with the rank-and-file rebels in the New York local. They worked steadily on him to repudiate his vow to the Catholic Church, to accept their explanations of the Hitler pact and the Soviet "defense" against the "invading" Finns. Though they made no headway, they depressed Broun and wore down his vitality. They deepened his feelings of guilt. Toward the end, some who had been his most trusted companions but who were also fellow-travelers, cut him cold. To a large-hearted man like Broun, this was the most grievous blow of all.

After his "eyes were opened" by what he saw in the Newspaper Guild, Pegler once told an interviewer from *Editor & Publisher*, he decided "to take a look at other outfits." Usually he scheduled two or three cross-country jaunts a year in search of columnar material. These focused more and more on the trade-union field. On November 1, 1939, Arthur Ungar, editor of Hollywood's *Daily Variety*, reported: "Westy Pegler making the rounds." For once, the columnist did not object to being called out of his name. He was on the trail of his biggest story.

For months, Ungar had been writing critically about Willie Bioff, West Coast leader of the International Alliance of Theatrical Stage Employees and Motion Picture Operators, known as IATSE. Since nobody had paid much attention, Ungar was glad to turn over to Pegler everything he and his staff had been able to collect on Bioff.

From Ungar, the columnist went to Carey McWilliams, who had been advising an insurgent group of IATSE members. While conferring with McWilliams, Pegler kept his columnar pot boiling with articles on a Cleveland old-age proposal, which was defeated at the polls, and the gambling hells and divorce mills of Reno, which he had visited on the way to California. He liked Nevada, he declared, because it harbored no radicals. According to the Chamber of Commerce, he noted approvingly, the CIO had been "run down the road."

Because he lacked any consistent philosophy, the columnist found himself approving in California what he disapproved in Nevada. Under the influence of McWilliams, he produced a column accusing the Associated Farmers of California of terrorism against seasonal field workers who had formed a union.

"The Associated Farmers deny that they have acted as vigilantes, and perhaps they can defy proof that they did in any official sense," he wrote, "but it is a waste of white paper and an affront to intelligence to say individuals belonging to the group haven't strong-armed strikers and organizers."

Bioff's trail led Pegler finally to Robert Montgomery, the actor who had read his column on the German Jewish children over the air. For four controversy-ridden terms during the 1930s, Montgomery served as president of the Screen Actors' Guild, fighting the studio bosses, the Communists within his own union, and the outside racketeers in the industry. In 1937, Montgomery had asked his union board of directors for a mysterious $5,000 appropriation. He refused to say what he would do with the $5,000, but he made a promise that if the board was not satisfied with his eventual explanation, he would pay back the money personally. With this $5,000, plus $9,000 out of his own pocket,

Montgomery hired private investigators to look into the criminal background of Bioff. This dossier was available when Pegler reached Hollywood.

Beyond doubt, the Hollywood producers had created the menace of Bioff. Back in 1933, their powerful Motion Picture Producers Association virtually forced IATSE out of business on the West Coast. In 1936, IATSE was moribund, with only thirty-three dues-paying members. Then the companies became concerned over the country-wide upsurge of unionism under the New Deal.

Out of a clear sky, Bioff and George E. Browne, IATSE president, were handed a closed-shop contract requiring 12,000 workers to join IATSE or be fired. This was a deliberate collusive act by the producers to guard against any chance that a decent union might capture their studio workers and increase operating expenses.

Rank-and-file members of the union protested to the California legislature in 1937, that they were being forced to turn over two per cent of their pay to Bioff-Browne for unknown purposes. This illegal assessment, for which no accounting was ever made, alone gave two million dollars to the racketeers. The rank-and-file group also revealed that the IATSE never held any meetings. The legislature appointed a committee which checked carefully with the producers before filing a whitewash report. Carey McWilliams persuaded two members of the IATSE to bring a suit over the assessment. The only effect was that those who brought the suit were fired by their studio.

By the time Pegler arrived on the scene, some producers who had been on intimate terms with Bioff were beginning to weary of his extortionate ways. But that was not the whole story. As Sidney Lens, a Chicago AFL leader, wrote in his labor history, *Left, Right and Center,* the Bioff-Browne case was "something entirely different from the shakedown tale given by the movie magnates. It is a story of employers who found it expedient to utilize unscrupulous racketeers and then to sever their relationship, through the instrumentality of the Browne-Bioff case. It is a story of employers becoming concerned about the inexorable pressure of rank-and-file employees who were determined to end the situation foisted upon them by the major movie companies and the Bioff-Browne racketeer combination."

Robert Montgomery invited Pegler to his home. There he and Kenneth Thompson, executive director of the Screen Actors

Guild, showed the columnist the evidence they had collected including copies of material already sent to Treasury Secretary Morgenthau, who was about to start income-tax–evasion proceedings against several of the IATSE officials. "Pegler's questions showed he had done a hell of a lot of digging," Montgomery said later, "but we gave him the basic facts long before he wrote anything on the subject in his column."

On the way back from Hollywood, Pegler stopped off in Chicago, to verify personally Montgomery's information on Bioff's early criminal record. A card index at police headquarters showed that a William Bioff had been convicted of pandering in 1922 and given a six months' sentence. Bioff had appealed the sentence and been released pending the decision of the higher court. A phone call to the clerk of the Supreme Court in Springfield, Illinois, established the almost incredible fact that the appeal had never reached there. The case had simply been sidetraceked and forgotten.

The crucial question remaining was whether Chicago's William Bioff was Hollywood's Willie Bioff. Always an indefatigable legman, Pegler went from precinct to precinct. At last he located a detective who had known Willie Bioff as a young muscle man. This detective had recognized Bioff during a recent trip to Hollywood and had actually chatted with him about the good old days in Chicago. That ended the problem of identification.

On November 29, 1939, the first Bioff column appeared. It was written in flat simple newspaper style with none of the convolutions the public had come to expect from "Fair Enough." It continued for several days and then on and off during the rest of that year and well into 1940. The central revelation was that "a Chicago pander who muscled into control of the moving picture projectors throughout the United States and of the studio trades and crafts in Hollywood" still owed all but eight days of an old six-month jail term in Chicago. In a delightful aside, Pegler explained to the customers that "pander is Ritz for pimp and not a comical Chinese bear, as you might think."

Not long after Pegler began his installment-by-installment exposé, Bioff was arrested. When Governor Horner of Illinois delayed extradition, the columnist denounced him so strongly that the Governor sued the Chicago *Daily News*, which carried the column, for $25,000. The suit was soon withdrawn. Bioff was returned to Chicago and required to serve the rest of the sentence which had been conveniently forgotten for seventeen years.

Nailing George Browne was more complicated. After referring cautiously to the IATSE president in print, Pegler had lunch with Browne at the Hotel Astor in New York. "I was starting to think he was a nice enough guy and probably not a thief after all," the columnist revealed later in an interview, "but the tipoff was when Browne said that all he wanted was to be let alone to run his union. He wouldn't even stand for a retraction. He was too anxious to hush it all up. That convinced me and I began to dig all the harder."

Back to Chicago went the reporter, in search of evidence that Browne had been a gangster before he gained respectability as a union leader. He finally located a hospital record showing admission of Browne for a gunshot wound and interviewed the patrolman who signed in the patient and the doctor who operated on him. That did it; Browne eventually went to prison for ten years under an anti-racketeering law.

Westbrook Pegler was criticized later for not stressing the responsibility of the moving picture producers for the racketeering in their studios. However, his reasearch had been crammed into a period of less than a month while he continued to produce his regular columns.

Checking the role of the producers would have taken much longer. Hasty references to the producers might have proved libelous. In short, from a hard-boiled journalistic point of view, the exposé was sufficiently sensational. Why go farther?

Treasury Secretary Morgenthau, whose tax suits ruined the whole Bioff-Browne gang and even unearthed evidence which brought some producers into court, met Robert Montgomery at a public affair some years later. They agreed it was amusing that Pegler got all the glory while the two of them, who had done the basic work against the racket, received no public credit. Friends of Carey McWilliams and Arthur Ungar also registered belated claims to fame. This kind of jockeying develops in the wake of any large newspaper story. A reporter needs news sources. In this case Pegler had three chief informants—Ungar, McWilliams and Montgomery. None of them enjoyed a national audience and none of them could have done what he did.

In one 1940 extension of the Bioff gambit, Pegler exposed George Scalise, president of the Building Service Employees International Union. According to the columnist, his tip came from an "exploited scrubwoman." Federal courts in Brooklyn soon verified that a George Scalise had spent time in Atlanta Federal

Penitentiary for white slavery. Was it the same Scalise? In his capacity as an influential labor official, it was rumored, Scalise had angled for a presidential pardon to wipe out his criminal record. Phone calls to Washington confirmed this. Having eliminated any concern over libel, Pegler proceeded to rip Scalise for operating a racket. Thomas E. Dewey, the able and ambitious young District Attorney of New York County, indicted Scalise on a charge of squeezing one hundred thousand dollars from hotels and contracting firms. Crying that he had been "peglerized," Scalise resigned his union office. He was subsequently sent to Sing Sing for ten to twenty years for forgery and embezzlement.

The columnist's added prestige led him to tackle the Newspaper Guild with fresh vigor. Picking up a leaflet signed by two founding fathers of the union, Lewis Gannett and George Britt, asking better attendance at New York Representative Assembly meetings to prevent a recurrence of an unrepresentative vote against conscription in case of war, Pegler tried to persuade them over the telephone that the Guild was "rotten with communism." When they declined to make any such public concession, he trounced them in his column. He had no way of knowing that Gannett and Britt were cooperating secretly with the Guild Progressive caucus which he continued to praise. Next he addressed an open appeal to Mrs. Roosevelt to help "the American members of the Guild"—as he had dubbed the Progressives. But she was already in contact with the caucus and had made the largest single contribution to its overdue printing bill.

In the course of his fulminations, Pegler did arouse some uninformed Guild members. He became a particular hero in Youngstown, Ohio, a company union town if there ever was one. Early in 1940, the progressive caucus in New York circulated a petition for Kenneth Crawford, Washington correspondent of the New York *Post*, as Broun's successor for president. The Communist faction hesitated and then decided to go along with Crawford to avoid an immediate test of strength. That made Crawford's election virtually unanimous, but after the official deadline for recording votes, the Youngstown local weighed in with a single honorary ballot for Westbrook Pegler for president.

The doorbell was ringing at the castle in Pound Ridge, flowers were arriving, and the lawn was filling with neighbors. Earlier in the day, Westbrook Pegler had been incredulous when a telegram from Columbia University informed him that he had won a $1,000 Pulitzer prize for "articles on scandals in the ranks of organized labor . . . a most distinguished example of a reporter's work." Recalling the old story of Corbett staggering out of the ring after his fight with Sullivan and saying that he would not believe he had won until he saw it in the *Police Gazette*, the columnist sent an exuberant return wire to the university, reading: "I won't believe it until I see it in *Editor & Publisher!*"

The later afternoon papers of May 5, 1941 confirmed the glad tidings. Only then did Pegler accept the inevitable. He slipped upstairs where his wife was in bed and took her hand shyly. "Mom, I didn't mean to do this to you," he said. Julie Pegler said she thought she could stand the excitement for once.

Walter Winchell, with whom Pegler had been feuding, was morose. "Westbore Pigler," he wrote the next day, "took another guy's scoop . . . Pigler's story was bravely dug up by an obscure feller on the Hollywood *Daily Variety* a year before he ran it."

It remained for General Hugh Johnson to produce an official accolade in the form of a Barrack Room Ballad of praise for Pegler on his own *World-Telegram* split-page. "After reading that," commented the proprietor of "Fair Enough," "There is nothing left for me to do but die."

13. WAR GARDEN

Substantial tax reductions could be anticipated in running a farm at a loss. Within easy reach of New York City, Connecticut offered more desirable farm sites for sale than New York State. Furthermore, Connecticut, unlike New York, had no income tax of its own. These were the familiar arguments. As the United States drifted toward participation in the European war, a new one was added: farmers, however amateurish, classed as a patriotic necessity. President Roosevelt and several members of his cabinet took pride in the fact that they were tillers of the soil, part-time or by proxy.

Westbrook and Julie had other, more personal reasons for deciding, soon after he received his Pulitzer Prize, to make their long-contemplated move to Connecticut. Pound Ridge was so much more crowded and noisy than it had been when they arrived in 1929. In search of quieter pastures, Jack Pegler and his family had already shifted across the state line to South Salem. Other old-timers were leaving. The social atmosphere in Pound Ridge seemed less friendly. Except for the rather atypical Gene Tunney and one or two others, the whole Broun crowd had turned a cold shoulder after Heywood's death. In the sense that his ideas and his friends survived, Heywood Broun haunted the Peglers.

The rundown hundred-acre farm which the columnist and his wife purchased at an undisclosed price in the summer of 1941 was located in Ridgebury, an outlying section of Ridgefield, only fifteen miles away from Pound Ridge across the state line but a world away in purpose and atmosphere.

Modernization of the place was to cost $50,000 before it was completed. Everything took longer than expected; it was not until November of that year that they got around to knocking out partitions, the first step in transforming a rambling old farmhouse into a modern dwelling.

Putting planning in the hands of a Ridgefield architect named La Caya and construction in the hands of a Ridgefield dealer named Martin under a cost-plus contract, the Peglers departed in search of balmier weather, isolation and peace of mind. Instead

172

of the familiar Florida sun-spots, they tried the Arizona desert this time, setting down at the Rancho Rezhone near Tucson, the only walled town in American history. By the time they returned to Ridgebury in the early summer of 1942, the United States was at war, and the central section of their farmhouse, which was to have nine large rooms and four or five bathrooms, looked as if it had been bombed.

From a nearby rented house, Julie and Westbrook tried to speed up the work. Priorities were being slapped on scarce materials like copper piping, plumbing fixtures and lumber. In the midst of experimental gasoline rationing, thirty to forty workmen arrived at the farm every morning in from fourteen to twenty cars and left every evening. The members of this imposing motorcade were drilling a 220-foot artesian well, installing a furnace with automatic stoker, five water closets, an electric pump, electric conduits, and metal lathing.

At this delicate juncture, Pegler was publicized nationally as a patriot. A local committee started a scrap-metal drive. At its request, he drove to Ridgefield. There, at the busiest point on Main Street, he allowed the bumpers to be detached from his car so that they could be contributed to the war effort. He posed for pictures alongside his naked vehicle. *Life* and other publications carried layouts.

People did not respond to the drive; they were reluctant to go bumperless. Eventually Pegler purchased new bumpers for his car at a cost of $125, to replace the seventy-five pounds of scrap metal which he had given away. The experience aroused his grumpiness. On the ground that "a man from Washington" first mentioned the drive, he blamed the administration for a "hoax." Reminded that he was one of the hoaxers, he changed the word to "mistake."

The fact that scrap collection and gasoline rationing during this period were designed primarily to bring home to the public the seriousness of the war effort did not impress Pegler. He was being personally deceived, he felt, particularly on gas rationing. Everybody knew that Treasury Secretary Morgenthau flew home from Washington to Dutchess County on weekends and that CIO President Lewis drove his car everywhere—supposedly on union business!

When a salesman phoned about war bonds, Pegler was agreeable, but by the time the salesman reached the farm, the columnist had changed his mind. The income tax had strapped

173

him, he said. He was not going to put any more of his cold cash in Treasury Secretary Morgenthau's hot hands until he received assurances that there would be no more free yachting parties on Coast Guard cutters in the Gulf of Mexico for Harold Ickes and Harry Hopkins.

There had been considerable local gossip about the strange doings out at the Pegler farm. This erupted in exposés by the Bridgeport *Herald*, a newspaper circulating widely in Fairfield County, and *PM*, an experimental tabloid in New York, to the effect that the columnist was circumventing, if not violating, various war regulations.

Pegler blamed the stories on a local builder. Original plans had called for eight bathrooms. Under war conditions, bathtubs were difficult to find. This builder, who had some bathtubs left over from a contract to build cottages, offered them to the Pegler work force. When a hitch developed over transfer of title, according to Pegler, the builder "went to *PM* and for fifteen dollars sold them a story insinuating that I was violating priorities when he was the one who sold the material."

The Bridgeport paper called the farmhouse "Scab Manor." Pegler replied that the selection of employees was up to the contractor, that it would be silly for him to go around looking for union cards and anyway there might well be some unionists on the payroll.

He was never a man to laugh off minor charges. On the curious and unconvincing ground that Sam Karp of Bridgeport, a brother-in-law of Molotov, once told a Congressional committee he would not allow the Bridgeport *Herald* in his house, Pegler called the paper Communist. He made a similar assertion about *PM*, which was owned by Marshall Field, the Chicago millionaire.

Enemies of the columnist, including some communists, spread the story of the luxurious farmhouse. Asked mischievously in public on one occasion whether he thought building homes with copper pipes and sheets was causing the wartime copper shortage, Pegler retorted: "No, but union sabotage might have a lot do with it!"

Though the journalistic excitement over the farmhouse faded away, local gossip did not subside. After the Peglers took possession of the remodeled structure in November 1942, a Connecticut group called at the New York *Post* to suggest an investiga-

174

tion of the whole non-essential project. A preliminary check with Pegler brought a reply telegram:

"Job has been inspected twice by government representatives since the Communist smear and an offer to abandon work forthwith voluntarily was rejected. This is not an estate but a farm like the farms of President Roosevelt, Secretaries Morgenthau and Ickes and Wendell Willkie and is producing meat under the guidance of the county farm agent, a federal officer. The construction is minor by comparison with that of an entirely new building which is being put up by the Labor Temple Association of Seattle as a clubroom and hiring hall costing $150,000 with plans for annex to cost $80,000 additional, for which an officer of the Labor Temple Association plans to ask priorities, all of which undoubtedly is according to law and regulations."

A *Post* reporter specializing in labor matters phoned Pegler, who claimed to have a blanket authorization on War Priorities Board stationery for whatever strategic materials he needed. This would have been unusual. It could not be confirmed.

On the other hand, Raymond L. French, an assistant to E. J. Huss, WPB official in Bridgeport, revealed over the phone that the columnist had been given permission to finish remodeling since the work began before WPB regulations went into effect. French would not discuss a report that Pegler had broken a promise to keep subsequent expenditures down to $1,000. French did say that the government contemplated no formal complaint against the columnist.

The explanation put the matter in reasonable perspective. The only way to probe in greater depth would have been to visit Ridgebury. The *Post* reporter doubted whether such a trip could be justified in wartime, and upon his recommendation the city editor ended the investigation without any story.

Meanwhile Westbrook Pegler was emulating Markham's man with a hoe. Until it got too cold that fall, he cleared brush and stretched wire in his spare time. He sawed some cedar posts. He learned to plow with a Ford-Ferguson tractor plow and he did a little harrowing. He was a flabby forty-eight, without agricultural experience, so the work was uphill all the way. He watched Daniel Merritt, his regular farmer, and Merritt's assistants, Johnny and Ed, but their capacity did not prove contagious. Julie did what she could. Despite her frailty, she took brief turns at harrowing and plowing. On one occasion, she served as midwife to a sow.

Thereafter she retired to the porch. Westbrook persisted longer, with short wind, aching muscles and a nagging suspicion that he might be more of a hindrance than a help to his own eight-dollar-a-day hired hands.

The Peglers had planned to live on their farm at least from June through September every year but as the war advanced, they stayed away more and more. Relaxation proved difficult for Westbrook in Ridgebury. He had a dog on the place, a dachshund of uncertain antecedents named O'Brien. Westbrook was fond of O'Brien, but when his mind turned elsewhere he was often rude and rough. O'Brien took revenge in the presence of visitors by cringing in a corner to indicate that his master beat him. After the visitors left, the dog would lick his master's hand in search of forgiveness.

The columnist realized he was a failure at farming. Formerly he would bridle at a joke that all guests were entitled to free rides on his rubber-tired tractor. It was a working, not a playing farm, he would stress. Now he poked fun at himself by declaring that his farming consisted of an occasional stroll across the fields during which he came up to a vaguely familiar farmhand and inquired what was wheat and what alfalfa.

Though the farm did not make money, it continued to yield potatoes, hay, beets, soybeans, tomatoes and corn in variable quantities. Sometimes it was difficult to dispose of the produce. Pegler frequently gave away his hay. One year all his potatoes fetched less than two hundred dollars. He presented corn to one neighbor who had helped harvest it and who had made his brother-in-law and another man available for work on the estate. The brother-in-law used a sidehill patch on the property for silage. The columnist kept one hundred sheep for their wool, but he never cared much for sheep. He owned twenty-five head of cattle which nobody wanted to buy when he wanted to sell them, despite all his earlier talk about operating a rural meat factory.

For four successive years, Pegler took income tax deductions on his losses. On some of these returns he was reported to have paid additional assessments. In 1944 he washed the soil from his hands. "Farming is like playing a violin," he concluded ruefully. "You have to devote a lot of time. I don't have the time." Eventually he sold the place to a Danbury grocer named Marshall who had been buying his potatoes.

A poll conducted by the University of Wisconsin School of Journalism among five hundred editors of daily newspapers in 1942 named Westbrook Pegler as the "best adult columnist"—whatever that meant—with Raymond Clapper, the Washington news analyst, a poor second. Knox College in Galesburg, Illinois, made him an honorary doctor of laws in 1943 for "speaking up for the common man." According to an estimate by John McCarten in the *American Mercury,* his salary jumped from $75,000 in 1941 to a breath-taking peak of $90,000 in 1945.

Since by popular standards he had become the champion in his field, the pundits gathered around to feel his muscles. Gerald W. Johnson, editor of the Baltimore *Sun,* wrote in the New York *Herald Tribune* that Westbrook Pegler had succeeded "because he has voiced more adequately than anyone else the deep resentment of a people tortured through ten weary years by the necessity of thinking unfamiliar, not to say original thoughts every day . . . His main business is relieving the hypertension of a public that has been compelled to think too much. He does it so well that I am inclined to think he ranks as a rough but effective corrective of public disorders only a little lower than the grand old trinity of hell, hanging and calomel."

In a biographical magazine called *Who,* J. P. McEvoy hailed the columnist as "a saltier Billy Sunday" and a "secular Savonarola with a sports-page vocabulary." In *The Sign,* a Catholic publication, John B. Kennedy suggested that Pegler was paying for controversial success in the form of "a nervousness not due to living mode—it's the knowledge that he is constantly under surveillance by those who love him not." In the *New Leader,* a social-democratic organ, Ferdinand Lundberg concluded that the columnist's mind was just a feather in the whirlwind of his emotions and that he frequently used a machine gun to kill mosquitoes because he could not control his strong but primitive sense of justice.

Sterling North, a syndicated critic reviewing the third book of collected Pegler columns, dismissed the author as "a case of indecent intellectual exposure."

Despite all the articles pro and con, the man whom they described did not come into clear public focus. He seemed content to leave it that way. He commented cryptically that people could find out what he stood for by studying what he was against. On the ground that his newspaper work kept him fully

177

occupied, he refused to lecture, write articles or appear on the radio. Once, early in the war, he felt obliged for patriotic reasons to break his rule against speech-making. A meeting had been called in Boston to raise funds for John B. Powell, the anti-fascist newspaperman who lost his feet in China. Pegler memorized a talk and practiced it before his mirror and before Julie. When the crucial day arrived, however, he couldn't eat for nervousness or remember what he wanted to say, and the result was embarrassment to his listeners as well as to himself.

Look arranged an interview with him in 1944 by promising that he would not be quoted directly and that he could make corrections in the margins after the article was completed by Glen Parry and Roscoe Drummond. The title was: "Westbrook Pegler, Tonic or Poison?" The writers had no point of view, and their subject gave them little help. Where they mentioned his "Fine, that's swell" reaction to a California lynching in 1933, he noted in the margin that those three words did not represent his attitude. "You have to read the story to know what it said," he added noncommittally. He did not change references to himself as "James Westbrook Pegler," indicating that in private, at least, he was still Poppa's boy. He showed concern over one small statement that his schooling ended after two years at Loyola Academy. "What? That's only a high school!" he scribbled in the margin. To some readers the implication may have been that he went to college.

There was no great mystery about the origin of most of the themes used by the columnist during the war. They came from the constitutionalism which the Liberty League spent so much money to popularize during the mid-thirtys. According to this doctrine, all reforms, particularly those involving large-scale federal expenditures or an unbalanced budget, were likely to harm the ordinary citizen. The preferred alternative was voluntary cooperation in the traditional American way of life. Since liberalism was tinged with Communism, the issue, as Al Smith put it long before Pegler did, was "the clear, pure, fresh air of free America versus the foul breath of Communist Russia." For the rest of his political approach, the columnist shopped around at the journalistic delicatessens operated by William Randolph Hearst, Colonel McCormick and Captain Patterson. He was not an original thinker.

It was not so much what Pegler said as how he said it. Under the incitation of success, he went considerably beyond the range of invective normally permitted in public discussion. He discovered he could denounce whole segments of the population—unionists, politicians, artists, entertainers, educators, intellectuals of all sorts—without alienating too many of them indefinitely, and sometimes with surprising recruits from these very groups. He learned how to inch toward a target and how to ease back from an exposed position. Sometimes he wasted a whole column just to launch a pet impertinence or a devastating phrase toward the end.

As though by instinct, he reached for the reader's subconscious with rags and tags of seemingly disconnected phrases heavy with emotional impact. And the magic with which he played on the reverse connotation of words!—leaving a deliberate impression opposite to what he was saying, like Cicero forbearing loudly and at length in public to discuss his rival's lewdness and general corruption.

Pegler's verbal tricks may have grown partly out of a feeling that he had to move deviously to fool his enemies. Yet his caution was only relative. Despite his contention that what he wrote sounded more angry than he felt, many of his columns gave the reverse impression. An impulse arose irresistibly within him to obliterate the objects of his righteous wrath. Like Carlyle, he had a fire in his belly.

Perhaps because of his disillusionment with the Newspaper Guild, Westbrook Pegler pursued his vendetta against organized labor with particular excitement. He may have sensed a greater personal menace to himself in this field than in any other. As early as 1940, the Scripps-Howard newspapers felt obliged to feature three bylined articles by AFL President William Green to show that they did not share the anti-labor hysteria of their leading columnist. Subsequently Pegler popped up at a press conference held by Green in Washington. He listened carefully while the ordinary labor reporters posed questions and received answers. As the conference was about to end, Green remarked that he was pleased to see Pegler present. Did the columnist have any questions to ask? Pegler said he had none.

"There are several members of the executive council present," Green continued. "Perhaps they would like to ask you some questions. Would you mind answering them?"

Pegler shook his head. "I'll do my talking in print, not from the witness stand," he said pleasantly but firmly. He was soon hitting the AFL again in print as a "great, arrogant, corrupt, hypo-

179

critical, parasitic racket, a front for panders, thieves, extortioners and thugs."

Philip Pearl, the AFL press agent in Washington, retaliated with an anecdote in the AFL Weekly News Service, which he edited, about an alcoholic weekend cruise in Long Island Sound on Roy Howard's yacht. In the middle of the night, he reported, a guest awoke to the sound of excited talk on the quarterdeck, got dressed and went up to find Westbrook Pegler engaged in debate with himself.

"Would it be unkind to suggest that Pegler in his ravings against the AFL will have about the same audience and the same effect as that memorable night aboard the yacht?" suggested the unkind Mr. Pearl.

Postponing a vacation, Pegler stalked his prey by long-distance telephone in the middle of the night. How much did Pearl get paid? What were his duties? When did he last get a raise? The spate of questions continued until the yawning laborite remembered to hang up. When the phone rang again, he didn't answer. Subsequent columns on Pearl were rough, but no rougher than those on the whole labor press in Washington. Edwin Lahey of the Chicago *Daily News* finally responded to the charge that he and all his colleagues were spineless and subservient. "A discussion of Peg at this stage of his career properly belongs to psychiatry," said Lahey.

Many labor reporters felt that Pegler got undue credit for his exposés. Since he had no staff, a racket had to be well-wrapped up in advance for him to handle. In one conspicuous case, a rank-and-file group appealed unsuccessfully to Pegler before turning to George Hartman, labor editor of the Chicago *Tribune*. Hartman traveled to Minneapolis, Miami and elsewhere to establish the unsavory record of Max Caldwell, who held twelve thousand grocery workers in thrall under a closed-shop contract guaranteeing sub-standard wages and no strikes. Caldwell escaped jail, but his labor grip in Chicago was broken. In a less significant case, Pegler won national acclaim for hounding Mike Carrozzo, a union mobster facing a federal indictment, until Carrozzo died unexpectedly of a heart attack.

There was, to be sure, more racketeering in AFL unions and more communism in CIO unions than the leaders of the federations conceded. The late Edward Levinson estimated that the Communists controlled a 20 per cent slice of the CIO at their peak in 1938 before rank-and-file rebellions with some help from the CIO leaders reduced their influence to negligible proportions.

The percentage of racketeer-influenced unions in the AFL was harder to estimate. Most business unionists were far from racketeers. They might lack any particular social or political consciousness, but they managed to secure economic benefits for their members. Even a racket-run union might do more for its members from a dollar-and-cents point of view than no union at all. It was possible for a racket-run union, or a company union, to convert itself into a bona-fide union as its leaders acquired the techniques of collective bargaining. It was also possible for a union to be reformed after an exposé. Pegler had no time to waste on subtleties. Long after the Building Service Employees had straightened out as a union, for example, he continued to refer to it in terms of its jailed ex-president, George Scalise.

In the fall of 1943, CIO Secretary Carey and Pegler agreed to a debate in the *Ladies Home Journal*. In his opening statement, the columnist conceded that the Newspaper Guild was no longer controlled by Communists. When Carey noted in rebuttal that Pegler had never previously mentioned this, though the takeover took place in 1941, the columnist cut out the reference to the Guild in his opening statement. He then used "Fair Enough" to denounce the magazine for various sins and to declare that he had trampled all over Carey in an article not yet available to the public.

The Newspaper Guild fought back. For a while it ran the columnist's name entirely in lower case. It tried unsuccessfully to prevent his syndicated material from appearing in *Stars & Stripes*, the Army newspaper.

Guildsmen on *Mid-Pacifican*, the Army newspaper in Hawaii, conducted a purposeful survey among soldiers on Pegler, to the effect that he was promoting disunity between the fighting men overseas and the working people back home.

Members of the merchant marine, whom Pegler had belittled as "riff-raff getting fantastic pay," sent him a jagged hunk of a Liberty ship with a note to remind him that six thousand men had already perished as a result of submarine warfare. Printers from the *World-Telegram* composing room joined merchant seamen for two hours in a picket line outside the plant, chanting: "We're out to win the war. What the hell is Pegler for?"

Letter-writing campaigns were organized in a number of cities to get "Fair Enough" dropped as prejudicial to the war effort. Some were inspired by communists, who by this time put Pegler on a par with Hitler and Mussolini. Where Pegler was dropped, as the Richmond *Times Dispatch* and other papers discovered, a substantial protest developed. In restoring Pegler at the *Times Dispatch* after an absence of several weeks, editor Virginius Dabney explained that readers asking for the columnist said in effect: "Yes, maybe he did misrepresent; probably he did. But we think we are entitled to read the column and judge whether or not he is misrepresenting."

In 1944, Roy Howard visited David Dubinsky to suggest that he was publishing a liberal paper which deserved a better circulation in the labor field. How could he get it? "That's easy," said Dubinsky. "Fire Pegler!" Roy Howard suggested that the three of them get together for an intimate chat. They did get together. Pegler shrugged. "If the sun shines, is there any news in that?" he asked. They parted without mutual understanding.

Politics is like an escalator in a department store. A man may assure himself that he is not moving while he is being carried slowly from one floor with varied displays to another with an entirely different layout of merchandise. Westbrook Pegler's point of view underwent a gradual transformation during the war. In 1940 he turned against the New Deal on the ground that it had instituted anti-capitalistic reforms instead of repealing prohibition and going about business as usual. By 1944 he was so far to the right that the Republican party could barely hold him.

After the fall of France in 1940, England stood almost alone against the enemies of democracy. A Committee to Defend America by Aiding the Allies, formed to support President Roosevelt's views, was offset by the America First Committee, which marshalled Charles Lindbergh, Senator Burton K. Wheeler and others to denounce the allies in the name of isolation. Pegler felt free to pound both sides at whim. Isolationist Representative Hamilton Fish threatened a libel suit after one attack, whereupon the columnist noted acidly that congressmen had the advantage of being able to berate ordinary citizens with impunity from the House floor. He rebuked Senator Wheeler for hating F.D.R. to such a degree as to lose his sense of balance. The Senator in turn denounced "evil journalism" and demanded greater respect for elected officials "in times when there is a trend toward totalitarianism through the country." When Wendell Willkie, the unsuccessful GOP candidate for President in 1940, came out for aid to England the following year, Roy Howard turned on him in a fury, and Westbrook Pegler promptly denounced Willkie as "a fake Hoosier."

The columnist began to backtrack on his own suggestion that the United States get into the war on England's side. If the United States did take part, he wrote, "civil liberties would be suspended and win or lose the cost would be so great that capitalism would be unable to pay off and therefore would perish."

This was also Colonel McCormick's opinion. When Roosevelt met Winston Churchill on a warship off Newfoundland to draw up the Atlantic Charter, Pegler snapped that people "toying" with the idea of a postwar association of nations were "either crazy or just politicians." If families couldn't get along, he pointed out, how could nations? After the war, he predicted, the United States would be "more nationalistic than ever. As a nation we just aren't inclined to world brotherhood. We are strictly loners."

At the insistence of the President, the first peacetime draft had been authorized. If millions of Negroes were to risk their lives for their country, they could not be denied equality in other directions, various Negro newspapers emphasized. Pegler charged abruptly that the Negro press was undermining the loyalty of Negro soldiers. Such papers, he wrote, should be given the same treatment as Father Coughlin's *Social Justice*—that is, suppressed. "A more Fascistic method for dealing with papers which are attempting to voice the opinions of an exploited minority would be hard to imagine," commented the *Christian Century*.

Pegler's posture became more complex after Pearl Harbor. All the America First arguments against President Roosevelt were true, he said. The President had tricked the country into war.

On the other hand, he wrote, "It is well to have a man in the White House who will not bother to break clean or keep his punches up. A better fighter to conduct this war could not be found."

The columnist did not hate Roosevelt, he stressed in a dispatch from Tucson in the spring of 1942. No loyal American could hate the President in wartime. "The Roosevelt-haters are the Coughlinites and their clamorous but not very numerous kind whose daggers thirst for the blood of Americans and, lately, the Communists who hated him with equal fury while Russia ran with Hitler."

Since the Coughlinite movement had disintegrated and the

183

Communists were already trying to convert trade unions into company unions so as to speed help to the Soviet Union, the President, according to this analysis, faced no domestic dissidence at all.

Pegler was even prepared to gather Mrs. Roosevelt into his patriotic embrace. "She knows the country better than any other individual including her husband. I think we can take the wraps off and call her the greatest American woman." Naturally, letters poured in inquiring whether Pegler's conversion to the First Family was real or forced. He had not been gagged, he announced. Going a step farther, he volunteered: "I will say that I have never been conscious of any attempt by the New Deal to shut me up."

Such unnatural amity could not long endure. In Chicago, Colonel McCormick supported the war effort for exactly one month after Pearl Harbor. Then he began to recall publicly how much smarter the country would have been to heed his isolationist slogans. In New York, the Colonel's cousin, Captain Joseph Patterson, opposed gas rationing and other war measures in a tone which suggested that he was angrier at his old friend Roosevelt than at Hitler. In Washington, the Captain's sister, Eleanor M. (Cissy) Patterson, having acquired two papers and merged them as the *Times-Herald* at the start of the war in Europe, did her sniping closer to the White House.

The Hearst and Gannett newspaper chains, even Scripps-Howard to some extent, joined in the Anvil Chorus. The mood of 1940, when 77 per cent of the press unsuccessfully opposed a third term for Roosevelt, was soon re-established with Pegler as chief critic.

By this time Mrs. Roosevelt was serving as director of the Office of Civilian Defense. She found that she could not endure the charges by Pegler and the three furies of isolationism (as *Time* described the Colonel, the Captain and his sister in 1943) that she was hiring Communists for the purpose of boondoggling. "Because people have fought for and stood for liberal causes," Mrs. Roosevelt said in her formal resignation, "they should not be branded as Communists." She defended calisthenics, acting, singing, dancing and other OCD group activities as "forms of civilized behavior calculated to offset the hardships of wartime living" and concluded: "Perhaps we must all stand up now and be counted, the virtuous Westbrook Peglers on one side and the so-called boondogglers on the other!"

It took the columnist a while to devise what he called an appropriate riposte. His opportunity came when a deportation order was issued against Harry Bridges, a West Coast Communist union leader. Pegler simply suggested that something similar be done about Mrs. Eleanor Roosevelt.

Once again the column known as "Fair Enough" reeked with epithets old and new for President Roosevelt. In the fall of 1943, the columnist served as best man at the wedding of his favorite nephew, Arthur James Pegler, II, who had just been graduated from the naval reserve midshipman's school at Columbia University. A foreboding (which turned out to be wrong) that Ensign Pegler would "die in Frank Roosevelt's war" impelled the columnist to new anti-administration extravagances.

When the government tried to steer manpower into war plants under closed shop contracts, Westbrook Pegler wrote that an attempt was being made to set up a dictatorship and that the workers should revolt. He still considered Hitler an enemy of mankind, but "when I get thinking about this dangerous union thing, this empire of the irresponsible which President Roosevelt has set up in this country, I find that I am more afraid of that than of Hitler."

To protect the President's life in wartime, a voluntary press agreement had been reached against revealing any precise advance information about his personal movements.

In January 1945, Pegler threatened publicly to break this agreement. About this time, two FBI agents came to call on him. The columnist was taking a bath in his Waldorf Astoria suite when the government men arrived. Since he had recently cracked three ribs during a fall at the farm (as he was carrying a case of bourbon to a closet) he asked them to strap him up. One FBI man held an end of an eighteen-inch roll of flannel against the columnist's side while the other started walking around with the rest of the cloth. Suddenly, the walker was inspired to skip, chanting: "Here we go gathering nuts in May, nuts in May, nuts in May!" The others joined in. After the May dance, the three men sat down for a serious talk. According to Pegler, "some fellow" had expressed "subversive sentiments about the Commander-in-Chief." Whether the threat to President Roosevelt emanated from the columnist or from somebody else, neither he nor the FBI ever disclosed.

185

14. TURN TO THE RIGHT

The powder train for the explosion which blew Westbrook Pegler out of his comfortable middle-of-the-road journalistic seat with Scripps-Howard and the Chicago *Daily News* had been sputtering for years. It was laid in 1940 when Frank A. Knox, the Chicago publisher who had been Landon's running mate in 1936, became Secretary of the Navy. Another prominent Republican, Henry L. Stimson, became Secretary of War at the same time. The appointments represented an effort by President Roosevelt to forge national unity in the face of the worsening situation of the country's European allies. Westbrook Pegler thought that the two Republicans had betrayed their party, but he kept this view to himself at first.

As publisher of the *Daily News*, Colonel Knox held almost half of Pegler's contract. He tried to stay aloof from the columnist's crusades, but he was too deeply involved with administration policy to escape embarrassment. Though he had taken leave from his newspaper to serve the President, the *News* was still close to him and associated with him in the public mind. One of his complaints was that Pegler's roar drowned out the relatively quiet *News* editorials.

Early in 1944, Pegler produced a series asserting that wartime inheritance and income taxes were striking at the existence of marriage and the family. Nathan Robertson, *PM* tax expert, took these columns sentence by sentence under a heading of BUNK and explained errors of fact and logic under a heading of BECAUSE. It made the *World-Telegram*, the Chicago *Daily News* and the other subscribing newspapers look ridiculous.

Lee Wood, executive editor of the *World-Telegram*, hinted at embarrassment in an April 1944 interview with *Editor & Publisher*. "Columnists have been over-rated," he said. "Though they write and speak for themselves, readers believe they speak for the newspapers publishing them, creating confusion."

Marshall Field had been publishing *PM* in New York to acquire journalistic experience. His real purpose, he revealed in the spring of 1944, was to challenge Colonel McCormick's long-established supremacy in the Chicago morning newspaper field. While a plant was being constructed for his new paper, the Chicago *Sun,* Field rented space in the Chicago *Daily News* building.

With the memory of his *PM* grievances fresh in his mind, Pegler wrote a column complaining that the Chicago *Daily News,* an afternoon newspaper, should have remained neutral in the morning paper fight. The *Daily News* omitted subsequent columns praising Colonel McCormick and insulting Marshall Field on the ground that it was, in fact, neutral.

On April 25, 1944, Paul Scott Mowrer, *Daily News* editor, notified Pegler he was being dropped as a columnist. Pegler reacted with a column roasting the *Daily News* and its absent publisher. Surprisingly, the *News* printed this, along with a Mowrer note that a local writer, Phil S. Hanna, would henceforth fill the space occupied by syndicated Pegler material from New York.

Mowrer wrote that the blast at Colonel Knox "serves notice on other purchasers of the Pegler column that if they ever, for any reason, wish to discontinue it, they must expect to be attacked and misrepresented by Mr. Pegler in other newspapers." He continued:

"We have spoken highly of Mr. Pegler in the past . . . If his judgment equaled his courage, he would be a great newspaperman. It was when he began writing about things he obviously didn't know about that we began to lose confidence in his judgment. In the course of the various controversies in which he has been engaged, Mr. Pegler has developed antipathies of such violence that he has allowed his feelings to overcome his reasoning powers.

"Take, for example, the Pegler column today. Mr. Pegler recalls that the *Daily News* was formerly opposed to the New Deal. If he had gone to the trouble of informing himself, he would know that the *Daily News* is still opposed to the New Deal. He asserts that Colonel Frank Knox, publisher of the *Daily News* on leave of absence as Secretary of the Navy, has 'surrendered' to the New Deal. The fact is—and Pegler knows it—that Colonel Knox answered the call to take charge of our Navy only after long hesitation and searching of heart, as a patriot, putting country above partisanship in time of great national peril . . .

"Goodbye, Mr. Pegler."

The New York *World-Telegram,* the Cleveland *Press* and other Scripps-Howard papers omitted the Pegler column attacking Colonel Knox. Other Pegler subscribers, with no such

187

well-timed kill order, ran the column. The Colonel, who was 70, died of a heart attack the next day.

Visitors from Tucson drove out along Oracle Road—an appropriate touch considering the pundit at the end of the road—until they saw "Casa Cholla" ("House of the Jumping Cactus") prettily painted pink and yellow on a wooden placard by a gate. The main adobe-type stucco house, white with blue trim, was a small but luxurious two-bedrooms-and-bath affair. The wire-enclosed forty acre estate included another small building of similar construction used as a writing office, a separate chalet for a caretaker and his wife and their dog, and a swimming pool in the open. Spotted neatly around the grounds were such desert blooms as the ocotillo, the yucca and the century plant.

The Southwest and its flowers had charmed the Peglers on sight in 1941. Instead of going again to a tourist ranch the following winter, they had purchased their own place in the shadow of the lordly Santa Catalina Mountains outside Tucson. Though they spent parts of 1942 and 1943 in Connecticut, they had felt increasingly uncomfortable in their farmhouse there. On the other hand, they felt at home in Arizona. The climate, at least from November through June, seemed ideal for Julie; the relative peace, quiet and isolation pleased Westbrook after the noise and strife of the big city. In 1944 they established legal residence there, on the edge of the desert.

One warm evening in May, 1944, Casa Cholla had late visitors. It was somewhere between 2:00 and 3:00 o'clock in the morning when Westbrook Pegler appeared at the bus terminal in downtown Tucson with his guests, two young officers in uniform and two young ladies. His car had stalled, and his party wanted a place to sit and talk pending the arrival of a garage mechanic who had been summoned by phone.

Cranford Holly, a young bus driver in uniform, his girl and two bus company clerks came out of the terminal just as the visitors arrived. The bus terminal was closed, they said, and could not be reopened. They were tired and they were going home.

The Pegler party, which had obviously been celebrating, refused to accept the explanation. One of the girls with the naval officers made a saucy comment to Holly, who retorted in kind. Then she grabbed his shirt and he pushed her back with his hand. At this point, Westbrook Pegler weighed in with a wild swing.

Holly was something of an athlete, having been high school diving champion. He simply yanked his head out of reach and countered with a right hand punch to the columnist's chin. Pegler went down with a thud. By the time he arose, one of the naval officers was striding rapidly down the street toward the Santa Rita Hotel. Pegler set off in pursuit, but one of the girls ran alongside him, screaming: "He didn't hit you, it was the bus driver!" Pegler stopped, turned and saw the other girl, the one who had heckled Holly in the first place, belaboring the bus driver with her purse. Pegler returned and tried another punch, and he was dropped to the sidewalk again. This time he rested on one knee until his head cleared. Suddenly he made a dive for Holly's legs. The younger man stepped away and kicked him in the face.

Police arrived. They included a captain, a sergeant named Seymour Ryan, and three patrolmen. The captain questioned the naval officers on the street while Sergeant Ryan listened to the bus company men. Pegler did no talking, and Sergeant Ryan, who later transferred to the Phoenix police force, got the impression that the columnist's jaw had been fractured. The captain stared at Pegler, a man of almost fifty with disarranged clothes and a black and bloody face. "He's an old man," said the captain with distaste. "Things like this can't go on."

The captain wanted to prefer charges against Holly. Respectfully, Sergeant Ryan pointed out that the bus company men seemed to be minding their business when the trouble began. The captain shrugged his shoulders. He was going back to the station house, he said, and the others could talk it over and decide what was to be done. Westbrook Pegler classed as an important person in Tucson, but there was no disposition to please him by keeping the fracas off the police blotter. The point was that he had received a beating at the hands of a young, strong and entirely sober opponent. Since he did not wish to prefer charges or even to accept medical attention, everybody went home.

The next day, the girl who had slammed Holly with her pocketbook made several threatening phone calls to the bus terminal. As a precaution against a possible suit, Holly made a formal statement to the Arizona Adjustment Bureau, which handled claims against the bus company, but no suit was filed.

After a lapse of time, during which Tucson gossiped avidly, the brawl at the bus terminal received limited attention in one newspaper. Friends of Pegler wanted him to protest, but he declined to do so. He could see no damage to his reputation, he said, in an account which depicted him as fighting for a lady's honor.

Of all the physical encounters involving himself which he wrote about constantly in anecdotal form, this was the only one which could be documented. And it was never mentioned in his column.

Westbrook Pegler's relationship with Roy Howard had become frayed, but the break did not come until August.

To judge by reports and photographs, the columnist wrote, President Roosevelt might not be able to serve out a fourth term. His reelection would therefore serve only to inflict Henry A. Wallace on the country as president. (This was before Senator Harry S. Truman replaced Wallace on the 1944 Democratic national ticket.) Roy Howard objected to speculation over the life expectancy of a public official; it was unethical, he said. Pegler was already dickering with Hearst. Making an abrupt decision, Howard agreed to accept token columns, which he had no intention of printing, until November 23, when the Pegler contract expired. This had the effect of releasing the columnist for immediate service with Hearst's King Features Syndicate.

Howard and Pegler exchanged parting salutes in *Editor & Publisher*. "It long has been and continues to be our opinion that Mr. Pegler is one of American journalism's most colorful, conscientious and effective craftsmen," said Howard. "Those of us who have been closely associated with him and who have enjoyed his sense of humor and his comradeship wish him all the best wherever he elects to pitch his tent."

Pegler said: "I'm switching because I have a better job."

One formality remained before the columnist could emerge as a Hearstling. He had to be blessed by the Banshees, a captive group of sports, theatrical and political celebrities operated by the King Features Syndicate in the interests of publicity for its headliners. More than one thousand guests, including Roy Howard, Robert (Believe It or Not) Ripley, James A. Farley and former Mayor James J. Walker, gathered at the Waldorf for the stag luncheon and its customary affectionate ribbing of the guest of honor. Bugs Baer, the humorist, was toastmaster. Introducing Pegler, he said: "If genius is an infinite capacity for taking pains —and giving them—then Pegler is a genius!"

Clutching the microphone desperately, the columnist got a

laugh with an obviously rehearsed reference to the way President Roosevelt had launched his fourth-term campaign with an appeal for help at a Teamsters Union convention in Washington. "President Dan Tobin, ladies and gentlemen of the Teamsters Union," he began.

He had planned a non-controversial discussion, Pegler said, of Thomas E. Dewey's presidential campaign swing around the country. Dewey would not convert any New Dealers nor would the New Dealers convert any Republicans, he declared. Dewey would not do so well in states with large union organizations. The columnist's voice was trailing off. "Louder!" somebody shouted. "It's not so good anyway," said Pegler, moving on to California.

Northern California, he said, was more hopeful than Southern California, though perhaps Northern had made a mistake making a to-do about the open shop at this time. Southern was stuck with a Democratic candidate who turned out to be a former Kleagle of the Klan from Long Island. He had missed Dewey's best speech in Oklahoma, Pegler said, and he had not been able to catch a re-broadcast of the speech. Suddenly, he was finished.

Jimmy Walker tried to liven up the atmosphere. "That *nonpartisan* talk of Peg's was a gem!" he shouted. To friends around him, he added: "I don't know anybody who can be so interesting when he's wrong."

Bugs Baer closed the meeting. "I introduced Pegler when he made his first speech at the National Press Club in Washington," he said. "I'm glad to see he hasn't improved a bit. A good many of us writers become talkers—and that's the end of us."

15. OUT IN THE DESERT

One advantage of living in Arizona, Westbrook Pegler pointed out, was the relief it gave from foreigners. "In New York and vicinity, and especially in the political atmosphere," he wrote, "a hundred varieties from other parts of the world are whetting knives and cherishing old hatreds, all to the effect that the whole mass of people lives in a spiritual tension. Not until you get away from New York do you fully realize that practically all the claptrap about 'groups' and 'minorities' and 'democracy' which beats on people's ears and jabbers at them from the pages and the stage is professional propaganda to keep hateful men on the payroll of societies which would expire if they didn't stimulate hatred."

Employment by Hearst gave full scope for the columnist's xenophobia. He had begun to shout about foreigners during the war. At a time when China was an American ally, he urged the exclusion of all Asiatics from American immigration. Except for the few Negroes already here, he wrote, "this is going to be a white man's country." He was soon urging the exclusion of white immigrants from citizenship. "Our country belongs to us and not to everyone who wants to come in," he declared. When the United States tried to absorb some of Europe's displaced persons after the war, he objected on the ground that they would not be refugees unless they were communists in the first place.

Racial and religious bigotry, Pegler argued, was "as American as ice-cream soda." The domestic fair practices committees which had grown up during the war, he predicted, would force the great majority in the United States to "join the minorities" to get a fair break. He defended the use of derogatory tags like "Dago" and he began to stress the national origin and religion of his enemies.

Thus Supreme Court Justice Felix ("Old Weenie") Frankfurter came from Austria, he noted, and Sidney Hillman, a labor leader and politician, was "an ex-rabbinical student from Latvia." He even applied this kind of classification to his mail. Early in 1947, he received a complaint over one of his columns from a Dr. Benjamin Gilbert in New York. According to his old enemy

PM, which reprinted the letter, he returned it with a scribbled message near the doctor's signature: "Is this your original name? Mine is Pegler."

Leaving Scripps-Howard had the effect of drying up some of Pegler's news sources. Those who came forward now with tips were often more reactionary. In February 1947, for example, the columnist devoted several days to Michael Joseph Deutch. On information from Senator E. H. Moore of Oklahoma, Pegler stressed that Deutch, a native of Smolensk, Russia, had not yet been naturalized when he worked on federal oil programs during the war. It was hard to understand why a man's life should be exposed so mercilessly—until the Toledo *Blade* noted that Deutch had infuriated the oil lobby by agreeing to become the lead-off witness against Senator Moore's bill to turn tideland oil over to the states.

That same year, Pegler produced the exposé which he always maintained should have netted him a second Pulitzer Prize. This tip came from William Griffin, publisher of the New York *Enquirer*, who had been among the Axis sympathizers indicted for sedition during the war but who had escaped trial because of a faulty indictment. Griffin's story was that Elliott Roosevelt, one of the late President's sons, had welshed on three hundred thousand dollars in loans from John Hartford of the A & P store chain and several other men. Pegler showed that the President had tried to help his son in ways which were at least indiscreet, but the exposé got less attention than he expected, possibly because it broke in the Hearst press, where this sort of thing was almost routine.

Fritz Kuhn, who had led the German-American Bund in the United States before Pearl Harbor, told an American interviewer in his German prison camp that "the only American reporter who ever gave me a break was Westbrook Pegler." This upset readers who did not realize how ambiguous some of the columnist's attitudes had been in those days.

By now, however, he was finding excuses for former enemies ranging from Axel Wenner-Gren, the blacklisted Swedish industrialist, to the late Benito Mussolini. Commentators who were still thinking in war terms found this distasteful.

Out in the desert, Westbrook Pegler found Walter Winchell's weekly radio chatter particularly galling. Having committed himself not to reply personally to "the rogue," as he called Winchell, the controversialist trifled with the idea of building up somebody else as a counter-weight on the air. Early in 1948 he began a campaign to rehabilitate Gerald L.K. Smith, a Midwest racist who had learned his trade as a lieutenant of Huey Long. Smith had been "denied the right of free speech," Pegler declared in one of several syndicated columns on the subject, "whereas Communists, Zionists and Propagandists of all grades have had the full use of all propaganda and meeting facilities of the United States."

Since Smith was the best known Jew-baiter in the country at the time, protests soon forced Pegler to abandon his campaign. Religion played no role in it, he insisted subsequently under oath in a court proceeding. He wished merely to find somebody, he said, whose views would lead him "to attack and abuse the adherents of Winchell's political devotion."

His passing infatuation for Gerald L.K. Smith and a variety of references in his columns were cited frequently by small local Jewish groups and individuals as signs of religious prejudice, but Pegler was never accused publicly of anti-Semitism by any of the national Jewish defense groups. In denying prejudice, the columnist usually quoted from anti-fascist columns he wrote during the mid-1930s, particularly his famous piece on the plight of Jewish children in Hitler's Germany.

Viewed from Arizona, developments in the labor movement seemed particularly ominous to the columnist. Walter Reuther had played a decisive postwar role in routing the communists in the CIO by taking control of the huge United Auto Workers, and David Dubinsky of the International Ladies Garment Workers had started a drive against racketeering elements within the AFL. Reacting as if he were displeased on both counts, Pegler focused his anger on Reuther as a supposedly unreformed radical and on Dubinsky as a leader who still harbored a few racketeers in his own union. When Walter Reuther and his brother Victor were wounded seriously in separate attacks by underworld assassins after they moved against policy-gambling rings which had begun to utilize union shop stewards in the big auto plants, Pegler suggested that public sympathy for the brothers was "inappropriate." Considering their participation in sit-down strikes which won the union's first contracts, he continued: "The Reuthers had it coming."

An intensifying feeling for violence gave a febrile tone to many columns. Pegler was no admirer of Ickes but when a Bridgeport editor made an invidious comment on the New

Dealer's wife, Pegler wrote that he thought Ickes should have "gone right up there to Bridgeport and shot that editor dead . . . . I say this seriously." He hailed isolated killings of pickets as "salutary." In one newspaper strike, he justified the use of sufficient force "to bat the brains out of the whole mass of pickets, if necessary." Recalling Chicago's Memorial Day massacre, he expressed the view that the "good Chicago cops stood fast and killed no more than they had to." When New York police staged a roundup of vagrants, he suggested that "cops must be allowed to beat up the kind of vermin who were rounded up in the Broadway zone the other night." He deplored Dept. of Justice intervention in local affairs "under the pretext of maintaining the 'civil rights' of rodent characters who ought to be clubbed on sight and run out of gas."

Pegler's new verbal recklessness, derived from relative isolation and his own internal urgencies, seemed to attract more readers than it alienated. The columnist found justification and consolation in his increasing mail. More than a thousand letters a week arrived at Casa Cholla, many of them written in black pencil on ruled paper and seven out of eight approved of what he was writing.

By constant querulousness and his choice of targets, Pegler was tapping veins of interest enlisting the sympathy and to some extent the support of thousands of ordinary citizens. These were chiefly people who, in varying degree, despite the highest levels of pay and conveniences ever achieved in any country, felt restless, rootless, disappointed, inadequate, insecure, suspicious, abused or persecuted, and who were related to each other in a curious psychological kinship.

These were the anonymous men in the crowd on whom potential dictators rely. They were the authoritarians of the United States and Westbrook Pegler had become their preferred mouthpiece because he was one of them. The common rancor of the discomfited kept him company out in the desert.

From Casa Cholla on March 11, 1947:
"The paper says two below zero in Denver. Storm in New England. Roads blocked again. Outside here the sun is bright and soft and the kids are tanned a biscuit color and the flowers are blooming. It is as if our nation had been saving Arizona for a treat to the people, but still, don't look for guaranteed freedom from want and fear and work."

195

Despite the placid tone of the column, Westbrook Pegler was making heroic efforts at self-reform. Earlier that year he had spent several weeks in Presbyterian Hospital in New York for rest and a general checkup. During a period of a year or two, he had been required to make several visits to the Lahey Clinic in Boston, where the famous Dr. Sara Jordan ministered to his duodenal ulcer with medicines and common sense. If a man had an unconquerable habit, she did not demand the impossible, but she missed no chance to remind her patient that smoking and drinking irritated the colon. Letters came to Pegler regularly from Gene Tunney in the East, denouncing smoking as a poison but conceding some merit to the reasonable consumption of alcohol—as a food. Julie tried to be helpful by stressing her distaste for the mess and reek of smoking around the house.

Though he had made many unsuccessful efforts to swear off in the past, it happened this time by accident. One morning in the spring of 1947, the columnist did not smoke until noon, and then he did not smoke until evening, and when it came to bedtime and he still had not smoked, he was almost afraid to think about it.

It went on that way. After the second day, he ignored what was happening. When Julie complimented him on his will power and mentioned the comfort of a cleaner house, he said he did not wish to discuss the matter. Not until four months had elapsed did he feel safe enough to write Gene Tunney. After a full year, he began to calculate how many cigarettes he had smoked before he stopped. Considering the early years when he only consumed fifteen or twenty a day, it worked out to an average of thirty a day. Counting in leap years over a thirty-year period, he arrived at a total of 328,500 cigarettes, each two and three-quarters inches long, which if laid end to end would have stretched fourteen miles.

To placate his ulcer, he was not allowed by Dr. Sara Jordan to eat homemade bread, which he loved. He was required to eat boiled rather than fried fish or meat, to shun butter and crackers and to select fruit for dessert instead of pastry or ice cream. He did all right on the diet after a while. Drinking gave him more trouble. Trying to stay on the wagon for specified periods of thirty to sixty days proved difficult. Restricting intake to two drinks an evening worked better, particularly when he followed the W. C. Fields system of making each drink a double. If he slipped one night, he made a doubly determined effort the

196

next. He reported progress; by 1949 he could boast that in deference to his "gum-boil or blister" he had been avoiding bars entirely.

The columnist's higher standards for himself were accompanied by increasing impatience for the foibles of others. His puritanic tendency was not new, merely more pronounced. Public officials of whom he disapproved were often criticized in his column on moral grounds. Chief Justice Henry Vinson of the Supreme Court, he reported, had gone "to a drinking bout which took a revolting turn when an obscene phonograph record was played through to the last foul phrase," and Justice William Douglas had "read an obscene homemade doggerel" at a gathering of male correspondents in Washington.

While in this judicial vein, the columnist recalled that the late Supreme Court Justice Frank Murphy had gone dancing with young women in public as an old man "with far from stately mien." Pegler himself did little dancing in public. When Morris L. Ernst, the liberal lawyer, produced a book in 1948 containing a reference to celibates as "the most dogmatic expounders of the normal and moral," Pegler pounced on the phrase as if he had been personally offended.

At the age of fifty-five, which he reached in the summer of 1949, the celebrated journalist cut quite an imposing figure. The unfinished look which characterized him in the forties had yielded to grimness. He was heavier than he had been—"running to fat" was how he put it—and the flesh bulged around his collar and at the waistline. He stood almost six feet tall and he held his spine with such stiffness as to suggest early military training. He had a flushed countenance, from sun or alcohol or both, salt-and-pepper hair and tufted John L. Lewis-like brows over very nervous blue eyes.

Julie served increasingly as his social buffer. Since she had learned to handle her angina attacks with nitroglycerine, she was able to be more frequently at his side. If he went merely to a Tucson Press Club affair and rustled notes, stared at the ceiling and clinked a pocketful of keys in search of an opening sentence, she would be near enough to say: "Put your keys down, honey," and he would obey amid laughter and somehow find the words he was seeking.

When Westbrook went to Washington under subpoena in 1949 to testify before a House labor subcommittee, Julie accompanied him as moral support. He was supposed to present new

197

evidence of union mismanagement, but he had little to offer beyond the tips he received by mail and he was unwilling to jeopardize his tipsters by turning these over to the committee. During a recess, a reporter unknown to her remarked that Westbrook was as inept a witness as Willie Stevens in the celebrated Hall-Mills murder case.

"Willie Stevens was no dope," she interjected sharply. "I covered that trial and I know." Then she introduced herself and smiled, to let the abashed reporter off the hook. When Westbrook stepped down after a gruelling day on the stand, he was amazed at the cordial reception he received from the reporter, whom he had always assumed to be unfriendly.

Pegler's social appearances were limited, even in Tucson. He came to feel at home at the Press Club among the lesser practitioners of his trade in a town lacking a Newspaper Guild. He delivered formal and less successful talks at the Princeton and University Clubs. Occasionally he attended a cocktail party given by a local industrialist, and he was known to pay off accumulated social debts with a whisky-pouring on his own estate.

Tucson boasted a sizable literary colony, including Erskine Caldwell, Elliott Arnold and other well-known writers, but they rarely saw the occupant of Casa Cholla. His unlisted phone number was known to very few and a post office box concealed his exact address.

At one non-literary party, a writer noticed Pegler's secret smile when listening and his way of ducking his chin down and sideways every few minutes, usually with a deprecatory laugh. The sight reminded him of Sir Thomas More's description of Richard III: 'He was never quiet in his mind, never thought of himself as secure. His eyes whirled about, his body was privily fenced, his hand ever on his dagger, his countenance and manner like one always ready to strike again."

The columnist tried to conform to local mores. Along with other wealthy Republicans, he registered locally as a Democrat on the theory that this was the way to bore from within the dominant party. Though he confessed he could still be beaten "by women and cartoonists," he played a little golf at the Tucson Country Club. When it came time for the annual rodeo (Fiesta de los Vaqueros), he allowed himself to be displayed in the large portable jail which a Junior Chamber of Commerce group called "The Vigilantes" always parades through town. Snapshots of the

198

columnist with an oversized cowboy hat popped on his head and a rope around his neck caught him in an almost happy mood.

One evening he was driving home along Oracle Road when a Mexican woman hailed him. She was sick and wanted to go to the hospital, she said. Obviously she was pregnant. The super nationalist obligingly turned his car around and drove to the best hospital in Tucson. He engaged and paid for a private room. He didn't have long to wait for the news. The Mexican woman had been delivered of a large and healthy boy whom she named, out of gratitude to her benefactor, Westbrook Pegler Gonzales!

Word spread in Tucson of Pegler's unusual generosity toward his father, who had followed him to Tucson. Arthur Pegler and his second wife lived in a colony of modest ranch houses called Pioneer Village. It became known that Westbrook had selected the house and paid for it. He paid the taxes and allowed his father, who was now in his eighties, one hundred dollars a week for expenses. Even so, they rarely saw each other. Arthur Pegler's almost total deafness and blindness discouraged social intercourse, and Westbrook's column received priority over everything else. For six months a year, he traveled around the country in search of material, and sometimes Julie traveled with him. When they were in residence at the House of the Touchy Cactus, as some neighbors called it, Westbrook maintained a rigorous writing schedule.

If possible, he tried to start typing by mid-afternoon. With luck, he finished by dinner, which Julie planned for ten or eleven o'clock. The temptation to relax over a drink or two after dinner was always strong. Julie had trouble breathing at night and her sleep was always a furtive thing. Usually she did not get up until noon. Westbrook, who arose somewhat earlier, would come in then with a tray containing a hot cup of coffee and a couple of the brightest blooms from the desert. He made a ceremony of waking her up with a kiss.

There was a tendency for a while in Tucson to stress that Pegler was kinder in his person than in his column, but the final verdict had to be that he was unpredictable. A routine announcement by the Tucson Community School that it planned to raise funds by showing some old Charlie Chaplin films aroused him to nationally syndicated rage. Chaplin was a rotter, he wrote, a demagogic beast and a detestable alien guttersnipe whose politics were as red as his liver was white. The school authorities and

199

the community at large were startled by this outburst, but the movies were shown anyway and were well attended.

If a man hates at all, Samuel Johnson once said, he will hate his next neighbor. Westbrook got along all right with his next neighbor until noises in the night came between them. Raymond P. Fowler was a zealous Colgate alumnus, a former newspaper proprietor and retired investment banker from Buffalo with conservative views. He and his wife lived a half mile down the road with their dogs, cattle and six-car garage on an estate considerably larger than the Peglers'.

As early as 1947, Westbrook began to complain about the Fowler's four Norwegian elkhounds and one mongrel. Red Fowler rejected the complaint. His dogs barked only when disturbed by other dogs, cars or coyotes, he said. Nobody in a constant flow of visitors from the East had ever found them objectionable.

Since sound travels a long way on the desert, finding the culprit was not easy. The Fowlers decided that the barking came from boxers owned by another neighbor, a former Russian Czarist officer who had changed his name to Thompson after marrying an American woman. They almost proved their theory one night when they were waked up and discovered that their own dogs were locked up and quiet.

The Fowlers drove to the home of the Guy Curriers, who had expressed sympathy for the Peglers. They invited Mrs. Currier out into the starry night to hear for herself, but she said she would rather sleep. Suddenly there was silence. The barking had stopped, so there was nothing to do but return to Rancho el Palmar del Telecote.

Another night, the Peglers played detective. Driving out from Casa Cholla at 6:00 A.M., they claimed to have caught the Norwegian elkhounds of the Fowlers in full tongue. The Fowlers replied that their dogs had been stirred into barking by Thompson's boxers, which were fed about that time.

The exurban aristocracy of the desert tried to dismiss the feud as a joke. There was so much nocturnal prowling, they said, that the woodpeckers and elf owls who made their homes in the saguaro, or giant cactus, were putting up Do Not Disturb signs. Told that malicious rumors were being spread by the Peglers that he was a real Democrat as well as a nominal one, Red

Fowler invented a joke that the three great aggressors in the desert—the rattlesnake, the gila monster and Pegler—were alike in that they looked shy until they decided to bite.

Pegler's caretaker came over to the Fowler estate one day in 1949 to register a complaint and got bitten. The Fowlers blamed him for attacking one of their dogs with a club. The dog showed good judgment, they added. Soon after this, Julie made an effort to heal the quarrel by sending over a bouquet to the Fowlers with a note: "Love from Julie and Peg." Westbrook followed her lead by presenting his next neighbors with a pair of salt-and-pepper owls, with a card reading: "Thank God, these don't bark."

Grasping the extended olive branch, the Fowlers invited the Peglers over for dinner. Unfortunately, Red Fowler told an anecdote about the red tape involved in getting a calf slaughtered in Tucson. Westbrook became so upset over his neighbor's easy-going toleration of what he considered to be unforgivable bureaucratic fumbling that he and Julie soon cut their visit short.

Two weeks later, the phone rang at 2:30 A.M. Mrs. Fowler took the call in her bedroom. Putting a hand over the receiver, she told her husband: "It's Pegler again, about the dogs." Fowler groaned. "Is Peg crocked?" he demanded. She nodded. The previous dinner table conversation came into Fowler's mind. "Tell him to go to hell, and hang up," he said, and Mrs. Fowler obeyed instructions.

Pegler sued for $1,000 damages and a temporary injunction to stop the Fowler dogs from barking. He ridiculed the Fowler counter-claim about the Thompson boxers, saying that one breed barked tenor and the other baritone and he could certainly tell the difference. Supreme Court Justice Lee Garrett of Tucson tried to make peace at a preliminary hearing which settled nothing. The trial itself had to be postponed because Julie had broken both of her legs in a fall in New York while making an Eastern trip with her husband. When she and Westbrook returned, the Thompsons and their boxers had moved and an enduring peace had settled on the desert.

When Pegler's suit was finally withdrawn in 1951, he had to pay court costs. The Tucson *Daily Citizen* could not resist the temptation to run an imaginary interview with Yuma, one of the victorious elkhounds, in which she promised to bark endlessly and also to bite if anybody ever again referred to "that ob-noxious character in Casa Cholla as my handsome mother's son —or even offers to give HIS mother a bone."

More than once over the years, the columnist had referred to son-of-a-bitch as "the unforgivable American insult," yet here it was thrown in his face with obvious relish and malice. Except, however, for a furious phone call to William A. Small, pub-lisher of the newspaper, Pegler did nothing about it. Asked by neighbors why he took no direct physical action, the columnist quoted a Supreme Court decision to the effect that S.O.B. was a biologic impossibility, hence no insult at all. The neighbors could never figure him out.

16. SETTLING AN OLD SCORE

Quentin Reynolds, who was known to the public as the greatest, bravest war correspondent since Floyd Gibbons, stared out of the window of his apartment on the fashionable East Side of Manhattan. He had been staring out of the window for almost two days. In a column by Westbrook Pegler, he had been called Ferdinand the Bull, an artful check-dodger, a coward, a slacker, a war profiteer, a snob, a four-flusher and a nudist, with various physical and moral defects to match, including a protuberant belly filled with something other than guts, a yellow streak and a mangy hide. The column had come in retaliation for his review in the New York *Herald Tribune* of a biography of Heywood Broun by Dale Kramer. What should he do about it?

The book review had ended with these words: "Broun . . . could talk of nothing but Pegler's attack on him. He returned to his hotel, but not to sleep. It seemed incredible that he was allowing Pegler's absurd charge of dishonesty to hurt him so. But not even Connie could make him dismiss it from his mind. The doctor told him to relax; he'd be all right if he could get some sleep. But he couldn't relax. He couldn't sleep.

"And he died."

Pegler interpreted this conclusion, which went beyond anything in the book under review, as a charge of homicide. In a literary quarrel, it had always been his practice to whale away verbally in confidence that he would not be the first to cry foul. Except for the case of the barking elkhounds, which was different in that he considered himself the spokesman for like-minded neighbors, he had never run to a court for protection or relief. This time he minced no words in his portrait of his old friend from Pound Ridge.

Now it was up to Reynolds. Ordinarily he was an effervescent man. His wife, Virginia Peine, the actress, let him alone on the theory that his brooding over the Pegler column would work itself out. Finally he turned to her. "Ginny," he said, "would you mind if I sued?" She was delighted. "I'd have divorced you if you didn't," she said. "I thought you'd never get angry."

Pegler showed no concern over the resulting $50,000 suit.

He had been brushing aside libel actions for years. Harry Bridges, the Communist labor leader, had sued for $600,000 and others had sought similarly imposing amounts, but as yet nobody had collected a cent. In a single instance involving Abram N. Spanel, president of the International Latex Corporation, the columnist had been forced to apologize. Spanel used newspaper advertising space to reprint articles he considered notable. He then armed his salesmen with stacks of reprints with which to cajole larger orders from their customers. Because of his choice of material for reprinting, Pegler had called him a "pro-Red editorialist." This was ridiculous; Spanel was simply a shrewd business man. A formal retraction soon led to the withdrawal of suits amounting to millions of dollars.

The filing of a libel suit normally imposes silence upon a defendant pending trial. Pegler, however, had tried something new when Drew Pearson, the Washington news analyst, served a complaint on him in 1949 shortly before Reynolds brought his suit. In his legal answer to Pearson, Pegler asserted that the original actionable adjectives (liar and blackguard) were applicable "from A to Z." He thereupon appended twenty-six fresh examples of what he had in mind, one for every letter of the alphabet! Shuddering at this unprecedented behavior, Pearson's lawyers got a judge to strike out the answer.

When Pegler tried similar tactics on Reynolds, Louis Nizer, Reynolds' lawyer, allowed the deliberately insulting answer to stand.

Since it compounded the libel, it gave Nizer the right to peer into every corner of Pegler's life. During the next four years, while the case languished on an overcrowded calendar, Nizer took full advantage of the opportunity.

The pre-trial examination sessions were private but formal, before an official stenographer. Each session had to end by 4:00 P.M., so that the columnist could get to work on the short essay which would appear coast to coast in precisely three days. Sometimes Pegler would arrive in a diffident mood and give almost apologetic answers. At other times, he would toss a sardonic "Hello, Mr. Lipschutz" at Nizer and snarl at everybody present. The Lipschutz reference meant he was feeling persecuted; Isidore Lipschutz was a rich emigré diamond merchant from Belgium whom Pegler was currently accusing in his column of "operating a private gestapo" through the Non-Sectarian Anti-Nazi League.

204

Sometimes the sessions would be held as often as three times a week. Then the columnist would bring up illness of his father in Tucson or some new complaint on the part of Julie to secure a recess which might last several months. Regardless of delay, the sessions always resumed. In addition to the career of Quentin Reynolds, which was the basic issue, and the "inter-racial orgies" at Broun's Sabine Farm which were beginning to loom large in his mind, Pegler got a chance to discuss at length his own attitudes and associations. He referred, for example, to the *Herald Tribune,* which had carried the Reynolds review, as "a pro-Communist newspaper—always has been and still is." The *Herald Tribune*'s support of President Eisenhower, he said, was merely "evasive action."

He himself had never been pro-Communist or a fellow-traveler, the columnist declared. He recalled getting in touch with the *Daily Worker* around 1935 or 1936. He visited Earl Browder at Communist headquarters in New York "to see the cut of his jib, the same as I am going to call on Frank Costello (the gangster) and some other people to see what they look like."

Brought abruptly up to date, he acknowledged receiving various anti-Semitic rabble-rousing propaganda sheets without asking for them. They included Gerald L.K. Smith's *Cross and the Flag,* Conde McGinley's *Common Sense,* Curt Asher's *X-Ray* and Leon de Aryan's *Broom*—but not Gerald Winrod's *Defender.* He knew about Winrod's paper, which was published in Topeka, Kansas, but he did not get it. He conceded that he had tried to build up Gerald L. K. Smith "as a counterweight" to Walter Winchell, who took an aggressively pro-New Deal attitude on the radio. He thought better of this idea after awhile, he said, and asked Smith to cease quoting his "greatest orator of the age" phrase of praise. Among lesser ultra-rightists, he particularly remembered George Sylvester Viereck. They had discussed poetry, he said. He once received an exposé of Winchell from Joseph P. Kamp and he had talked to Kamp on the telephone by mistake. He had corresponded with Merwin K. Hart and he had encountered Edward Rumely in a coffee shop. He was uncertain how much contact he enjoyed with the Columbians, an anti-Negro outfit down South which he had defended obliquely in his column.

Any suggestion that he was "a poison-pen artist" was just a Communist smear, Westbrook Pegler informed Louis Nizer. He denied, for example, that he had been unfair to President Eisenhower. A woman who had known the General during the war had written a book and he had sent questions about the book to the White House without receiving an acknowledgment to his letter. "He impugned his own morals," Pegler said. "I merely commented on disclosures by a lady . . ."

Over the years, it was true, he had "attacked many scoundrels." Any others? asked Nizer. "No, I did not," said Pegler firmly. "Everyone I attacked was a scoundrel."

The occupational disease of commentators is the illusion that they can significantly influence events. By stressing his preferred role as a shoe leather-and-telephone kind of reporter, Westbrook Pegler had resisted this sickness, but now he was beginning to show signs of infection. He liked to explain how he put Harry Truman on the presidential ticket with President Roosevelt in 1944 and how he almost defeated Truman for President in 1948. His first achievement was based on a series of columns revealing the "Dear Guru" letters written by Vice-President Wallace to a Far Eastern cult operator on Riverside Drive in New York. These revelations might well have affected some delegates to the 1944 Democratic national convention. "I didn't know my own strength," crowed Pegler in 1950. "The silly, sordid story of Henry's infatuation with a grandiose sideshow character in Chinatown getup cut down Eleanor Roosevelt's candidate just enough to let Truman in."

The 1948 situation revolved around Bernard Baruch, a retired financier known as an adviser to Presidents. Baruch refused an appointment that year to the Democratic finance committee; he always refused such appointments. On a mistaken notion that the refusal showed sympathy for the growing anti-Truman campaign being conducted by the Hearst–McCormick–Scripps-Howard journalistic axis, the President wrote Baruch one of his impulsive bitter letters. Word of the letter soon got around.

Westbrook Pegler at this time was undergoing another course of treatment for his ulcers at the Lahey Clinic in Boston. From a fellow patient, financier Joseph P. Kennedy, he received a fairly accurate account of the Truman letter. The columnist was always working. With Kennedy lounging nearby, he reached Baruch on the telephone and needled him about the rebuke from the White House.

In a similar vein, Baruch said he didn't want to talk to anybody who obviously had been taken in by the President. He had said some favorable things about Truman, Pegler conceded, but not recently. He persisted until Baruch burst out abruptly that the President was "a rude, ignorant, uncouth man!" This was off the record, he added, but Pegler was receiving nothing in confidence. Pegler hung up and used the remark precisely as he had heard it.

After the column appeared, Baruch denied making any statement for publication. The damage had already been done, since the column goaded President Truman into releasing a version of his original letter. Baruch was a Jewish layman of sufficient importance to swing votes, particularly in New York. New York did go for Dewey that year, thereby almost but not quite terminating Truman's White House lease.

When President Truman made his decision to buck Communist aggression in Korea and won UN support, Pegler urged the country to pull out on the ground that the United States could not cope with oriental hordes to whom death meant nothing. The American strategy, he said, should be to assassinate the one hundred leaders of Soviet Russia who were backing Chinese aggression. America had accomplished greater feats than this in the past, he said, implying as an after-thought that it might be well to handle the one hundred leaders of the domestic labor movement in the same fashion.

When two Puerto Rican nationalists made an unsuccessful attempt to assassinate President Truman, John O'Donnell of the New York *Daily News* grumbled in his Washington column that the pools of blood on Pennsylvania Avenue would certainly carry the upcoming Congressional elections for the Democrats. O'Donnell was wrong; other factors proved more influential, including the deep freeze-and-black market perfume scandals of the administration, economic dislocation at home and, of course, the Korean War. The result was a national Republican sweep.

On December 2, 1950, King Features Syndicate inserted a large and unusual advertisement in *Editor & Publisher* attributing the spectacular GOP victory at the polls to "the courageous columnist, Westbrook Pegler." It continued: "In such key states as Pennsylvania (Pegler circ. 1,315,000), Illinois (Pegler circ. 650,000), Connecticut (Pegler circ. 2,585), and the majority of all other states the results were the same—the people and Westbrook Pegler were amazingly close together—convincing

207

proof that Westbrook Pegler's courage in choosing his ground and standing firm—despite wide criticism—has now been justified by the vote of the people of the U.S."

Quentin Reynolds told Virginia Peine he wasn't sure he could hold out until the libel case reached trial. He was facing economic strangulation. The first effect of the columnar attacks by Westbrook Pegler had been to cut off his major source of income. Between 1933 and 1949, *Collier's* magazine purchased three hundred ten articles from him at prices ranging up to $2,500 an article. After the so-called libel column appeared in 1949, the magazine bought no new material from him; he was too controversial.

Retreating from a high standard of living is never easy. Reynolds used what money he earned as it came in and then had nothing left for taxes. After several years, a federal tax lien in excess of forty thousand dollars was standing against him. Before the Pegler blast, the foreign correspondent was in demand as a radio personality. Now his agent, Mark Hanna, found he had become "poison" on the air. He could still do moving picture work and deliver lectures, but Pegler was working to discredit him in those fields.

Hearing that Reynolds might go to Hollywood to work on a picture about General Jimmy Doolittle, the columnist made a visit to Lowell Thomas, who was associated with the celluloid epic.

Pegler revealed that Thomas assured him he felt "shocked" over the choice of Reynolds and added that the General himself considered it "inappropriate." Nevertheless, arrangements had been completed, so Reynolds kept the job. Pegler was unaware at this time that Lowell Thomas was friendly enough to Reynolds to use him as an occasional replacement on his radio show. He did not even realize that the book on which the movie was based had been written by Reynolds.

Early in 1951, Pegler heard that Reynolds might deliver a five hundred dollar speech before the New York Credit and Financial Management Association. He took drastic action. His February 1 column was devoted to the lack of qualifications for lecturing possessed by his old friend. He had consulted with Leslie Gould, financial writer on the *Journal-American*—"who maintains a vigorous anti-Communist theme in his copy," he noted significantly—and Gould had found that "no check had been made into Reynolds' associations." Pegler continued: "As a public service, I provide herein information concerning Quentin Reynolds, which may be a guide to any organizations which may desire to hire him . . . It may also help the radio and TV publics to evaluate his statements."

Among other things, mention was made of Reynolds' brief wartime service with the lend-lease exploratory mission to Moscow headed by Averell Harriman and Lord Beaverbrook. The purpose of this mission, growled Pegler in print, "was to thrust on the Soviet dictator the riches of the U.S. including, in the long run, vast amounts of stuff which was used to build up industrial Russia after the war." The columnist then provided a list of various stands taken on Russia by Reynolds over the years which he said paralleled the arguments of "Communist traitors" in the United States.

Stunned by the ferocity of this assault, Mrs. Reynolds rushed to Pegler's office at King Features on East 45th Street in New York. Weeping, she demanded: "Why don't you let up? Do you want to destroy us?" The columnist said he had nothing against her. If the suit were dropped, he promised, he would never write another word about Quentin. Mrs. Reynolds agreed to let him know, but when her husband heard about the visit he said he had no intention of being bludgeoned into submission. To Louis Nizer's relief, he decided that the suit must go on.

Pegler's effort to blacklist Reynolds as a subversive character did not prevent the former war correspondent from making his scheduled speech before the New York Credit and Financial Management Association. He made other speeches. In one case, he was invited to address an Amateur Athletic Union dinner in New York. Though not an AAU member and not invited to the dinner, Pegler made it his business—"as a public-spirited, anti-Communist American," he explained—to expostulate privately with Gene Tunney, James A. Farley, former State Boxing Commissioner Eddie Eagan, Robert Moses and Jimmy Powers, sports editor of the New York *Daily News*. He "gave the facts" on Reynolds to these influential AAU members, leaving the decision whether to exert pressure for cancellation of the arrangement "to their patriotic judgment." He was baffled when Reynolds made the speech after all.

For some time, Pegler had been considering an appeal to Pope Pius XII. The decrease of Communist strength within the

CIO had involved him in acrimonious debate with some influential spokesmen for the Catholic Church in the United States. The CIO had no more right to expel Communists than Democrats or Republicans, Pegler wrote in 1949, echoing unconsciously, perhaps, Heywood Broun's old argument. CIO President Philip Murray was "a sanctimonious hypocrite who still owed retribution, restitution and public contrition," he declared. As for Catholic labor leaders like Joseph Curran and Michael Quill, who had turned against the Communists in the National Maritime Union and the Transport Workers Union respectively, they deserved no trust, Pegler said, because they had given him no help when he "fought Communists—red-baiting, they called it" back in his Newspaper Guild days.

"When you try to make me yield and trust these men, whether by abusive language or sacerdotal authority," he wrote defiantly, "I don't trust you . . . The fact that the veritable Moscow bolos were betrayed by a small set of double crossers who heard the whish of angels' wings and got afraid of dying unshriven, only proves again that this monstrous power has neither principles nor conscience."

Westbrook Pegler was not an active Catholic though he had priests among his friends. He believed he understood the fine shades of Catholic opinion on all matters. Words like "encyclical," "synod" and "sacrament" rattled like hailstones through his copy as he asserted that labor priests were taking moral shortcuts and shaking hands with union racketeers and murderers. This last charge involved him in a series of quarrels with Catholic publications. At one point he yielded his column for a day to the only guest writer he ever entertained, the Rev. William J. Smith, director of the Crown Heights Labor School.

The *Wage Earner*, published by Detroit Catholic unionists, announced a day of prayer for Pegler. This was just "a piece of pietistical cant," he retorted, urging prayer for Philip Murray instead. When Ed Marciniak, editor of *Work*, a Chicago Catholic labor publication, noted that nobody proposed to abolish marriage because of instances of adultery, Pegler's typewriter smoked with fury over the idea that unionism could be compared with the divinely ordered institution of matrimony. His Catholic critics were being "personally spiteful," he said. "The poor dear boy," mocked Don Capellano, columnist for the New York Association of Catholic Trade Unionists, "Imagine anyone being personally spiteful to such a hatchet man!"

The Hearst columnist became more insistently theological. Father Smith and other labor priests, he argued, did not speak for the entire cloth nor with clear authority from the Vatican, since they were interpreting advisory writings of the Pope which were not dogma. *The Sign,* a national Catholic magazine published by the Passionist Fathers, devoted several issues during 1950 to refuting this view. Father Ralph Gorman, editor of *The Sign,* discovered to his dismay from a flood of mail that many Catholics were "in abysmal ignorance of the social teachings of the church," and that some "preferred Mr. Pegler to the papal encyclicals."

If heresy, by dictionary definition, was unorthodox religious opinion tending to promote schism, Pegler was rapidly building himself up into a heretic. Some sense of religious peril may have been among the reasons for his pilgrimage to Rome. Early in March 1952, he reported that he had just delivered an "eye-opening report to the Vatican's highest authority on union labor" about "the criminality and autocratic rule of American unions." Furthermore, he said, he had been asked to "write for the Holy Father a statement of the truth in care of the Papal Secretary of State."

After checking hurriedly, the Catholic Welfare Conference News Service in Washington wired a hundred newspapers in the United States and Canada that the Vatican disavowed "any Holy See association with the Pegler attack on unions." The Jesuit magazine *America* cleared its skirts with a similar statement. Those responsible for the denials were either bad reporters or liars, raged Pegler. "I will stake my word against any man, whatever his office," he wrote.

The burning of heretics being unfashionable in the twentieth century, Pegler escaped with a slap on the wrist. An official spokesman of the Vatican declared in Rome that nobody there was designated as a special authority on union labor or had any right to negotiate with Pegler. The American visitor, it was suggested, might have spoken with some priest or monsignor "who either shared his view or was just trying to be polite, and asked for a report on labor to get rid of him."

Pegler reiterated in his column that he spoke to "the official adviser to the Pope on union matters," that this adviser listened to his account, exclaimed that the Pope was being "imposed upon with false representations"—presumably by others—and asked for a written report. The columnist, however, never got

211

around to submitting such a report to the Papal Secretary of State.

Both were large and impressive, though Quentin Reynolds was the larger, more relaxed and eight years younger. Both had formerly been sportswriters and foreign correspondents. Both were Catholics of Irish extraction, though Reynolds had more Irish in him than Westbrook Pegler. They looked well-matched in court, yet their purposes were different. Reynolds, who had a resonant voice, a courteous manner and curly iron-grey hair, reached out deliberately for the jury's sympathy and support. He focused on winning a libel suit to the exclusion of anything else. Pegler, on the other hand, wanted chiefly to deliver a few more telling blows at Reynolds and, through him, at the late Heywood Broun.

He faced a more immediate enemy: Louis Nizer. At first he fenced rather successfully with the celebrated lawyer. When Nizer asked if he had "any explanation locked up in breast or mind" for charges against Reynolds which he could not support factually, he snapped: "Don't get anatomical; I knew a great deal about Quentin Reynolds." When Nizer did not hear clearly the word "strafe" during a discussion of the Dieppe raid which Reynolds had covered during the war, Pegler explained that this was "a German word, meaning rake." Pressed for a definition of honor, he said it was "each man's rag doll, to do with as he pleases."

Nizer asked Pegler many questions about "an all-day carouse" which allegedly occurred at a war plant after a ceremony in which Reynolds participated. Producing a photograph taken at the ceremony, the lawyer asked if the smiles on the faces of the officials were any indication of carousing. "I believe the angels smile," Pegler replied loftily. "I never heard of them carousing."

As the trial wore on, the columnist's hostility toward the lawyer began to break through his self-control.

The questions asked were tricky, insolent and unfair, he complained. "You will have me hanging myself with these shotguns!" he shouted once with an uncharacteristic confusion of metaphor. When Nizer charged that he had contradicted himself under oath in 130 instances, this was due, he said, to Nizer's "exhausting brain-washing tactics." He began to mimic Nizer from the witness stand. When the lawyer drew near to hand him a

212

document, he shrilled unexpectedly: "Get away from me, get away!" Thereafter a court attendant was designated to hand exhibits back and forth between the men.

Early in the trial, Dale Kramer appeared. Heywood Broun's biographer sat quietly in a rear seat among the spectators. As the crowd thinned at the end of the day's session, he approached Pegler, who was stuffing papers in the yellow briefcase which was his constant companion. "You said in your column you wanted to meet me," he said, offering his hand. "I'm Dale Kramer." Pegler shivered. "I won't shake hands," he muttered agitatedly. "You're a bastard."

"What did you call me, a bastard?" roared Kramer, a two hundred pounder, white-haired at the age of forty-two. "Then you're the same!" The two men were so excited they hardly knew what they were saying. Kramer recovered first. "I won't hurt you," he said. Pegler replied: "You dirty bastard, I'll say you won't hurt me!"

The columnist took eight or ten little scampering steps over to a court attendant. "That man was threatening me," he cried, pointing a melodramatic briefcase. "I mean it. He was threatening me!" The court attendant ran to find the judge, who had left the courtroom. The judge called an immediate session in chambers during which he warned Kramer and Pegler to stay away from each other, not only in the courtroom but throughout the Federal Court building.

The next morning, Westbrook Pegler showed up early. He and a clerk were the only ones in the courtroom when the first of the reporters covering the trial arrived.

The reporter exchanged a few sentences with the columnist, who was in a prickly mood, and then went out of the courtroom into the corridor. There he encountered a sturdy young man wearing a black sports shirt, one of a group of idle persons known to reporters as professional jurors, who shop from one trial to another in the building in search of free entertainment.

The professional jurors usually travel in a pack, but this time the young man was alone. He and the reporter exchanged expert opinions on the progress of the trial until the courtroom door opened abruptly and Westbrook Pegler strode out. His eyes almost popped from his head. In a letter to the reporter years later, the columnist revealed that with the Kramer incident still fresh in his mind he had jumped to the conclusion that "the man in the black shirt" meant him physical harm. When a photographer

213

snapped Pegler's picture on the steps of the Federal building during the noon recess that day, the startled look was still on the controversialist's face.

The trial lasted eight weeks. Pegler never relaxed. He sat with ramrod stiffness in his chair when he was not testifying, his choleric jowly face pointed straight ahead, his eyes nervous as butterflies. Each time the sound of chimes sifted through the ninth-floor windows of the courtroom from the steeple of a nearby church, he jumped as if he were hit, then glared around him. If he noticed anybody favorable to him sitting near somebody on the Reynolds side, he at once asked him to move. His chief associates were his wife Julie, a stocky, determined but not unpleasant-looking woman with dyed reddish hair, and his secretary since 1947, Maude Towart, a tight-lipped, tall, angular Frenchwoman.

From time to time, persons favorable to Pegler came into the courtroom. They were quiet and aloof and relatively few in number compared to the constant influx of persons of importance from the theatrical, sports, and literary worlds whom Reynolds and his wife seemed to be always welcoming.

"It's just like being on shipboard," chattered the statuesque blonde Virginia Peine during an intermission. "One meets all one's friends here!"

Reynolds was the kind of foreign correspondent who called First Lords of the Admiralty by their first names. He liked almost everybody except vegetarians and teetotalers. At the time of the Nazi aerial blitz of London during the war, he had abused Hitler and praised British courage so successfully in broadcasts from London that an English poll placed him second in popularity only to his good friend, Winston Churchill. At the request of another close friend, the late President Roosevelt, Reynolds had returned from abroad in 1944 to deliver one of the roundup orations at the fourth-term Democratic national convention in Chicago.

This personal background Louis Nizer laboriously put into the record. The attitudes of distinguished friends ranging from Averell Harriman and Senator Taft to Viscount Mountbatten and Lord Beaverbrook were duly impressed on the jury. Famous war correspondents including Walter Kerr, Ken Downs, Lionel Shapiro, John Gunther and Edward R. Murrow took the stand personally to pay tribute to their colleague: Quentin Reynolds had almost died in the Libyan desert from exposure to the sun after crawling through the enemy lines. Quentin Reynolds had broken several ribs in London, throwing himself away from an exploding bomb. Quentin Reynolds was almost the last correspondent to leave Paris before the German troops moved in. No other correspondent could match his 30 months at various fronts during the war. His reputation was genuine enough. In the face of it, Pegler's charges of slackerism, war profiteering and cowardice fell flat.

On the issue of communism, Pegler's memory had betrayed him. Reynolds had worked for *Collier's* for years after Pegler imagined he had been fired for holding radical opinions. When his name was finally dropped from the masthead, it was at his own request so he could be free to take on outside work while continuing to contribute to the magazine. Any remaining doubt in this area was resolved by a letter from FBI director J. Edgar Hoover certifying Reynolds as the sort of "confirmed liberal" who constituted the country's best bulwark against communism. Peglet himself, after testifying that the war correspondent was "so far to the left as to be almost out of the Democratic party," wound up by conceding grumpily: "I don't say he is not loyal and a good American. I say he is a dope!"

That left only Sabine Farm and Heywood Broun, which lay at the heart of Westbrook Pegler's hatred for Quentin Reynolds. Here the columnist let himself go. Disregarding the fairly innocuous pastimes in which he himself had engaged, his inflamed memory now focused on the unmarried couple that reportedly lived together one summer in a shack on the Broun estate, the Negro singer who was credited with seducing "a susceptible white girl" up there and the whole "parisitic, licentious lot" around Broun who were reported—though Pegler never saw it himself—to swim together in the nude.

Broun's Sabine Farm was "a low dirty place," insisted Pegler, "which he shunned" whenever he could. Broun himself went around "filthy, uncombed and unpressed, with his fly open, looking like a Skid Row bum." He added carefully: "I didn't say he *was* a Skid Row bum. That is different." Making another fine distinction, he asserted that Reynolds "imitated but did not exactly emulate" Broun's sartorial carelessness. "He wore laces in his shoes."

What did he mean by saying Reynolds had a mangy hide, Nizer asked. "Well, he wasn't clean," said Pegler, screwing up his face, "but I didn't say literally, I didn't intend to say he literally

215

had the mange, because I don't think he could have the mange any more than he could have dysentery or the pox . . ."

Some of the more worldly spectators gasped. Dysentery required intestines, and pox had become a vulgarism for syphilis. Pegler seemed to be hinting that Reynolds was physically incapable of contracting either disease. Nizer kept pressing. "You intended to be hateful with that word 'mangy' didn't you?" he demanded. Pegler half rose in the witness chair. "No," he said excitedly. "I don't hate anybody, not even you!"

It may have been his glare or Nizer's slight, seemingly involuntary withdrawal, but chuckles and snorts burst from the rear rows of spectators and swept forward through the courtroom until reporters, attendants, trial counsel and stenographers were roaring with laughter. Even the jury was smiling. Judge Edward Weinfeld pounded for silence, threatening to clear the court. The laughter stopped, but it left an impact.

Reynolds had testified he was allergic to the sun. That killed the columnar charge that he had once gone "nuding along the public road with his girl friend of the moment." Pegler then rushed into the breach with two incidents which he now considered, in the perspective of twenty-two years, to have been scandalous. Returning in 1932 from the Democratic national convention which nominated F.D.R. for the first time, Pegler testified, Reynolds, then unmarried, had shared his compartment on the train with a girl. He offered her name for the record, but it was rejected.

That summer, he went on, Reynolds and this girl—again he volunteered the name and again it was stricken—shared the same shower up there in the country and slapped each other's bare buttocks merrily in full sound if not sight of others! From these two incidents, which Reynolds did not bother to refute, Pegler went on to a story which Heywood Broun's wife Connie, he said, had told him. She had been rowing on one of the two lakes at Sabine Farm. Seeing Quentin Reynolds standing in shallow water, she invited him for a ride. When he hauled himself in over the stern of the boat, according to this story, he proved to be wearing no trunks—"not even a hairnet," said the columnist. There he sat "with his lavalliere dangling while she looked at the sky and the trees."

The court recessed for lunch. Afterward, Mrs. Pegler, smart in a black and white hat and pearl earrings and a dress to match, testified to hearing the same story from Mrs. Broun. Julie's account echoed her husband's to a word. Asked if she had discussed the case with Westbrook at lunch, she replied: "Mr. Nizer, we haven't discussed anything but the case for the past five years!"

Mrs. Broun was next. She never told such a story to the Peglers or anybody else, she said. She never went rowing, she added, because she dreaded the water, not being able to swim. While on the stand, she took occasion to deny two other points. There was no mixed nude bathing at Sabine Farm, she said; it was simply not true. Furthermore, Pegler's statement that Reynolds had proposed marriage to her in the funeral coach on the way to Broun's grave was silly as well as untrue, she said. Bishop Fulton J. Sheen, who converted Broun to Catholicism, and Broun's son Woody were with them during the entire trip to the cemetery.

Charles Henry, a leathery-faced, sardonic, elderly Southern bachelor who handled all the important Hearst libel matters, had long since abandoned any effort to curb his obstreperous client. He did not cross-examine Mrs. Broun. In summation, he did his best to put a favorable gloss on an almost totally unfavorable situation. It was a simple case, he declared. Reynolds had been overmatched in a spat between prima-donnas and had come squealing to the courthouse for undeserved relief. One of the twenty-eight character witnesses for Reynolds, he noted, had said that the war correspondent's reputation was unimpaired. This proved that the Pegler columns did no damage, Henry argued.

Louis Nizer in his turn noted that there had been not a single character witness for Pegler. Why? "There isn't another writer that has a worse reputation for inaccuracy, indecency, for recklessness, for malice, for hatred, for viciousness, for besmirching people's characters and destroying them," he said.

Judge Weinfeld's charge was stern and clear. He left no doubt that the Pegler column was defamatory. The jury, eight men and four women, deliberated for thirteen hours, during which it filed back into the courtroom four times for advice on complicated points. It returned a verdict of $175,001. Exhausted physically and emotionally by the long trial, Quentin Reynolds understood the foreman to say $175. He almost collapsed. But Virginia Peine heard clearly. She burst into tears, then ran across the courtroom to kiss in turn each of the four housewives on the jury. The Peglers were not in sight. Anticipating an unfavorable verdict after the severity of the Judge's charge, they had long since left the courtroom.

Jurors revealed later that the vote at one time was eight to four for a $475,000 verdict, of which $300,000 would have been in compensatory damages and $175,000 in punitive damages. To get a unanimous verdict, as required by law, the majority agreed to whittle down compensatory damages to one dollar and to hold punitive damages at $175,000.

In a 1930 case, a jury had awarded $100,000 in compensatory damages and $100,000 in punitive damages for a libel appearing only in the Kansas City *Post*, which had a circulation of 150,000. On appeal, this verdict was reduced to a total of $125,000. The Reynolds libel had run in 186 newspapers with a combined circulation of 12,000,000. Despite a series of appeals, the verdict was not reduced. With the addition of interest and other charges, Reynolds won almost $200,000, the largest amount ever collected in an American libel case.

17. BANSHEE AT BAY

The Hearst brass decided to use the Banshees to rehabilitate their soiled champion. Westbrook Pegler did not like the idea. He said he had never expected to win the suit anyhow. He told friends that he was more upset over the death that summer of Mabel Pegler, Jack's wife, than he was over the Reynolds verdict. His mail indicated that the denunciations in court had aroused more sympathy than distaste among his readers. He was not hurt financially. He was one of two American journalists—the other being Walter Winchell—strong enough to insist on contractual exemption from any libel payments. The entire amount was therefore absorbed by the Hearst Corporation and Hearst Consolidated Publications, Inc. Syndicate sales were good and his five-year contract had three years to run.

The Banshees designated Pegler as the outstanding reporter and columnist for the year 1954. They did not delimit the area of the award. Since the two hundred or so papers using Pegler comment at this time were located not only within the continental area of the United States but also in such spots as Mexico City and Honolulu, a world title was conceivably involved. Westbrook Pegler frequently noted in his column "how utterly worldly and worthless" most journalistic awards were, "how sordid the motives for bestowal in most cases." It was the duty of an honest newspaperman, he said, to reject such "tainted baubles." Nevertheless, he was in no position to resist indefinitely the honor which was being thrust upon him.

Banshee awards were signalized by the presentation of a Silver Lady, a twelve-inch statue of a scantily clad blonde wearing a large plume. Presumably the plume was designed for writing, but the pose of the Silver Lady recalled Sally Rand behind her fan at the 1933 Chicago World's Fair.

The membership of the Banshees did not vote on Silver Ladies—that was up to the Hearst authorities. According to Webster's Intercollegiate Dictionary, banshees are fairy visitants of Scotch ancestry who come to warn a family of approaching death. These particular Banshees would have resented any such definition. Except possibly in their drinking habits, they were not Scotch. They were not tourists or fairies and they were far from gloomy. The worst that could be said about them was that they enjoyed publicity and were not averse to genial association with top-rank newspapermen who could provide it.

The ceremony was duly held at the Waldorf on November 18. On the cover of the Banshees' program, alongside a lunch menu starting with mock-turtle soup, appeared a caricature of the columnist as a knight in medieval armor, wielding a ten-foot pen as a lance. "His targets are as numerous as the sandy hair on his well-covered head," declared an accompanying biographical note. "It makes no difference to James Westbrook Pegler if the object of his disaffection is a popular idol or a scapegoat. Like the famous umpire, Bill Klem, he calls 'em as he sees 'em."

Old friends rallying around the knight included Hamish Mc-Laurin, a journalistic acquaintance of forty years' standing who used to live out in the desert near Tucson and who was currently living on the West Coast; Garry Swinehart, a one-time neighbor from Pound Ridge who had testified for Pegler at the Reynolds trial; and Frederick S. Tisdale Jr., former newspaper editor of Milford, Connecticut, whose residence had been one of several utilized for the homeric poker games of Heywood Broun's rural intelligentsia.

Up from Washington had come anti-New Deal warhorses Walter Trohan and John O'Donnell. Roy Howard was on hand. So were John N. Wheeler, the syndicate man, and James L. Kilgallen, the International News Service veteran who always said Pegler took more pains with his copy than any other news-paperman he had ever met.

Hearst executives present included William Randolph Hearst Jr., inheritor-in-chief of the properties of the late William Randolph Hearst; Ward Greene, editor and general manager of King Features; J. D. Gortatowsky, general manager of the Hearst news-papers; W. A. Curley, editor of the New York *Journal-American*; and Richard E. Berlin, president of the Hearst Corporation.

Affairs of the Banshees are traditionally stag, but Julie sat at the most conspicuous table near Jack Pegler and Arthur James Pegler, who had come respectively from Connecticut and Arizona. Westbrook had insisted on the supporting presence of his wife, who showed no embarrassment at being the only woman among a thousand men. The columnist's brother and father had needed no urging to attend.

An unusual turnout of political primitives diluted the normal attitude of careless good fellowship at Banshee affairs. It was a moment of crisis on the far right. Down in Washington, the columnist's protégé, Senator Joe McCarthy, was under desperate siege. In an effort to prevent censure of him by the Senate, a committee calling itself Ten Million Americans Mobilized for Justice had established national headquarters in New York. From the nearby Roosevelt Hotel, where they were engaged in the feverish collection of pro-McCarthy petitions, the Ten Million had sent over their chief of staff, Major G. Racey Jordan, a former brewery publicist, together with a score of activists.

 Among the followers of McCarthy additionally gathered that noon in the grand ballroom of the Waldorf Astoria Hotel were John T. Flynn, the historian; Hamilton Fish, the prewar isolationist Congressman; Rabbi Benjamin Schultz of the American Jewish Committee against Communism; John Bond Trevor of the American Coalition of Patriotic Societies; William F. Buckley, Jr., McCarthy's biographer; and Roy M. Cohn, McCarthy's former counsel. These partisans were hoping that Pegler would use the national sounding board provided by the Banshees to rally support for their leader.

As usual at Banshee affairs, Bugs Baer presided. Without much preamble, he introduced Bob Hope as chief speaker. The visitor from Hollywood brought the Racey Jordan-Ham Fish-Roy Cohn contingent to the edges of their chairs by expressing gratification at being "invited to address this McCarthy rally." Hope, however, was joking, and many of the Banshees laughed. The humorist continued to make topical cracks in deadpan style. For a while his voice was drowned out with laughter. It emerged with a suggestion that the coat of arms of the brave knight on the program was two Rybutol tablets on a field of Serutan.

He was puzzled, Hope confessed, when they asked him to attend a lunch for "West." "West who?" he asked. "West Pegler," he was told. "Oh," he said. Pegler was glaring up at him from a seat directly below the rostrum, furious over being called out of his name. Obliviously, Hope rolled along. "You must come," they told him. "There must be something nice you can say about West." He said he had been trying to think of something for quite a while . . .

"I consider Pegler my friend!" said Hope. "He must be my friend, because he doesn't mention me in his column. It's nice to be on friendly terms with Pegler because he has so many ways of calling you dirty names." Other people besides himself liked

Pegler, he confided. "Eleanor likes him. She keeps a picture of him in her home. I can't tell you what room, but the picture blends nicely with the tile. Even enemies read Pegler's column. Quentin Reynolds buys two papers every day—one for each birdcage. By the way, I met Quent recently on the way to the bank . . ."

Hope had saved his best for last. There was great excitement in Minneapolis that hot August day in 1894 when Pegler was born he said. The complaining volume of sound emanated not from the infant but from the obstetrician. "They knew the baby was going to be a columnist because it bit the doc! They asked, 'Is it a boy or a girl?' and the doc said, 'I don't know, it won't let me look!'"

The hard-core Banshees loved it, but Pegler's political following drooped. "You can say what you will about Pegler," concluded Hope, having said it, "but he's a very potent force in our America, a very necessary force and a great American. I guess that evens me up. Thank you."

Applause lifted Pegler to his feet. Despite encouraging nods and smiles from Julie, his manner was sheepish as he moved to the microphone. He cleared his throat. "I know I'm going to blow up and trust a lot of people," he said. His voice lacked carrying power. "Speaking is a little out of my line. I'd like to say something about the responsibility of a newspaperman. It's not a matter of abusing individuals but of opposing people because of their stand on issues . . ." His tone dropped to a mumble. His concluding remark, relatively audible, was to concede that he was a bigot, as charged, since he had always been "governed by bigotry for the Constitution and the Nation of the United States."

The columnist received scattered applause as he dropped into his seat. The Hearst brass grinned at him and Julie gently massaged the back of his red neck with her hand. However, his ordeal was not yet over. Silver Ladies being suspect in New York, the King Features had contrived another climax to win newspaper coverage. They had rounded up Medal of Honor winners from all over the country to present an illuminated scroll to Pegler. Once again, the guest of honor climbed stiff-legged to the platform.

"You always had the courage to call the turn," declared Richard O'Neill, spokesman for twenty-five Medal of Honor winners. "Your ability to crystallize opposition is one of your assets."

The columnist was touched. Rolling the scroll nervously in his fingers, he replied: "I am simply without words. I am speechless. I can't say any more now." This time he received heavy applause as he left the platform. When he reached his table, he was furtively wiping his eyes.

Joe McCarthy was nursing a sore throat when he left Washington for a vacation in the Southwest. The Republican Senator from Wisconsin, a former poultryman with a law degree and a somewhat spurious war record, had built himself up into almost a second President. He was only forty-five that spring of 1954, at the peak of his capacity, yet he could not help feeling the strain of his indirect conflict with President Eisenhower. Since Senate hearings involving one of his former assistants were not due to start for a week or so, he told reporters he would rest until then in Phoenix, Arizona. However, he did not go to Phoenix. Nobody there could locate him. For a week he and his wife, Jean, who had been his secretary prior to their marriage the previous September, dropped out of sight.

When he next came to public attention, the Senator was riding with Westbrook Pegler through Tucson, which is a hundred miles from Phoenix. The two men had just made a quick trip in Pegler's car to the Mexican border town of Nogales, where residents in that part of Arizona go when they are bored and looking for a little excitement.

Earlier, the McCarthys had relaxed in comfort with the Peglers at Casa Cholla, twelve miles outside Tucson. Spring is the most beautiful time of year out there on the edge of the desert, with all the flowers in bloom. Lounging alongside the Pegler pool or sitting over drinks on the verandah facing the rugged Santa Catalina Mountains, the twin controversialists had plenty of time to discuss past, present and future encounters.

Joe McCarthy had been taking guidance from the columnist on issues ever since he first hit the front pages in 1950 with his inflammatory Wheeling, West Virginia speech that there were 205 communists in the State Department. Each new Pegler campaign, from the supposed Soviet infiltration of the Central Intelligence Agency to the imaginary menace of foundations organized for public research, drew quick support from the Senator. When the State Department disclosed that it had discharged some employees as homosexuals, the two men sang exultantly in almost daily harmony.

During his 1952 European tour—the one in which he visited the Vatican—Pegler discovered that "a lot of La Boca's tripe

223

and a great deal of stuff by well known Communists and fellow travelers could be found in the Paris, Frankfurt and Berlin reading rooms of the U.S. Information Service." Pressure from Senator McCarthy soon forced Secretary of State John Foster Dulles to revamp the nation's overseas libraries. The Senator invaded other executive departments. He made the Voice of America purge its employes. When Mutual Security Administrator Harold Stassen objected to McCarthy's demand that he sign an agreement with 118 Greek shipowners, President Eisenhower nudged Stassen into acceptance. The New York *Times* warned editorially that the administration was "running out of opportunities on which it can grasp the initiative and fight it out once and for all with the Junior Senator from Wisconsin."

Joe McCarthy's power base was his chairmanship of the Senate investigations subcommittee. In the spring of 1953, he sent two committee assistants on a flying tour of Europe. They were Roy Cohn, his counsel, and G. David Schine, a strikingly handsome youth from a family of considerable wealth, who was supposed to be an expert on communism.

These brash youngsters, each twenty-seven years old, spent seventeen hours in Bonn, nineteen hours in Frankfurt and twenty hours in Berlin, making wild statements about American policies and officials. They demanded among other things that Samuel Reber, U.S. Deputy Commissioner for Germany, publicly denounce a subordinate, Theodore Kaghan, who after a radical past had become one of the most effective organizers of anti-Communist propaganda in Germany. Reber refused.

That July, Schine was drafted. Joe McCarthy sought a commission for him through Major General Miles Reber, Army chief of legislative liaison at the Pentagon, a brother of Samuel Reber. Meanwhile, Private Schine was being treated at Fort Dix as no other private was ever treated. During basic training, he left on weekends with or without passes. He avoided onerous duties like peeling potatoes on the ground that he had to answer important long distance phone calls. He posed for a picture with Defense Secretary Robert Stevens when Stevens visited Fort Dix. He patronized mere captains and majors. Then Drew Pearson, Pegler's old antagonist in Washington, produced a column detailing the Army's delicate handling of Schine. In self-defense, the Army charged formally that it had done so only because it had been threatened with persecution by McCarthy, Roy Cohn and the executive director of the McCarthy committee, Francis Carr. The

224

three men filed forty-six counter-charges to the effect that the Army was trying to avoid exposure of Communists within its ranks.

The Senator returned from Arizona for the hearings full of health and arrogance. On the opening day he said that General Reber's failure to get Schine a commission was explained by the retirement of Samuel Reber from government service as a security risk.

Actually, Samuel Reber had retired for age. There was no doubt about his loyalty or that of his brother. However, the chairman of the military subcommittee holding the hearings was Senator Karl Mundt of South Dakota, an admirer of McCarthy, and the committee counsel was an inept Taft Republican from Tennessee named Ray Jenkins. Because of their hesitancy in the face of McCarthy's bluster, days were required to get the facts about the Rebers into the record, and by then McCarthy was starting other rabbits.

Joe McCarthy was projecting a comic-strip fantasy about Communist sympathizers helping Communist spies in the highest reaches of the Pentagon. He had no real case, but he was helped by an incident he had exploited the previous winter: Filling out the routine Army questionnaire, Irving Peress, a dentist commissioned in 1952 under the doctor draft law, did not answer questions about his political affiliations. No regulation required him to answer. The dentist was advanced automatically in rank until Army officials began to suspect him of Communist sympathies. A court martial would have been possible but he had committed no overt crime so it was decided to discharge him as part of a reduction of force.

Tipped off to what was happening, Senator McCarthy brought Dr. Peress before his committee. The dentist declined to incriminate himself. The Senator then demanded within twenty-four hours the names of all Army personnel concerned with the promotion and honorable discharge of Irving Peress. The commanding officer at Camp Kilmer, where Peress had been discharged, was Brigadier General Ralph Zwicker, a close friend of President Eisenhower and one of the heroes of the Battle of the Bulge.

On instructions from the defense department, General Zwicker refused to give any names. Senator McCarthy then haled Zwicker as a witness before the Senate investigations subcommittee and berated him in public for not having the brains of a five-

225

year-old child. "Any general who says he will protect another general who protected Communists is unfit to wear the uniform," the Senator concluded.

Though he was not presiding over the Schine hearings, Joe McCarthy continued to act with the same recklessness. He was not held down by the rules of evidence and order which govern a courtroom. Without adequate control, the Schine hearings became a vast disorderly drama whose plot could be shaped by any actor able to command the stage. Realizing this, the Senator raised issues and asked questions not to elicit information but to convey insinuations to the untrained minds among the millions of Americans watching the show on their TV sets.

Like Westbrook Pegler, who was simultaneously sparring with Louis Nizer in a New York courtroom, McCarthy made the eventual mistake of focusing his fury on his chief legal opponent —Joseph Welch, sixty-three, a dry and watchful Bostonian serving without fee as special counsel to the Army. Welch was a lifelong Republican known to the Pentagon as a brilliant trial lawyer, although he lacked political experience. He behaved with such diffidence and courtesy that the Wisconsin Senator decided to move against him on a personal level. With dramatic emphasis he revealed that one of Welch's former legal assistants had once belonged to the National Lawyers Guild, a Communist front. He named the young man.

Joseph Welch seemed stunned by the malicious irrelevancy. "Until this moment, Senator, I think I never gauged your cruelty or your recklessness," he said. His one-time assistant's association with the National Lawyers Guild, well known to him, meant nothing, he continued, since the young man was never a Communist or a fellow traveler, yet the accusation would haunt him and his family for the rest of his life. "I like to think I am a gentle man," said Joseph Welch, near tears, "but your forgiveness will have to come from someone other than me." Then he sat down and buried his head in his arms.

More than 10,000,000 Americans were watching by television that day, with other millions listening by radio and reading the newspaper accounts. To many this revelation of personality came as the climax of the hearings. When the session ended, spectators who normally crowded around McCarthy to get his autograph or shake his hand turned away in silence. Reporters followed Welch out of the Senate caucus room. "What did I do?" the Senator asked a friend, in anguish. "What did I do?"

There had been only one other possible revolution in his time. Pegler had missed it: because of confusion in his thinking and an inability to transcend his journalistic frame of reference, he had failed to take a stand alongside the prewar isolationists. In the McCarthy movement, history gave Westbrook Pegler a rare second chance. He reacted with a zeal which exceeded that of the Senator himself.

Mutual friends liked to retell what happened on election night in 1952. Joe McCarthy had the support of Dwight D. Eisenhower that year and he could have won re-election to the Senate on his own account. It was a walkaway, but when the columnist reached him by phone to inquire anxiously about the returns, the Senator kidded him for ten minutes to the effect that he was losing. This lack of seriousness handicapped McCarthy as a mass leader. He didn't trust his future sufficiently or hate his enemies enough. In a crisis he was curiously hesitant, unsure how far he really wanted to go.

The Schine hearings having produced no clearcut decision, colleagues of McCarthy moved to censure him for bringing the Senate into disrepute. By now it was clear that White House assistant Sherman Adams, Attorney General Herbert Brownell and other administration spokesmen were working for a solution which would remove the Senator from the President's path.

Six months of hearings, reports and floor debate were required to bring the censure motion to a head. Meanwhile the Senator's followers, including Westbrook Pegler, took his case to the public.

An early manifestation of crusading spirit came at a July dinner in New York honoring Roy Cohn, who was retiring from the McCarthy committee. The Senator himself, William F. Buckley, Jr. and Fulton Lewis, Jr. (whom Pegler praised as the best broadcaster in the country) were present to whip a crowd of two thousand five hundred into a frenzy over what a lesser speaker called "the criminal alliance between the Eisenhower-Dewey Republicans and the leftists."

Pegler, whose columns in those days were chock full of historical references to dastardly, unreliable and subversive behavior by the United States military forces, was in the audience. Introduced in a flowery fashion by Rabbi Schultz, who was presiding, the columnist stood up and nodded bashfully as the grand ballroom of the Astor rocked with applause. A minute later, a movie cameraman came over to snap Pegler's picture. In an abrupt change of mood, the columnist made violent gestures of protest, growled, and hung a handkerchief in front of his face until the cameraman left.

George Hamilton Coombs, a radio commentator and former Congressman, described the Cohn dinner as the agitational debut of "the rabidly anti-Eisenhower wing of the Republican party, buttressed by the wild fringe crowd which is usually found fighting on the side of the Gerald L. K. Smiths, the fanatics of the extreme right, some fascist-minded, some philosophic royalists, some religious zealots of all shades of belief." Pegler retaliated with a column denouncing the radio station which carried the Coombs report. The columnist was particularly incensed over Coombs' remark that McCarthy was "building a nationalist movement based on hate." Nationalism was a synonym for patriotism, declared Pegler. "What is wrong with hating traitors and those who protect them?" he demanded.

Pegler's commitment to the cause grew. At the next large McCarthy rally, held in Baltimore, he actually appeared as a nationalist orator. None of his friends expected such a development, since over the years he had refused offers running into thousands of dollars for a single radio or television appearance. His brother Jack used to explain: "Bud doesn't think a white man should be a gabber," but the columnist's reluctance might also have been due in part to previous failures as a public speaker.

Pegler opened his Baltimore speech with a promise to be brief. He would not make a single reference to Eleanor Roosevelt, he said. This was a good relaxed start, but he spoiled it by assuring his audience that he had timed his talk in advance and that it could not possibly last more than ten minutes. His general approach was historical. He mentioned the pre-Eisenhower betrayal of Republican principles by Frank Knox and Henry Stimson. He cited Wendell Willkie as a Trojan horse within the party. He branched off into an account of Freedom House, which had been founded in honor of Willkie and which had recently given a George Foster Peabody award to some commentator named "Egbert" Murrow. It should be called the George Foster Nobody award, he suggested, since Peabody was an obscure contemporary of Colonel Edward M. House, a sinister backstage figure in the Wilson administration.

Partly because of his apologetic manner and his high, conversational and often indistinct voice, he lost his audience. They applauded when he finished but friends suggested that he be less polite next time and let go with the righteous indignation which marked his column. Actually column and speech were compounded of the same material; he was simply no orator.

A great popular march on Washington was announced at the Baltimore rally. Squads of Wisconsin lumberjacks in working clothes were being organized, it was revealed, to throw out those who tried to spy upon or disrupt subsequent rallies. This was news.

Would the march on Washington resemble Mussolini's famous march on Rome? Would the lumberjacks be an American version of storm-troopers or black-shirts? How would steps like these affect the Senate hearings? Joe McCarthy temporized. The lumberjack squads never materialized and the march on Washington dwindled to "a dignified convocation" by train and bus to form a united front against communism.

With Joe McCarthy wavering between rival cliques of advisers, the contours of his movement changed from day to day. Westbrook Pegler was too preoccupied with personal problems at this time to be available for advice. If he had been asked, it was reasonable to suppose that he would have plumped for lumberjacks.

The Washington rally took place in Constitution Hall on November 11. As usual, Pegler was present. Called upon for a greeting, he stalked to the microphone and growled that all he wanted to know was the name of the Army officer who promoted Major Peress! He was learning: the reference aroused a full-throated howl from the crowd. Many former isolationists like Ham Fish were there to retaste the heady old atmosphere of hate. American flags hung everywhere, and posters reading: "For McCarthy: for America!" A variety of nationalist orators worked on the emotions of the crowd and then the Senator himself, in a low-registered, choked scream: "I make you this solemn promise—regardless of anything—the fight will go on and on and on and on!"

The deadline for Senatorial action was fast approaching. Ten Million Americans Mobilized for Justice had been organized to bring pressure on the Senate from the outside and its petitions were being circulated frantically. The Senate had already begun its final period of debate on the censure motion when the climactic McCarthyite outpouring took place in Madison Square Garden on November 29.

Major G. Racey Jordan, presiding as chief of staff for Ten

229

Million Americans, made a special point of introducing West-brook Pegler as one who had long borne the burden of the fight. Pegler took a bow. Jordan next turned to "this towering giant behind me on the platform, Ham Fish, who was the first . . ." Ham Fish took a bow. Lieutenant General Pedro del Valle, who had urged the 1952 GOP national convention to consider seriously the program of Robert H. Williams, one of the country's most virulent anti-Semitic pamphleteers, also sat prominently on the platform. Racists in the audience, each with his own group of supporters, included Joseph P. Kamp, the expert on Walter Winchell, and James V. Madole, who had replaced Joe McWilliams as the chief ultra-rightist in the Yorkville section of Manhattan.

Gerald L. K. Smith appeared in a ten-gallon hat. Greeted by a reporter who remembered him from isolationist days, Smith gave a false name and fled, explaining later in his newsletter, which was then distributed from Los Angeles, that he was afraid of being identified and "mobbed by hysterical Jews in front of Madison Square Garden." There was no crowd of any kind outside the Garden at the time.

A series of retired military men and nationalist orators roared about Communism and "the invisible government in Washington." Though Senator McCarthy could not appear, his wife Jean read a message from him, and the Garden crowd expended some of its suspicion and rage on Lisa Larsen, *Life* photographer screaming "Go Back to Russia" and other insults as she was escorted by the arm from the meeting for taking snapshots. It was the old Bund atmosphere of 1939 all over again.

Nevertheless, there had been only 13,000 persons in the Garden, which could accommodate 22,000. The slim turnout led to immediate cancellation of projected similar rallies in Chicago and San Francisco.

On December 2, 1954, along with wires from George Stretemeyer, one of its most important retired generals, urging detection of "the hidden force of government," the Ten Million sent armed guards with great stacks of pro-McCarthy petitions to the United States Senate. The guards had to check their pistols at the door before they were allowed to enter the Capitol. Later that day the Senate by a three-quarters majority voted to censure Joe McCarthy on two counts, for abusing the Senate's own elections subcommittee and for browbeating General Zwicker. At the White House next day President Eisenhower greeted Senator

Watkins, the Utah Republican who had led the fight for censure, and congratulated him significantly on "a very splendid job."

McCarthy was almost finished. Democratic gains in the Congressional elections that fall meant he must soon lose his chairmanship of the investigations subcommittee on which his capacity for political reprisal rested. In combination with this, Senatorial censure sufficiently blurred his image as a lone crusader to make his decline inevitable and predictable.

Westbrook Pegler gave up reluctantly. He was a featured speaker in place of Joe McCarthy himself at a New York nationalist rally on December 6 in honor of the late Senator Pat McCarran of Nevada. Senator McCarthy had sent a telegram expressing his "cruel disappointment" over the fact that his doctor would not permit him to attend.

The columnist lectured the audience. "The Garden rally was a turkey," he said. "Let's not kid ourselves, we've been laying some terrible eggs lately." The rallies he had been attending for the last few months had been "melancholy and depressing" to him, Pegler declared. "I don't know why we can't turn out a good crowd," he cried, noting that there were only nine hundred present in Lost Battalion Hall, which could easily handle two thousand. "If Eleanor Roosevelt were speaking in this hall tonight, she could have filled it twice over!"

18. MISOGRAMMARIAN

A conference on "Anti-Intellectualism in America Today" was held one Sunday afternoon in January 1955, at the Carnegie Endowment Center in New York. It was sponsored by Goddard College, whose campus is located in Plainfield, Vermont. Panelists included former Tennessee Valley Chairman Gordon Clapp, Paul Blanshard and Dr. S. Stransfeld Sargent, a professor of psychology at Barnard College. Norman Thomas and Mrs. Eleanor Roosevelt were among the three hundred specially invited guests.

Attacks on professors were a phase of McCarthyism, declared Dr. Sargent. Behind the sneers at "eggheads" and "double-domes," he said was a desire to infect people, particularly young people, with the idea that intellectuals could not be trusted "because of a fatal tendency to indulge in subversion." "I myself," concluded the professor with annoyance, "was labeled by Westbrook Pegler as one of 'four pretentious windjammers' when I appeared on another conference panel!"

Dr. Theodore Brameld of New York University served as the conference reporter. During his own panel discussion, he did not mention Pegler, but in the summary prepared for the press he said that "the commonest kind of anti-intellectualism was exemplified by McCarthyism, Chicago Tribunism and Peglerism." This was his only reference to the columnist, but it sufficed to ignite one of Pegler's most prolonged rages.

Though all the New York City newspapers, including Hearst's *Journal-American,* carried stories about the conference, the columnist singled out the *Times* for retaliation on the ground that the *Times* had been "picking" on him. He threw down the gage of personal literary combat to Arthur Hays Sulzberger, who he described as "the salesman who married the boss's daughter and became publisher."

When Sulzberger did not acknowledge the challenge, he began to bomb the *Times* at measured intervals, the way the Red Chinese bombed Quemoy and Matsu.

A full year after the conference, Benjamin Fine, educational editor of the *Times,* told a Congressional investigating committee that he had once been a member of the Communist party. Pegler was jubilant. "At this stage of the game," he wrote, "the *Times* is stuck with its director of education, Doc Fine, and I am going around unbearably swollen with pride in my anti-intellectualism . . . Like J. Robert Oppenheimer, double-dome protégé of Egbert Murrow and Ford's Fund for the Republic, Doc Fine is so intellectual that he don't know from nothing. Thus he couldn't see anything in Communism inconsistent with loyalty to the U.S. We anti-intellectuals are contending in our dumb, ignorant way that this proves that ignorance is very desirable from the standpoint of Old Glory. Anti-intellectualism usually means anti-Communist."

Westbrook Pegler's real target was Theodore Brameld, but first he delivered a few absent-minded slaps at his old enemy, Eleanor Roosevelt. Noting that Mrs. Roosevelt had been present "at a little dance of the double-domes in New York," he had flirted with the idea of challenging "Dreamie" to a contest at from 500 to 5,000 words, against time or within a period of weeks, he said, until he realized that she had not yet received her diploma from kindergarten.

In the playful tone which often disguised extreme anger, he dismissed "anti-intellectual" as a "homemade word that the double-domes are bandying about with the earnest self-consciousness of a sea-lion trying to thread a needle with a one-inch rope." Actually, he said, he was a misogrammarian. The dictionary defines misogrammarian as a person who despises learning, but he provided his own definition as "a dummy who does not know nothing, does not want to know anything and does not like intellectual people."

As for Theodore Brameld, who had set him up as an ism, here was "a character who teaches politics and other theoretical propaganda at New York University." Notified that Dr. Brameld's subject was the philosophy of education, he questioned whether there was or could be any such subject. Anyway, he said, the social sciences—"socialistic as the title suggests"—were "clap-trap and quackery" hostile to the Constitution.

"I don't want to be unfair to Brameld," he added with an invisible grimace, "but if he wants a piece of my play, well, give the man room. I will write him lopsided, sight unseen!"

With the help of his readers, who frequently did free research, Pegler devoted his next few articles to background information about the professor, ranging from alleged earlier pro-

233

Communist views to the stray fact that his second wife was previously his "student assistant." When the barrage let up, Dr. Brameld sent a statement to the columnist through a lawyer asserting that he was not a Marxist and making one or two other minor points. He was immediately lambasted all over again in print with something new added: a hint of complicity in murder!

Twenty-three-year-old Anne Yarrow had been strangled and mutilated in her Greenwich Village apartment. The police were questioning various suspects. "I will observe that he (Dr. Brameld) was vice-chairman of the Mayor's Council on Human Relations in Minneapolis in 1946-47," wrote Pegler, "and that 'human relations' was the subject which a young woman was studying for a 'master's degree' at New York U. when she was murdered last week in a Greenwich Village hideaway. It came out that as a practical experiment in human relations, the girl had been cutting up with a social worker . . . who is married and a Negro." To this amalgam of reform, miscegenation and crime, he added a slow insinuation: "I wish I knew whether this co-ed had been one of Brameld's students . . ."

When no reader came forward with the desired information, Pegler began to belabor New York University for "bashful evasions" as to whether Miss Yarrow ever studied human relations under the professor. The fact was that by this time the university press agents were refusing to talk to the columnist. Some two hundred newspapers from coast to coast were soon reporting that a New York professor named Brameld—shorn as usual of his title—would not "volunteer" the degree of intimacy existing between himself and a brutally murdered girl student.

Abandoning any idea of rebuttal, Dr. Brameld dropped out of sight in New York City to accept appointment as a visiting professor at the University of Puerto Rico. He later taught at Boston University. Learning of his whereabouts at one point from a letter to the New York *Times*, Westbrook Pegler promptly reviewed his scandalous misapprehensions about the professor who had questioned his intellectual horsepower.

Theodore Brameld was never cleared of suspicion of homicide in Westbrook Pegler's column. The professor told friends that he never had Anne Yarrow in any of his classes. Certainly he did not kill the girl. Her murderer turned out not to be a teacher or a fellow student in human relations and not even the married Negro social worker whose name was dragged into the proceed-

234

ings, but an unbalanced twenty-three-year-old wood-finisher from Brooklyn named Farrell who was duly sent away to the Matteawan State Hospital for the Criminal Insane.

Drew Pearson was an educated man with a genuine social viewpoint. He had been a student of Phi Beta Kappa caliber in college and later a college teacher.

For a couple of years after World War I he deserted the campus to help rebuild devastated Belgium villages as a volunteer with the American Friends Service Committee at six dollars a month. He broke into journalism not at the cityroom level but halfway up the ladder, by undertaking to interview the "twelve greatest men in Europe" on a shoestring for an obscure syndicate. This paid off with a job as Washington correspondent. Co-authorship of a book of acidulous depression era sketches called *Washington Merry Go Round* then led him into writing a widely syndicated column out of Washington under the same title.

Being a newspaperman requires both a thick hide and some sensitivity, and working in the glare of public attention imposes extra strain. Pearson schooled himself to live quietly despite the sensation and intrigue which engaged him. A tall, tweedy, balding man with wary blue eyes and a superb coat of mental armor, he regularly produced more news beats than all his competitors put together. He recognized few sacred cows. Men like Walter Lippmann, Marquis Childs, and James Reston might win polls among their peers as the best Washington correspondent, but none possessed more national influence than Drew Pearson. He often made mistakes through not verifying the tips which bounce in and out of every correspondent's office in the course of a day, but his batting average on predictions was high.

Pegler had begun to jeer at journalism as "a loosening profession" and "a simian cult." Writers generally, he declared in one column, were "ridiculously self-important. Books generally are flashy emphemera, without stamina, grace or taste. The vilest get the best reviews and sell best. Money is all that interests writers, not courageous truth-telling. Fiction is a cowardly medium . . ." Actors could not possibly be intellectual, he ground on, entertainers were usually smut-artists and virtually the only movie worth remembering was "The Birth of a Nation," seen on the silent screen decades before.

Because Pearson approached his journalistic task with discriminating seriousness, Pegler was bound to distrust him. He had other, broader grounds: Pearson combined high-voltage broadcasting with journalism. On the air, Pearson became almost as aggressive as Walter Winchell. These two focused more attention on themselves than on the news in their broadcasts. They often exaggerated trivia and paraded gossip as fact. They reversed Dale Carnegie's classic formula for success by cultivating and keeping enemies, particularly large ones like Pegler whose reputation made him an attractive target. Pearson or Winchell could swing from column to kilocycle and back again, getting an extra cut at an enemy with each swing, whereas Pegler fought with one arm behind his back. Sometimes the unfairness of the competition drove him frantic.

When Joe McCarthy came along, the New Deal crusading spirit of Walter Winchell evaporated overnight. Winchell established himself as a syndicated defender of the Wisconsin Senator and a journalistic scourge of McCarthy's enemies. Other admirers of McCarthy had difficulty in adjusting to this development.

"Winchell has been converted," trumpeted Gerald L.K. Smith in *The Cross and the Flag*. "He's breaking his neck to get on the McCarthy-Gerald Smith-MacArthur bandwagon. This does not affect my attitude toward Winchell. He is still a scoundrel . . ." Westbrook Pegler showed a similar reluctance to embrace Winchell. Upon his return from Europe in 1952, he was asked by *Editor & Publisher* about reports that he had received special courtesies in military outposts abroad. "I got no red-carpet treatment," growled the columnist, "and I expected none. After all, I'm no Winchell!"

Nevertheless, the similarity of views between Pegler and Winchell became more and more pronounced. Pegler had criticized J. Edgar Hoover mercilessly over the years on various grounds, but he could not ignore the fact that Hoover was proving to be an unobtrusive friend of Joe McCarthy. He had objected particularly to Hoover's intimacy with night club reporters like Winchell, but now he took a fresh look and discovered that the FBI chief had collaborated with reporters on articles dealing with every phase of bureau operations except prostitution. In this crucial area Hoover had "kept the act scrupulously nice," Pegler noted approvingly.

With Winchell dwindling as a threat on the air, Pegler found Drew Pearson more of a nuisance than ever. The terms of the settlement of their previous legal difficulty, however, stood between them. Pegler had described Pearson as a fake reporter and

236

a miscalled news broadcaster specializing in falsehoods and smearing people with personal and political motivation.

This clump of epithets led Pearson to file a modest twenty-five thousand dollar-suit and John Wheeler, president of the Bell Syndicate, which distributed "Washington Merry Go Round," to bring another suit for the same amount. Both suits were withdrawn within a year through an exchange of letters.

"Dear Drew," wrote Pegler, "I have had several conversations with Jack Wheeler and Gorty (J. D. Gortatowsky, general manager of the Hearst newspapers), and we all feel that the best way for all concerned would be to drop our little controversy. Let bygones be bygones and forget it. This is my sincere desire. I do not believe our present course, if pursued, would benefit anyone and I do think we might bring unpleasant public attention to the newspaper business which has been very good to both of us. In fact, I think it is wasteful to devote valuable space to personal controversies among columnists. Any attempt to review the circumstances would only lead to recriminations, so I suggest we just skip it altogether. I am sure it is an incident that we mutually regret. My feelings were hurt, too, but time is a pretty good healer and they are all right again. Now if yours are cured, what about a drink?"

"Dear Peg," replied Pearson, more curtly, "I appreciate the spirit of your letter and agree that columnists have more important battles to fight than among themselves. I am therefore asking my attorney to withdraw the suit as of this week. This will be a good way to start the new year."

Pegler chafed under the terms of the truce. He was furious when Pearson forecast correctly over the radio that the Supreme Court would reverse a deportation order against Harry Bridges. Since he could not hit Pearson in print, he wrote an indignant letter to Chief Justice Vinson. Obtaining an interview with Vinson, he proffered his suspicions as to which one of the Associate Justices had leaked the story to his rival. It became almost axiomatic that anybody exposed by Pearson could find comfort in Pegler. Strays taken under his wing included John Maragon, the fixer, and President Truman's bumbling military aide, General Vaughan.

When Chairman J. Parnell Thomas of the House Un-American Activities Committee went to jail as a result of a Pearson exposé of kickbacks to him by his employees, Pegler argued that Thomas had done nothing more than President Truman did, as

Senator, when he placed his wife on the payroll. Though the columnist dismissed Bess Truman's secretary services as "fictitious and imaginary," some Washingtonians asserted that she was conscientious in her work. In any case, her employment was legal, which Thomas' actions were not.

On May 22, 1949, James V. Forrestal carefully copied a Sophocles poem on death before jumping from a thirteen-story window of the Bethesda Naval Hospital. He had resigned as Defense Secretary two months previously after Drew Pearson revealed in a broadcast that the administration was concerned over his mental condition. Pearson had previously derided Forrestal's efforts to influence American postwar policy in favor of the Arab countries in the Middle East on the ground that he was more influenced by his financial interests in American oil companies than by considerations of military strategy. On one occasion, Pearson described a robbery at the Forrestal home during which Mrs. Forrestal was deprived of her jewelry, he said, while the man at the head of the country's defense establishment ran away.

Breaking the pact between them, Pegler accused Pearson of driving a patriotic American to his death by persecution. The Defense Secretary was not even home when the robbery described by Pearson occurred, he said. Forrestal was a war casualty, he wrote in his column, "a victim of the wanton black-guardism and mendacity of the radio, which has been a professional specialty of Drew Pearson." This time, Pearson sued for a more substantial two hundred fifty thousand dollars. Pegler multiplied insults in his legal answer and when the answer was stricken from the record he repackaged it for columnar use. Pearson in turn began to add suits against individual newspapers printing the new attacks— thus invoking the specter of chain libel which had been scaring syndicate men for decades—while Pegler took another unprecedented step by writing whole columns on the history and personality of Pearson's lawyers.

What was shaping up was nothing less than a threat to Pearson's professional existence. Senator Joe McCarthy took the Senate floor one day in December 1950 to urge a national boycott of Adams hats until the company manufacturing them ceased to sponsor "an agent of Moscow" named Drew Pearson on the radio. For a while the Senator made it look as if wearing an Adams hat was subversive. On the excuse that it had decided to dispense with Pearson prior to McCarthy's onslaught, the company soon eased him off the network. Thereafter Drew Pearson was in noticeably less demand as a radio or TV personality.

As Fulton Lewis, Jr. other Hearst commentators and Mrs. Eleanor (Cissy) Patterson of the Washington *Times-Herald* joined in the assult on Pearson, something of a lynching atmosphere was created. When Pearson tried to launch a newsletter for business executives at fifty dollars a year, Pegler promptly warned possible clients through his column that his rival was an inaccurate reporter with a defective character.

Several times during this period Pearson was attacked physically. Joe McCarthy himself came up to him on one occasion at the Sulgrave Club in Washington and either slapped him repeatedly in the face or kneed him in the groin—depending on whose version you preferred to believe. Pearson filed a $5,100,000 suit against Pegler, McCarthy, Fulton Lewis, Cissy Patterson and others, charging conspiracy to drive him out of business, which was transparently true, but enormously difficult to prove.

Somehow Pearson managed to survive as a syndicated news analyst out of Washington until the McCarthy tide began to ebb. Pre-trial examinations continued in the huge conspiracy suit, though none of the parties seemed anxious to bring it to a head. Eventually, in the fall of 1955, when Westbrook Pegler and his wife Julie were touring Europe, Pearson suits against Hearst newspapers in cities like Baltimore, Milwaukee, San Antonio and Albany were quietly withdrawn.

Simultaneously, Hearst began to carry "Washington Merry Go Round" in those cities. The obvious explanation was correct: the legal tangle had been cut behind Pegler's back by a deal giving Pearson considerable additional national circulation.

For the True Crusader, there were humiliating details. In the Albany *Times-Union,* the first Drew Pearson column ran directly above Pegler's column. While continuing to pay for Pegler, the *Times-Union* soon dropped him completely from the paper. This happened elsewhere. Moreover, the settlement of the big conspiracy suit specified that neither columnist would henceforth attack the other publicly, which gave Pearson protection against resumption of the feud.

The Hearst newspaper chain was having increasing difficulty in keeping Westbrook Pegler within bounds. Though William Randolph Hearst did not die until August 14, 1951, a reappraisal of his latter-day attitudes began in 1948-49. William Randolph Hearst, Jr., a trusted lieutenant of his father, realized that sensationalism, xenophobia and back-to-McKinley economics were no longer an adequate journalistic program for predominantly middle-class readers, many of whom bought cars on the installment plan or who owned heavily mortgaged homes. For guidance in shaping a new program, the younger Hearst dispatched Frank Conniff, a New York *Journal-American* columnist, to Washington on weekends. Conniff said what he thought. Unlike other subordinates who tried to guess what the boss was thinking or who reserved comment until the boss enunciated his line, Conniff started from the political premise that he had always been a Democrat and probably always would be one. He strove to produce recommendations for a gradual modernization of Hearst policy.

The big break came in 1952 when Senator Taft and General Eisenhower were vying for the Republican presidential nomination. Almost automatically the Hearst press exalted Taft and criticized Eisenhower until word came down that the General and the Senator were equally fine and distinguished Americans— either of whom would make an outstanding President. Some of the murkiest column-writing ever seen in America resulted from this confidential order, yet it enabled the Hearst papers to go along easily with Eisenhower when he won the nomination and later to support him as President on "modern" issues.

Westbrook Pegler pulled as much as he could against the new policy. In his coverage of the GOP convention, he slanted his columns overtly toward Taft. He acted as a persistent propagandist for the McCarthy-MacArthur wing of the party. When Taft's chances faded, the columnist was consulted personally by the MacArthur camp on a last-minute deal which might persuade the Senator to transfer his delegate strength to the nationalists. The deal fell through.

After inauguration, Pegler gave lip service to the Hearst swing toward political centrism by announcing that he was "going to start fresh and try being patient with President Eisenhower and kind to him." Within a few months, however, his patience and kindness wore thin. He fidgeted publicly over "the European-type social-democracy . . . taking shape under President Ike." He lambasted Arthur Eisenhower for calling Joe McCarthy "the most dangerous menace to America." He recalled gloomily that the President was "just a Lieutenant Colonel when Roosevelt plucked him from the file and started shoving him forward to the rank of five-star general" and that President Truman also respected Ike. Maybe Eisenhower should have run frankly for President as a Democrat, he suggested.

"I am not under-estimating Ike," wrote the columnist, more in regret than wrath. "He is a picnic pitcher in a world series . . . you will see."

Gradually he worked up a lather of rage. The President had appeared at an AFL convention to "wheedle a mob of goons." The President played too much golf and was untrue to the Constitution—a word always spelled with a Capital C. Maybe some Constitutional Republican like Senator Goldwater of Arizona or Senator Bricker of Ohio would make a better choice for President in 1960.

"I realize that many of us who are accused of McCarthyism because we fight against treason and for the Constitution have been dwelling in fear ourselves," Pegler wrote. "I am fed up with this cowardice and will not be guilty again. By God, I am going to be an American from now on! And be damned to anyone who tries to scare me. Life that way is not worth living."

In earlier days, the columnist had followed Walter Lippmann's practice of ignoring a small critic. This invariably drove such a critic frantic, he found. Now minor controversy seemed harder for him to resist. When a Tennessee newspaper printed some relatively mild criticism about him, he challenged the editor to physical combat "at any convenient place between Tennessee and Arizona," but the editor did not accept the challenge.

Grace Lewis, whose column appeared directly under Pegler's in the Syracuse *Post-Standard*, complained that his analysis of political conventions and national elections made her and her neighbors look like "a herd of slobs." Incidentally, she referred to the columnist's "daily flow of bile" and described him as a "human saddle-sore." In a nationally syndicated reply, Pegler wrote that it would be in poor taste for him to refer to Miss Lewis' glands. He was "in no position to speculate," he added. "The lady's personal hygiene, which I hope is of the best, is not a municipal issue." After this boorish opening, he restated his original thesis that the only superior quality about a delegate to a national political convention was an unlimited capacity to consume booze and that "the common man, that faceless object" was ordered to vote "by rich men sitting in a box." He then lectured his colleague on the Constitutional government which had vanished, he said, in the United States.

241

The Syracuse *Post-Standard* closed the controversy with an uneasy, conciliatory editorial awarding the decision to the local girl. "Come on, Peg," it concluded. "Calm down—take it easy!"

When two ex-Communists testified early in 1953 that a concealed party member had been retained in the office of the late Robert P. Patterson, a wartime assistant to former Defense Secretary Henry L. Stimson, Pegler promptly referred to Patterson in his column as "a renegade Republican who turned New Deal bureaucrat with a strong sympathy for the Communist treachery." He also accused Patterson of seizing opportunities to make Communist propaganda. A dozen men of importance, including General Julius Ochs Adler, publisher of the New York *Times*, wrote privately in concert to William Randolph Hearst, Jr. to protest that Patterson might have made a mistake or two but that these did not justify any implication of disloyalty.

Hearst wrote to Adler that he had been in Mexico when the column appeared, that he would not have let it go through if he had been around and that he would "talk to Peg about it when I see him in Washington next week." Hearst did talk to Pegler. The result was that Pegler intensified his attack on Patterson.

Hearst and his wife visited Supreme Headquarters of the Allied Powers (SHAPE) outside Paris in July, 1953. They chatted with General Alfred Gruenther, Eisenhower's former chief of staff who had become Supreme Allied Commander in Europe, and with Irving Brown, European representative of the AFL who had just returned from Germany with AFL President George Meany. The General complained that Pegler had been denouncing Brown and Jay Lovestone, two former Communists whose expert advice was often sought on the selection of labor attachés in the American embassies in Europe and who had helped the European labor movement break its Communist shackles.

"Irving Brown has done more to help us than anybody else," General Gruenther told the Hearsts significantly.

William Randolph Hearst, Jr. said he had missed the pieces but that he would look them up when he returned to the States. In this, as in other similar cases, nothing happened except that Pegler redoubled his abuse. Brown and Lovestone, insisted the columnist, were concealed Communists working for the "Central Intelligence Agency, a mysterious American gestapo . . . (engaged in) dirty work . . . mysterious under-handed activities." At least one such Pegler article was printed approvingly in *Pravda*.

Hearst was handicapped by a curious dispersal of authority

242

within the hierarchy. After the death of his father, he had been elected chairman of the editorial board of the chain of newspapers, but this did not give him control of the board. Some Hearst officials felt that Pegler should still be allowed a free voice in the vaguely re-oriented orchestration of columnists. Moreover, some of the individuals entrusted with enforcement of the new policy could not cope with the columnist's installment-by-installment approach to fresh heresies. In any case, Westbrook Pegler continued to slide into print his increasingly reactionary and violent ideas.

Early in 1954, when Frank Conniff turned sharply against Joe McCarthy for associating with fascist-minded and anti-Catholic Texas millionaires, Pegler hailed Generalissimo Trujillo of the Dominican Republic, chief dictator in the Western hemisphere, as a man "much more sensible, practical and helpful to his people than Roosevelt, Truman or Eisenhower." In one amazing column he compared F.D.R. to Hitler point by point—to the entire disadvantage of the late President!

In addition to his incredible Colonel House conspiracy, which put American Presidents from Wilson to Eisenhower at the mercy of sinister international forces, Pegler developed two pet theories during this period. One was that ultra-rightists were being railroaded to lunatic asylums for political reasons. The other was that the time had come for revolution. In support of his first theory he cited chiefly the cases of Lucile Miller and Ezra Pound. Mrs. Miller, a Vermont woman who regularly ground out an agitated propaganda sheet with racist overtones called the *Green Mountain Rifleman,* had been indicted on nineteen counts for urging young men to evade the draft. She was sent temporarily to a hospital for treatment so she could be tried. She and her husband Manuel were eventually tried, and convicted. He received a year in prison, and she was released on probation.

Ezra Pound, the poet, had collaborated clumsily with the enemy during the war as a radio commentator for the Italians. He was sent to St. Elizabeth's Hospital in Washington after the war, at the request of his lawyer, because he was obviously incompetent to defend himself on a charge of treason. In response to popular outcry based on his literary achievements, he was finally released on condition that he return to Italy. He signalized his arrival in Rapallo with a grotesque press conference during which he asserted that the entire United States was a lunatic asylum.

Revolution, almost forgotten as a word and as a prospect by

243

the zealots of the left in America, became a favorite subject for Pegler starting in 1954. He discerned a hidden partnership between federal agencies and union rackets so powerful that it could be broken "only by violent revolution, if at all." He reported hope among the Constitutional pro-American Republicans for a "political revolution" through alliance between anti-Eisenhower Republicans and conservative Southern Democrats. The coming revolution, he declared, might be "bloody or political" but it would certainly be non-intellectual—"the public is not intellectual but more nearly insensate"—and it would boil up in sudden mass anger over basic grievances.

Hearst policy was revised dramatically in 1954-55. David Sentner, the chain's Washington correspondent, tipped off the national office in New York that a friend at the Russian embassy kept suggesting that things in Russia had changed since Stalin's death in 1953. "'Enough to permit a visit to Russia by William Randolph Hearst?" inquired Sentner, and was told: "I don't see why not!" On the basis of this tip, Hearst, Conniff and Kingsbury Smith, the Hearst European editor, visited Russia in January, 1955, interviewing ranking Soviet officials. In the wake of these sensational interviews, which were ticketed for a Pulitzer Prize from the time they appeared, William Randolph Hearst, Jr. was appointed editor-in-chief by the board of directors of Hearst Consolidated Publications.

One of Hearst's problems was to erase the public impression that Westbrook Pegler spoke for the newspaper chain. In a similar situation in 1944, Roy Howard had dropped Pegler, but the internal solidarity of the Hearst organization militated against that kind of solution. Hearst focused on the New York *Journal-American,* where for years the Pegler syndicated material had been carried in a unique display down the entire left side of page 3—in double column—and running over to another page whenever necessary. Now the column was shifted to a rear page for contributors. It was carried in column and a half measure under a cartoon, where it frequently had to be trimmed to fit the page. Simultaneously, orders went to all Hearst editors giving them the authority for the first time to cut or kill any Pegler column they thought got out of line.

19. MAN OF THE UNDERWORLD

Julie Pegler died in Rome on November 8, 1955. For the next day or so, Westbrook acted almost as if he were demented, running in and out of the hotel where she had suffered her fatal heart attack, drinking heavily at times, talking wildly and gesticulating. Then he quieted down. The funeral service, he decided, must be held in New York—at the Church of the Blessed Sacrament where they were married thirty-three years before. The body could be sent to New York by plane. He himself would return on the liner "Cristoforo Colombo," leaving Naples November 18 and arriving in New York November 26, two days before the funeral. For the time being he had lost any taste for writing but by throwing together leftover European impressions during the leisurely European voyage, he hoped to stay within reach of his column-writing schedule. Actually, he missed publication only during the last two weeks of November.

Though the circumstances were tragic, there could be no guilt or blame—only loss. Julie was sixty when she died. She had survived twenty-one years since the first dreadful onset of angina in Pound Ridge. During part of that time, as one family friend put it, Westbrook had "carried Julie on his back" to Florida, to Arizona and any other place which promised relief from her frequent feeling of painful suffocation. She had gradually learned to live with her ailment. An old cardiac pro who carried nitroglycerine wherever she went, she had gone along on his 1952 tour of the continent and she saw no reason not to go along again.

Nobody could have predicted that Westbrook would be the one to become ill first and that his illness would coincide with the most crucial stage of the trip, the summit conference in Geneva, yet this did occur. Who could say what precise event caused the disabling flareup of his ulcers? He faced many pressures, some arising from the conference itself, others from his deteriorating relationship with Hearst. When Krishna Menon tried to mediate —successfully, as it turned out—in negotiations between the United States and Red China over the release of captive American fliers in North Korea, Pegler took it upon himself to inform the Indian foreign minister loudly and offensively in public that

245

he was butting in where he was not invited. This belligerent action alone involved considerable strain.

In general, Westbrook Pegler felt uncomfortable in the breezy climate of opinion created by William Randolph Hearst, Jr.'s expedition to Russia. He was unhappy over the way the Hearst chain, behind his back and to his competitive disadvantage, settled the long-standing legal quarrel with Drew Pearson. Finally, he was upset over the loss of several American newspaper clients through cancellations or refusals to resubscribe, one being the Tucson *Citizen*, his hometown outlet. Some years earlier his charges that the Connecticut countryside, where he used to live, was infested by Communists and homosexuals had turned the Ridgebury-Danbury newspapers against him. Now a similar press attitude seemed to be developing in Arizona.

As usual, when Westbrook became sick, Julie took over. Though the foreign field was new and tricky and extremely difficult for her, she kept the columns moving. She wrote sharply but she avoided her husband's moralistic weighting of sentences with words like "sordid," "snarling," and "loathsome." She had "a kind heart toward people, even bad people," Westbrook once said. As the unannounced guest conductor of the column she was not above relating a friendly anecdote about Einstein or trying semiseriously to explain a new atomic reactor which was exhibited in Geneva. With syndicated Pegler material under such heavy scrutiny at home, her less exciting copy probably conformed to the existing situation better than Westbrook's would have. Even so, some columns were shelved or killed, with a corresponding increase in her nervous strain.

The common effects of long and close marital association could be discerned in the Peglers. They often thought alike. Sometimes a reference to a familiar name or place would inspire them to start identical sentences simultaneously—only to break off in incredulous shared laughter. They leaned unconsciously on each other; when one became ill, the other seemed to generate extra energy for both. Thus, when Julie had a heart attack in Berlin after the Geneva conference, the convalescent Westbrook plunged into his neglected work while taking excellent care of Julie on the side. She soon rallied from the attack. She insisted on finishing the trip with him and there were no arguments in his mind sufficient to deter her.

Rome proved to be a hostile city. It was also noisy. Always neurotic about noise, Pegler reacted quickly with an entire column about the "horrible" and "maddening" abuse of auto horns in the street. Mussolini, he noted, would have remedied this condition "with an order."

Just as the Peglers arrived, the American Library put on a display of books and pamphlets on American labor with particular reference to Walter Reuther's guaranteed annual wage and David Dubinsky's social innovations. The columnist did a furious rehash of earlier exposés of American libraries abroad by himself and the Roy Cohn-David Schine team of investigators for Joe McCarthy, winding up with a charge that the current exhibition was false and dishonest and with the inference that it was also pro-Red and subversive.

The American colony in Rome was dominated by Ambassador Clare Booth Luce, Westbrook's former friend who had so unexpectedly filed an affidavit supporting Quentin Reynolds in the libel trial. Pegler discharged his animosity toward the Ambassador and her consort, publisher Henry Luce, in a series of venomous columns. He also tracked down and cross-examined various Americans of distinction who had come for a three-day "culturefest" at the Embassy, under the loudly announced assumption that they were internationalists or worse. Since the Vatican, that other great magnet in Rome for American visitors, recalled the columnist's sticky 1952 effort to influence Papal thinking on American unions, Julie found herself in an atmosphere of almost total social discomfort. Though she was no stranger to this kind of thing, it still bothered her.

The breaking point was reached in the form of a cable from King Features telling Westbrook to take a look at Russia before coming home. In view of the preceding visit of the Hearst task force to the Soviet Union, such a visit involved ideological difficulties, but Pegler decided it would provide a fitting climax for his European tour and also fulfill an impulse frustrated twenty-six years earlier by a quarrel over who should pay for some Moscow telephone calls. To his astonishment, Julie objected. She thought there were too many hateful connotations about the Soviet Union to make it a restful place for him to visit. As for herself, she was weary, she said, and she wanted to go home.

The issue between them was still unresolved several days later when they lunched in Rome with columnist Robert Ruark. In his presence they kept the conversation carefully casual. Westbrook talked about European tailors he had known and about the time Paul Gallico fell off an alp during the 1936 winter Olym-

247

pics at Garmisch-Partenkirchen and thereby became the involuntary ski champion of the world. Over brandy, he and Ruark discussed the degree of improvement in room service to be expected in Moscow now that almost anybody could go there. Julie said little, but she left a vivid impression on Ruark. "There was a woman a guy always would have liked to lunch with," he wrote after she died the next day.

Obituaries printed in the American press while Westbrook was still in Rome contained a number of annoying inaccuracies. Even those appearing in the New York *Journal-American*, the New York *Daily News* and *Editor & Publisher* declared that Julie had worked for the Chicago *Tribune* before coming to New York. One account listed her age as greater than her husband's. The columnist itched to straighten out the record but he was restrained by Julie's expressed desire for peace rather than for more controversy. There was no marker on the grave where Julia Harpman Pegler was buried in the Gate of Heaven Cemetery, Hawthorne, New York. She had forbidden it in her will.

"She felt that in twenty years nobody would know who she had been and that even in one year there would not be one in a thousand who would remember her name," Westbrook explained in a letter. "She wanted to be allowed to vanish from this world and from the notice of man."

One colleague suggested that Julie was what Pegler once thought of calling his column: "sweetness and light." She was his day off, his funny and kind side, another one wrote. He agreed with both; far from avoiding the subject, he was anxious to talk about Julie. "She did her best in life and she was very tired when she died," he told a newspaper acquaintance. To a friend who sent condolences, he replied: "She was indescribably good and generous and I hope she sleeps gently forever."

After he returned home, Westbrook Pegler suggested to King Features that his weekly output of columns be reduced from six to three; he wanted to take life easier. The suggestion was accepted. In his columns he still referred to himself as "a tireless crusader against sly crimes and political betrayals," yet he no longer sounded tireless. There was a new slackness in his style. After half a lifetime of building himself up as a bogeyman to adult Americans, he seemed complaisant over a last-minute attempt to convert him into an almost amiable legend. By order of management, the scowling Rhadamanthine visage which formerly illustrated Sunday pieces for the New York *Journal-Amer-*

ican had given way to a new sketch showing smiling eyes and puckish lips. A comparable transformation in reverse would have been to yank the false face off a department store Santa Claus and reveal the glowering countenance of Amos, the eighth century B.C. prophet of whom it was written: "The land is not able to bear all his words."

In the fall of 1956, a full year after Julie's death, Westbrook Pegler granted an interview to Lucy O'Brien of the Tampa *Morning Tribune* during a visit to Florida for a convention of Medal of Honor winners. Sipping his coke-on-the-rocks in the Tampa Terrace Bar as he waited for a plane, the columnist jumped at the chance to talk freely about Julie. She had been a reporter when they first met, he said, and he had let her hang on to her career for a while until she settled down to roaming the world with him. She was a creative writer as well as reporter, he pointed out, and she might have produced novels if she had not devoted all her energies to his career.

"How nice for you," remarked Mrs. O'Brien, drily, out of the unconscious superiority of a career woman who has also raised children.

"It was indeed," replied Pegler as if he were miles away.

Did he have any children? "We never had any; I wish we had," he said. He was weeping openly. Lucy O'Brien and her husband Michael, who had joined them at the bar, looked away so as not to embarrass the celebrated visitor.

Recovering himself, Pegler reminisced about apartments with a view—the view being Julie's invariable requirement—which they had shared in such diverse places as Davis Islands in Tampa in the 1920s and in Rome in 1955. He mentioned Maude Towart, his faithful secretary, who took guidance more from Julie than from him and who had been willed five thousand dollars and a diamond bracelet by Julie.

"Dames!" said the sixty-two-year-old columnist fondly, recalling one occasion when Maude and Julie maneuvered him into taking a trip in which he had no real interest. "They're all conspirators!" Reverting to the final trip, he said: "The only thing I owe the Russians is that they wouldn't give me a visa when my syndicate wanted me to go to Russia for a story. I couldn't get a visa so I was with Julie when she died. It was the only trip I ever knew Julie to drag her heels on."

Lucy O'Brien's two sympathetic articles about the columnist aroused wide interest. She had an additional impression which she did not commit to print. Westbrook Pegler was a lovable old man, now showing his age, she told friends, but he no longer cared much about anything and he was dangerously close to relinquishing his grip.

Willie Bioff was executed in gangland style at his home northeast of Phoenix on November 6, 1955. Somebody had studied his habits sufficiently to know that he drove off in his pickup truck every morning after breakfast. When he touched the starter button this particular morning, a number of sticks of dynamite planted under the hood exploded violently, blowing Bioff and the truck apart and showering Mrs. Bioff with glass from the window through which she had been waving goodbye. Some 125 windows in the luxurious home on East Bethany Road were shattered. Mrs. Bioff was not seriously hurt. A blackened finger of Willie Bioff wearing a $7,500 diamond ring was not retrieved from the grass 200 feet from the house until twenty-four hours later.

Westbrook Pegler was in Europe when it happened and he was not able to get back to Arizona before February. Then he took the trail without any apparent purpose except to relive past glory. It was an earlier series on Bioff which led to the Pulitzer Prize which was still his journalistic high-water mark. In 1939, however, he documented and organized his exposé before he began writing. Now he plunged immediately into reportage. Since he disclosed the day-to-day impact on himself of whatever facts he uncovered, this made for unusually exciting copy.

Willie Bioff first appeared in Phoenix early in 1950. He was then only fifty years old. By turning state's evidence against a half dozen leaders of the old Capone gang in Chicago, he had substantially reduced his term in prison on an extortion charge. He introduced himself in Phoenix as William Nelson, a retired businessman, Nelson being his wife's maiden name. He and his wife, a small faded woman some years younger than himself, lived briefly in Phoenix before acquiring an estate out of town in order to avoid a Phoenix law requiring the registration of ex-convicts.

Willie Bioff thoroughly hoodwinked Phoenix, Pegler indicated in the first columns of a series extending with interruptions over a period of a month. The pudgy ex-racketeer learned to dress Western style in hat, pants, boots and digbat necktie. He had an orange orchard and he specialized in growing plumbago plants and lantana flowers. Neighbors were impressed by his kindness toward their children—the Nelsons having no children of their own—and by the collection of nineteenth-century French paintings in his home. Mrs. Nelson proved to be a meticulous housekeeper.

Bioff seemed to have salvaged a good share of the thousands of dollars he had sluiced out of Hollywood. He carried a collection of diamonds with him in a small medical phial and a bundle of currency amounting to five or six thousand dollars. He did some trading in cotton, wool and grain through local brokerage houses. He took part in gin rummy and poker games at the Arizona Club and in other diversions at the Phoenix Country Club. He even joined Federal Judge David Ling and William Drew, the FBI resident in Phoenix, at a skeet shoot. The Judge never dreamed that his shooting companion was notorious for his use of human targets, but the FBI man must have been aware of Nelson's identity.

Journalistic experts on crime back East had theorized that Bioff was executed by the Mafia for his earlier betrayal of the Capone gang. Westbrook Pegler ridiculed this idea. In the first place, he wrote, there was no Mafia in America. Secondly, if the Capone gang had wanted vengeance, it could have moved much sooner.

The columnist interviewed a dozen associates of William Nelson. He learned that whispers about the criminal's background began to circulate in 1955 and that Nelson engaged in hazardous personal operations just before the murder. He tried to muscle in on a Reno gambling joint. "One of his most intimate friends reported that he reverted to his old abrupt customs to persuade the owners to sell the plant on his terms," the columnist informed the public.

Three weeks before the murder, Bioff and his wife and four Phoenix businessmen with underworld connections flew to Las Vegas. "The associated gamblers who run Las Vegas," disclosed Pegler, had asked Gus Greenbaum, a Phoenix gambler, to see "what could be done to persuade the big night-club acts to reduce their prices. Some acts were drawing up to sixty thousand dollars a week last year. These salaries were shaved in many cases under familiar forms of duress. In other cases, old-time professionals left over from the prohibition era voluntarily pared their pay in order to stay in action."

Gus Greenbaum, who had gone to Bioff for help, was further identified by the columnist as "one of the founding fathers of the

Flamingo, the pioneer plant of the Bugsy Siegel mob of New York and Hollywood. Siegal was murdered by rifle fire in Beverly Hills and the crime was never solved. Greenbaum got out of the Flamingo deal and went into another Phoenix operation. He is now one of the great captains of this weird industry in Las Vegas . . ."

The Bioffs stayed at a hotel in Las Vegas controlled by Gus Greenbaum.* In an effort to determine the outcome of their visit, Pegler consulted Harry Rosenzweig, a Phoenix jewelry store operator with extensive political connections. Rosenzweig, who borrowed fifty-five hundred dollars from Willie Bioff a few days before the murder and who repaid the money to the estate, said he had heard about a plan to cut salaries in Las Vegas by intimidation but he did not take it seriously. On the other hand, Barry Goldwater, the junior Senator from Arizona who lived in Phoenix and who was a friend of Rosenzweig, verified that Gus Greenbaum did appeal to Bioff.

To clear up some details, the columnist visited Mrs. Bioff. Having already gone farther than anybody else in tracing Willie's latter-day behavior, Pegler may have held some hope of solving the crime. Mrs. Bioff greeted him in a friendly fashion. He had always treated her husband fairly, she assured the columnist, and she was grateful for the fact that he had consistently omitted her name from his columns. She offered her visitor a drink, but he declined on the ground that it was early in the day and he was driving.

Was it true, demanded the columnist, that the Bioffs had flown back from that Las Vegas expedition in Senator Goldwater's private plane with the Senator at the controls? Not at all, said Mrs. Bioff indignantly. "Somebody is trying to smear Senator Goldwater," she said.

The columnist went next to the Senator, who had become his favorite American politician following the eclipse of Joe McCarthy. Goldwater revealed that Mrs. Bioff might have been more frank. "That was nice of Laura (Mrs. Bioff) to lie," he declared genially, "but I will tell you the truth. Peggy (Mrs. Goldwater), Laura and Bill were booked on a Bonanza Liner from

---

* Gus Greenbaum, former smalltime bookmaker who had become proprietor of the multi-million-dollar Riviera Hotel in Las Vegas, was eliminated in his turn by the underworld on December 3, 1958. He and his wife were trussed up in their Phoenix home and executed by knife slashes across their throats.

Vegas to Phoenix that night but an engine wouldn't start, so they couldn't take off. They asked me to take them and I said, 'Sure, if you don't mind flying at night over the mountains with me. Come on.' And they did!"

Pegler confronted Mrs. Bioff by telephone. "Did he say that?" she exclaimed. "Well what do you know? I just thought I ought to show respect for his office. He is a Senator. He is a wonderful man and he was a good friend."

Senator Goldwater was considerably more than a friend of Willie Bioff. He had been the mobster's employer right along. As head of the National Right-to-Work Committee, which wanted to outlaw the closed shop over as wide an area as possible, the Senator had been using Bioff as "an undercover informant," he told Pegler with no sign of embarrassment.

The columnist digested the new information. Senator Goldwater—"the most Republican Republican in the entire country," he sometimes called him—had been "making a specialty of exposing the criminality of unions," Pegler wrote, "in his campaign to uphold the open-shop or right-to-work laws of some eighteen states including Arizona." Pegler wondered whether the killing of Willie Bioff might not come closer home than he had previously suspected.

"The union rackets," he wrote, "with their millions and their great pool of criminal hoodlums or goons have declared political if not personal war on Goldwater. Perhaps they are not yet emboldened to knock him off but it is not straining to suspect that they could have procured the assassination of Willie Bioff for his traffic with Goldwater . . ."

The Senator's association with the criminal, explained the columnist, was "no reflection" on Goldwater but "a credit" to him. "Bioff educated Goldwater in the practical, coercive, terroristic and often criminal methods of union bosses all in strict accordance with their respective contributions which bar almost nothing. He concentrated on Walter Reuther and Hoffa, and Goldwater frankly acknowledges a debt to Bioff in the public interest. Certainly no other individual was better qualified to educate Barry. It is equally significant that not one of the qualified experts within the union movement has shown Goldwater anything but bitter, often vicious hostility."

The trail was still warm, but Westbrook Pegler was losing interest. What about "the respectable members of the Las Vegas and Phoenix underworld" who, he declared earlier, were con-

253

stant associates of Willie Bioff prior to the murder? Did Bioff stir up such trouble in Las Vegas that he had to fly back over the mountains with the Senator? What about Bioff's effort to crack the gambling combine in Reno? What if anything did Barry Goldwater have to do with these offside operations? To such questions and others which would be asked, Pegler provided no further answers. "There is no clue to the murderers," he wrote abruptly in conclusion.

In July, Pegler paid a visit to the Goldwater summer home in La Jolla, California, across the mountains from Arizona. Reporting on a social affair in nearby San Diego which he attended with the Senator and his wife, the columnist praised Goldwater as "the most promising citizen in public life" for predicting an eventual realignment in American politics which would pit a Conservative Party against a Labor Party.

"Barry voted against censure of Joe McCarthy," Pegler noted in his column, "and earned the loyal respect of Welker, Jenner and other dedicated Red-baiters who know that the real authors of the Joe-Must-Go campaign were conspirators in New York. Ike was just the agent of their design."

Goldwater, however, felt obliged to endorse President Eisenhower for another term. So did the Hearst newspapers. Still hoping for more radical developments, Pegler listed a few Republicans, including Clarence Manion and former Representative Thomas Werdel, who were still "faithful to the Constitution." In August he covered the GOP national convention at the Cow Palace in San Francisco. In one column which escaped censorship by praising Herbert Hoover, Pegler stressed the "disgust and almost desperation" in the minds of many Republicans over the activity of "secret forces fiercely loyal only to alien interests and no less hostile to the interests of the U.S." He added that "President Eisenhower's mysterious partiality to interlopers in the party and to Marxian heresies cribbed from Roosevelt had raised a degree of resentment close to personal hatred."

On September 11, the Hearst columnist made a quiet visit to the San Francisco "congress" of the Constitution Party of California, which voted to ratify and support a third party ticket organized by the new States Rights-Tax Reform Party, consisting of T. Coleman Andrews of Virginia, former Internal Revenue Commissioner, for President, and Thomas Werdel of California for Vice-President. The new party inveighed against things like the income tax, the peacetime draft, free trade and foreign aid, all of which were already anathema to Pegler. "No loyal Constitutional American," he wrote soberly in his column, could possibly object to the States Rights program.

The Andrews-Werdel ticket got on the ballot in only fourteen states. It did not appreciably reduce President Eisenhower's margin over Adlai Stevenson, who was again the Democratic presidential nominee. Actually, Andrews-Werdel polled fewer votes than the states rights ticket organized by Strom Thurmond of South Carolina in 1948 to fight President Truman's civil rights program. Undoubtedly, this debacle was responsible to some degree for the failure of the ultra-rightists to field another third-party ticket in 1960.

Frank Costello, the national crime syndicate manager, was ambushed in the lobby of his Central Park West apartment house in New York on the evening of May 2, 1957. A fat thug shouted: "This is for you, Frank," before he fired a .38 caliber revolver at close range and ran away. Miraculously the sixty-six-year-old gambler survived; the bullet merely parted his hair in a new place, leaving him groggy but intact. The police took him into custody for his own protection. Going hurriedly through his pockets, they noted memos indicating secret ownership of one of the Las Vegas gambling hells.

Nobody on the side of the law expected Costello to discuss the identity of his nervous assassin—and he did not disappoint them—but when he refused to discuss his gambling memos before a Grand Jury, he ran into contempt-of-court charges. Westbrook Pegler, whose extensive acquaintance with underworld figures dated back to his sportswriting days, rushed to the rescue. In copying memos from the pockets of a man whose only current crime was being shot at, the police had behaved outrageously, contemptibly and in violation of the Constitution, he declared in a column.

The crime syndicate manager appreciated this unsolicited defense. Talking for publication to another newspaperman a couple of months later, Costello described Pegler as "the only reporter with any guts," and added: "I'd like to do something for him some day." To those whose memories went back to the prohibition era when mobsters hobnobbed with columnists in the night clubs, this had a familiar ring. Sportswriters covering the baseball training camps down South in the mid-twenties used to describe the odd experience of Ray Long, *Cosmopolitan* magazine editor. Long visited Al Capone in the latter's home-in-exile on an island in Miami bay to discuss a possible article. Over a spaghetti dinner cooked by Capone, with plenty of wine, the pair became extremely friendly. "Look, Ray," the mobster said abruptly. "I like you and I want to show my friendship. *Who's your competition?*"

Standards, however, had changed somewhat in the course of several decades. *Journal-American* executives protested privately to Pegler that praise from Frank Costello in the year 1957 did not constitute the best kind of publicity. "I would rather have this fellow's good opinion than Earl Warren's," the columnist replied stoutly. "Or even Frankfurter's. He hasn't done half the harm in the world that they have."

When he repeated this conversation in his column, Pegler moved into dangerous territory. By implication he was linking the underworld to current agitation against Chief Justice Warren of the Supreme Court and Associate Justice Felix Frankfurter. The court had been under rising attack from the far right ever since its historic unanimous decision in 1954 that segregation of the races in the public schools was unconstitutional. Warren was singled out for abuse not only as head of the court but also as the decisive factor in several historic decisions on civil liberties. One decision upset the conviction of some Communist leaders. Another outlawed wiretap evidence and thereby led to the release of Frank Costello himself from prison in 1957 after he had served part of a five-year term for tax evasion. Some of the younger mobsters who had been running rackets in Costello's absence resented his unexpected appearance and it was they, according to the underworld grapevine, who organized an apparently foolproof assassination which was bungled.

Justice Frankfurter led a conservative minority on the Eisenhower court. Despite this fact, extremists continued to link him, rather than other Justices, to Warren in their denunciations of the court because he had been popularized as a symbol of supposed Jewish Communist conspiracy. Many fringe weeklies agitated persistently for the impeachment of both Warren and Frankfurter.

During the winter of 1957-58, those newly found friends, Frank Costello and Westbrook Pegler, lunched together in New York on occasion and were seen in restaurants like the Press Box in the evening. The columnist took to quoting the arch-criminal as an authority on juvenile delinquency. According to Costello, this was caused "by reformers who turned kids loose to run wild in the city streets." As an authority of sorts himself on youthful lawlessness, Pegler considered this a profound observation.

"I was the most delinquent little bum on Kenmore Avenue," he informed the amused Costello. "Stole milk. Smashed street lights. Jimmied penny gum machines . . ."

Pegler had a favor to ask. It was so large a favor that apologists for the columnist subsequently argued that he was joking. Pegler himself made no claim to being humorous. He did not sound humorous. Certainly his particular readership could have taken what he said at face value. He reported that he called Costello's unlisted phone and that the Prime Minister of the Underworld came around to see him. The following dialogue was carried in newspapers from coast to coast on April 11, 1958:

"I said, 'Can you kill a fellow for me?' He said 'Who is it?'

"I said, 'A crummy bum of a judge.'

"The P. M. of the Underworld said, 'What kind of a judge?' I said, 'Federal . . .'"

When it became clear that Pegler had in mind no mere local district Judge nor State Supreme Court Justice but a member of the United States Supreme Court itself, Frank Costello was startled. "Hey, you better go easy," Pegler quoted him as saying. "With those Federals, you can get into trouble."

He was "in the market for a murder," insisted Pegler. If Costello didn't want his business, he would go elsewhere. Costello was abashed. He had openly declared his intention of doing something for his journalistic protector and he did not propose to welsh on a promise. Outside of killing a judge, what could he do for his friend?

Westbrook Pegler had an idea. He had been working as a newspaperman since 1910, he said, and he was often "sick and tired . . . Hell's fire, I write twenty-five thousand words a month and I am always on the hustle. I want you to get together with Longie (Zwillman) and Meyer (Lansky) and all them, and make a big million-dollar foundation against subversiveness and make me director, fifty thousand dollars a year for life."

Frank Costello demurred. He did not want to deal with Longie and Meyer. Anyway, a foundation to combat juvenile delinquency would have more public appeal, he suggested. "Only fifty-Gs a year—for life," pleaded the columnist. "I haven't got too many many years. Maybe a quarter (of a million dollars) will see me there, so you talk it up—will you?"

257

Though Costello did not in the end establish a foundation on subversion or juvenile delinquency, the unvarnished dialogue between the criminal and the columnist, which set some sort of record for confessional literature, continued to disturb people inside and outside the Hearst organization. After renewed trouble with his ulcers put Pegler in the Leahy Clinic again for what he called the "standard indignities," he began to slide little gags into his column about Costello. FBI chief J. Edgar Hoover encountered the underworld czar on one occasion in the lobby of the Waldorf Astoria, he declared, and Hoover allegedly remarked: "I have sold you out, I want no part of you." Costello supposedly replied in surprise: "What did I do now?" and Hoover answered, "You are a phony; I just heard you didn't own the Waldorf."

Rounding off this anecdote, which was never confirmed or denied by Hoover presumably because nobody dared to question him about it, Pegler wrote: "There had been crazy rumors, some still persisting, that Costello owned J. P. Morgan and Company and Tiffany's." Now he was really joking. In similar mood, he quoted a paint store proprietor named Marcel to the effect that "Frank Costello, the Prime Minister of Crime," was hiring "old, broken-down, rum-dum painters" to work day after day in a cheap hotel and sign their canvases "with all kinds of names, Ike, DeGaulle, Judge Frankfurter, Judge Warren, Toots Shor, Ted Williams."

Pegler's defensive activity in relation to Frank Costello was combined with his customary offensive against the Supreme Court. The desegregation decision had "driven our people to violence," he asserted. He devoted dozens of columns to denouncing Earl Warren for accepting a California state pension on top of his salary as Chief Justice. He used terms like "loafers" and "bums" for the nine members of the highest court in the land, ridiculed their judicial habit of wearing robes and suggested that they did not even write their own decisions. He peddled an inflammatory myth to the effect that the desegregation decision was based on the testimony of social psychologists—"intellectuals," he pointed out—who were foreigners or radicals. Two senators took the myth seriously enough to charge on the Senate floor that the decision was Communist-inspired. Since professional legal analysis entirely disproved the idea, Congress and the public as a whole did not become upset.

Pegler suggested repeatedly in his column that he might be tossed into jail at any moment for contempt as a result of what he was saying about the Supreme Court Justices. The high court did not so much as acknowledge his existence. On October 21, 1958, however, it decided not to review Frank Costello's appeal. This had the effect of reincarcerating Pegler's friend in the Lewisburg, Pennsylvania, federal penitentiary, to serve out the remainder of his tax-evasion sentence.

Ultra-rightist outcry against the Supreme Court was getting out of hand. In November, a deluge of particularly threatening mail led the FBI to assign special guards to Earl Warren and Felix Frankfurter. The guards followed the justices night and day, as they worked in their marble court building, as they moved about Washington and as they rested at home. To Felix Frankfurter, who was getting on in years, the precautionary surveillance aggravated the distress he felt over the senseless campaign against him. He spent several weeks in a hospital that winter before returning to the bench, where he served until his retirement in the fall of 1962.

During his disoriented bachelorhood, Westbrook Pegler re-acquired the night club habit. As a café society celebrity in New York he ranked somewhere between Thomas Franklyn (Tommy) Manville, who at the age of sixty-five in 1959 enhanced his reputation for marrying by taking an eleventh bride, and Ernest (Papa) Hemingway, sixty that year, who was becoming a popular symbol of art just as his literary powers declined. Since Pegler had an odd sort of news value, the gossip columnists noted his movements carefully. At the Press Box, it was reported, Gene Tunney routed a group of four drunks who made threatening remarks to his friend. At the Stork Club, Sherman Billingsley introduced Westbrook (Peg) Pegler to the *New Yorker's* Lois (Lipstick) Long, whom he had known twenty years earlier and forgotten. At the Eden Roc Club, Pegler was seen dancing with illustrator Russell Patterson's young and charming daughter Russella.

Such trivial items were capped early in May, 1959, by news that the sixty-four-year-old controversialist had again found romance. Leonard Lyons scored the scoop: Seymour Weiss, the New Orleans hotel man who had once been treasurer of Huey Long's political empire, suddenly began buying champagne for all hands at Twenty One to celebrate the engagement of his friend Westbrook Pegler to Mrs. Pearl Wiley Doane of Hollywood!

Mrs. Doane, who was forty-seven, had been married twice, to Ernest Rue, from whom she was divorced in 1933, and to James Doane, from whom she was divorced in 1955. She had two children by Doane, an actor's agent who represented such well known Hollywood figures as Agnes Moorehead and Lionel Barrymore. A pretty woman of medium height and amiable expression, Mrs. Doane moved easily in the show business, night club crowd because her sister, Lee Wiley, was a popular singer. Eastern newspapers generally referred to Mrs. Doane as a "Los Angeles clubwoman." They did not know and therefore did not mention her record of off-beat political activity which qualified her as a helpmate for Westbrook Pegler.

Mrs. Doane entered California politics originally as a supporter of Thomas Werdel. In 1951, when Werdel was charging that a "Hitlerian" United States general staff was scheming, with help from Defense Secretary Marshall and General Eisenhower, to take over every phase of American life, she opened her Beverly Hills home for a garden party for Americans for MacArthur. The following year she was secretary of the Hollywood Committee for Joe McCarthy which raised funds for the Senator's reelection campaign in Wisconsin. In 1954, after Admiral Crommelin personally phoned Joe McCarthy to tell her to "get the ball rolling on the West Coast," she established a Beverly Hills office of Ten Million Americans Mobilized for Justice.

Mrs. Doane had earned a national reputation among conservatives through her work with the Wage Earners Committee, Students for America and Americans against Communism. She had won applause from the Hearst press and Gerald L.K. Smith's *The Cross and The Flag* for her crusade in the early 1950s against a genocide convention presented to the UN which she thought might try to tell the United States how to handle its minorities.

To a right-wing activist like Pearl Wiley Doane, Westbrook was more than a newspaperman; he was an elder statesman, a hero, of an entire movement. It did not get into the newspapers generally, but it was important news to her and her West Coast associates when he harangued the "Congress of Freedom" which convened in San Francisco in 1955 to plan, among other things, for the formation of a national third party the following year.

Pegler's minimal program on that occasion for the "American re-
sistance"—as he called it—included getting the United States out
of the UN (and vice-versa), the Bricker amendment restricting
presidential control of foreign policy, abolition of the Labor
Relations Board, control of private foundations "to forbid the
use of money for political experiments" and a 25 per cent ceiling
on the federal income tax in peace time.

The ideologically suited couple was united in holy matrimony on May 11, 1959, by Municipal Court Justice Pelham St.
George Bissell, III at the home of Dr. and Mrs. Thomas C. Case
in New York. Pegler kept to his usual working schedule in the
days immediately prior to the ceremony and he continued to do
so afterward with no break for a wedding trip. Friends considered this a favorable omen for the marriage. One flaw soon developed. Maude Towart, the columnist's faithful secretary, found
that she could not work with the second Mrs. Pegler as she had
previously worked with Julie. Her resignation left a painful gap
in his professional arrangements.

That summer, Westbrook Pegler took his often-postponed
trip to Russia but his wife was not able to accompany him. He
traveled with Vice-President Nixon's press party as far as Moscow, where he settled down for several weeks of hostile observation. Julie's concern lest such a trip prove unsettling to him was
fully justified.

For three days before he left by plane on what he called his
"greatest adventure," the columnist could hardly sleep because
of "shapeless apprehensions." He was "strangely upset," he revealed later, over the notion that Khrushchev might arrange the
liquidation of Nixon and himself. Since he believed that the
United States had "lost" World War II because American diplomats got "stumbling drunk" on vodka, he made and kept a
pledge not to consume a single drink while in Soviet territory.
Despite the Hearst task force discovery in 1955 that Russians
were also human beings, Pegler started his visit under the assumption that he was going to a "primeval murk where people
are only the biological result of lust." Naturally he did not find
anything to admire in the Soviet Union, not even the U.S. exhibition in Moscow, which displayed modern art which horrified him
and did not include books by John T. Flynn and "all the other
brave enemies of the great treason."

From Russia, the columnist moved into the Scandinavian
countries for extensive additional travel which delayed his return

to the United States. When he finally got back to New York, friends who visited him at the Park Lane Hotel noticed that Westbrook and his wife Pearl eyed each other like hostile strangers. Something was definitely wrong with the marriage.

When the weather turned cold, the Peglers left for Arizona. Even the relaxed charm of Casa Cholla did not suffice to ease the irritation between them. In January 1960, the columnist filed suit in Tucson for divorce on grounds of cruelty, asserting that his wife had prevented him from sleeping and had done other things which damaged his health. Mrs. Pegler denied the charges and indicated that she would fight him in court to the bitter end.

20. THE BROTHELIAN PRESS

In his sixth decade as a newspaperman, Westbrook Pegler again became a conversation piece at dinner parties. His name usually arose in connection with some rumor about his health, his marital status or his standing with William Randolph Hearst, Jr. Hostesses who had not given him a thought for years found themselves coping with a vague discussion of his role in American life. A decade earlier, bare mention of Pegler would have come close to disrupting any politically mixed social gathering. Now enemies praised him with faint damns and friends glorified him as if he were dead.

It was generally known that the columnist's career dated back at least to World War I, whereas Walter Lippmann his chief rival in length of journalistic service, did not begin writing editorials for the old New York *World* until 1921. Sheer survival might or might not be significant. How should Pegler, the Silurian, rightly be appraised? Was he that man-in-a-million who dared write precisely how he felt or was he just another smooth Tory? Was he a twentieth-century Carlyle or merely a kitchen scold? Since few of those taking part in such social discussions read his columns any longer, the talk was likely to trail off into anecdotal inconsequence. Any reference to the fact that here was the only nationally syndicated columnist in America openly advocating "Conservative Revolution"—in capital letters—was certain to evoke expressions of surprise and shock from the other guests.

Certain standard approaches to Pegler by his own crowd had helped him to blend with his surroundings. Ben Hecht, in his autobiography, *A Child of the Century,* had hailed him as a "one-man counter-revolution" and added: "He fought the mushrooming statism of the Republic and another concentration of power—its labor unions. He took swipes at the Catholic Church and even at a few Jews. He slipped occasionally, for he fought on muddy grounds . . . but when he finishes his stint and the editorial shears take him over, he will emerge as one of the brightest of the prose lighthouses in a time darkened by the pall of government."

That sounded like an obituary of a man without too much political influence. George E. Sokolsky, most wily of the Hearst columnists, provided another version. His colleague might have become successful as a satirist, he suggested, if he concentrated more on his George Spelvin pieces and devoted less white space to "telling the politicians to be decent, a most futile task and one bitterly unappreciated." Pegler himself revealed that he had consulted the Rev. James M. Gillis of the Paulist order on how an "uncompromising idealist" should behave when he "found himself too far ahead of his own artillery." Father Gillis replied that he should "drop back into the crowd lest he be crushed." The columnist said he had rejected this advice, but he did take refuge increasingly in Spelvin pieces when he ran into censorship.

It was odd how few intellectuals could trace the columnist's recent development. Some lost sight of him when he dropped down the Hearst chute in 1944. Others left him later with a feeling that he had failed to keep up with the times.

Opinion makers were by now inclined to dismiss him as a bore. Sydney J. Harris, a syndicated Chicago columnist, called him "a fading phenomenon like Winchell, soon to be remembered no more than Major Bowes* or Madame Blavatsky.†"

A few young iconoclasts theorized that Pegler was a good influence: a non-conformist in an age of regimentation. They felt queasy about some aspects of his non-conformity, such as his insistence that a racist was merely a harmless fellow who preferred his own kind, but even there, it was asserted, he might provide a counterweight to the nice-Nellyism of the day which had wiped dialect stories off radio and television, prevented legitimate criticism of various social and religious groups, and outlawed some excellent parodies of literary works. This group of defenders had recently discovered the columnist and did not read him steadily enough to appreciate the difference between non-conformity and revolution.

It was surprising how little notice the far left itself took of Pegler. The surviving handful of Communists, Socialist workers, Socialist Laborites and plain Socialists ignored him more completely than the middle-class intellectuals. Of course they no longer wrote, talked or even thought in terms of violent over-

* Edward Bowes, a major by courtesy, ran an amateur hour on radio circa 1935.
† Mrs. Helena Petrova Blavatsky, at fat theosophist, died in 1891.

throw of government. Before their very eyes a Hearst journalist was stealing their revolutionary argot, and not one yelled: "Stop thief!" They did not seem to appreciate that here might be a lowbrow Yankee variant of Pareto, the sociologist who laid the eggs of temporary fascism hatched by Mussolini in Italy, or the "fault-finding man of words" who according to Eric Hoffer generally prepares the ground for revolution.

Pegler's final reckless phase actually started April 22, 1959, when he concluded that revolution "must come because people who knew freedom must fight Congress and the courts to wrest that freedom back."

Adding the legislative branch of government to the judicial and executive branches, at which he had been tilting dangerously for decades, served to round off his personal rebellion.

How the revolution would unfold, he added, was "a mere detail." Since the Constitution had been "gutted" and Americans had become "slaves," he wrote a few weeks later in obvious parody of Karl Marx's Communist Manifesto, "what have we got to lose but our chains?" Any conjecture that levity hid in some remote corner of his mind was routed by subsequent labored columns including one to the effect that Americans were worse slaves, owing to an "act of lunacy" known as the federal income tax, than the Red Chinese in their communes.

The columnist's growing humorlessness was revealed in his relations with readers. During the 1960 presidential election, when he and the Hearst chain were temporarily in agreement to the extent that they both supported Vice-President Nixon for President, he carefully saved up letters of protest over his abuse of the Roosevelts until after the election. Then he sent out a form reply opening with Lord Macaulay's 1856 prediction that democracy was doomed and ending with several pejorative sentences of his own: "You grovel before the memory of a confidence man who dodged the draft in the war of his own generation and sold out your country to Russia. Quit slouching along. Try to walk tall . . . like a man."

When Major General Edwin A. Walker was removed as commander of the Twenty-fourth Division in Germany for indoctrinating soldiers with a "true-blue" political program which accused many prominent American citizens of being "pinko," Pegler used his column to thunder that a great heroic patriot was being framed by Communists concealed within the Federal bureaucracy. He stuck to this thesis even after the General exposed himself, at a Washington press conference, as a pathetically confused man.

When Robert Welch's John Birch Society, to which General Walker belonged, came under public scrutiny, the columnist wrote at first that he had not joined because he wasn't sure it was "far enough to the right." After satisfying himself on that score, he began to defend Birch Society insinuations about the loyalty and good sense of Chief Justice Warren and former President Eisenhower. His first two columns along this line, he reported, drew more than two thousand letters, "at least half of them from cities where my nice dissents have been suppressed." The John Birch Society, he said, was a "pro-American league of angry individuals" comparable to "the early Fascisti."

"John Birch may not be merely another murmur in the drugged sleep of a conquered people," he wrote hopefully. "It may be the first outcry in a grand revolution—led not by one general but by a hundred of the best generals and admirals that the country has yet produced."

From a professional point of view the columnist was running into shoal water. Enunciating national Hearst policy in January, 1962, Frank Conniff deplored "the nutty fringe of the American right," including General Walker and the Birch Society. Hearst writers generally fell into line, but not Pegler. In an article in *Esquire*, he gave his own Credo, from which he pledged he would not deviate: "A passion for truth, a hatred of deception and pity for The People in their contemptible submission to the fraudulent humaneness of the Roosevelt Myth. He (F.D.R.) was an unmanly Fauntleroy who ducked the draft in World War I, flinched before Stalin because he was tough, and threw our world away seeking the personal favor of a real man who despised him."

In succeeding months, Westbrook Pegler devoted solid weeks of columns to the gradual presentation of a theory that the Birch Society deserved credit for exposing Billie Sol Estes in Texas. Estes had created the biggest scandal of the Kennedy administration to date. On the basis of repeated personal visits to Pecos, Texas, and interviews with bankers and others caught in the promoter's rackets in grain storage and cotton-planting quotas, the columnist asserted that Dr. John Dunn, a thirty-four-year-old Birch Society member living in Pecos, had established himself as "the hero of the Conservative Revolution" by tipping off the FBI to Estes' manipulations.

Other reporters covering the Estes case did not mention Dr. Dunn. Since there must have been complaints from many quarters about Estes, Pegler's scoop seemed limited. The columnist insisted that the young surgeon's daring had aroused "terrible hatred" for the Birch Society at first but that the tide had turned now and that the "first major political breakthrough" for the Birch Society in the country could be anticipated in Texas. General Walker also made use of the Estes scandal in his campaign for the Democratic nomination for Governor in Texas, but in May he finished last in a field of six—"without enough votes to wad a shotgun," as one local observer put it. With no sign of discouragement, Pegler and the Birchites transferred their agitational interest and support to John Cox, the Republican candidate for Governor of Texas in the general election. He also was defeated.

Almost by definition, fascism constituted more of a threat to the American form of government than communism. Both were totalitarian, but one type seemed to afflict technologically advanced countries like Germany and Argentina, whereas the other fastened on poorer and less developed countries like Russia (as it was in 1918) and China. Such an expert as Professor William Ebenstein of Princeton University theorized that each had a revolutionary function: fascism to solve conflicts within an industrially advanced society; communism to industrialize a backward society.

By the early 1960's, the Communists were down to a few thousand members in the United States. Having served too long and transparently as the branch office of a Moscow concern instead of doing business on a domestic basis, they had alienated most of their sympathizers. They were unimportant in any political sense except as a scapegoat to rabblerousers on the right. So long as they retained their activist core, future growth could not be ruled out, but for the moment they were more nuisance than menace.

The tension and feeling of potential fascism, on the other hand, were on the upgrade in the country. There were several danger signals. One was an alarming, though perhaps temporary, increase in racism, stirred by school integration down South and

267

by shifts of population and changes in local customs in the big cities up North. Another was the increasing distress of white collar workers whose pay had fallen behind that of the blue collar workers for lack of unionization and who were becoming sufficiently unhappy and desperate to listen to suggestions that somebody else—the unions, business or government itself—should be blamed for their plight.

The incomprehensible struggle for outer space and the prospect of annihilation by the new weapons had created a curious numbness in American society. Contrary to Marx, who thought more leisure time would make workers more radical, most workers used the shorter work week to watch television or play games. They consumed newspapers, magazines and movies in the same abstracted and alienated way that they consumed commodities. Anti-intellectualism, always something of a problem in America, was becoming epidemic. The existence of so many millions of listless, bored, basically disgruntled persons, living in self-imposed conformity, conditioned to obedience and submission, was almost a standing invitation to a totalitarian movement.

Avowed fascists were still hard to find, since the designation had too many unpleasant connotations to be useful to an ordinary agitator. Many of the lunatic fringe outfits flaunting Hitler-ite swastikas or lightning bolts were—or at least had been, until quite recently—mere rackets. Over a period of decades, careless usage had diluted the meaning of fascism until it often seemed little more than an expression of distaste, yet no better term was available and a camouflaged neo-fascist could still be spotted by fairly objective standards as the genuine article.

Western culture rested on the Greek idea of reason, the Christian idea of moral equality, and the Jewish idea of mankind under one God. Promoters of neo-fascism rejected these guidelines. They distrusted reason; they glorified the instinctive, irrational impulses in people. They place taboos on subjects ranging from race to leader. They created historical fantasies for their own use.

In the domestic field, they turned their rage on organized labor, minorities, intellectuals and supposed traitors. They bridled at any mention of international organization. They encouraged attitudes which could be converted into aggression against enemies at home and abroad.

For organizational purposes, fascism has tended to exalt obedience and discipline in human relations at the expense of spontaneity. It stressed a supposedly natural hierarchical order: men over women, the strong over the weak, soldiers over civilians, one's own group over outgroups, one's own nation over other nations and the victors in war over the losers. It favored racism and imperialism. It practiced verbal violence and the more violent it sounded, the better chance it apparently had of attracting support.

A lot of new outfits with a fascist-like tone were breaking through the prosperous, determinedly bright surface of American life in the early 1960s. They included self-appointed America-savers, self-styled experts on communism and money-minded Crusaders. One group held periodic rifle practice with targets labelled Earl Warren and Dwight D. Eisenhower. Another skirmished grimly in the hills against the time when their rifles might come in handy. Some adopted protective coloration with names featuring "education" or "national indignation." Others marched loudly behind a cross or wrapped themselves in the flag, lending force to Huey Long's prediction that if fascism ever came to the United States, it would arrive in the guise of 100 per cent patriotism.

The fastest growing right-wing group—short of overt fascism was the Christian Crusade of Dr. Billy James Hargis. This was evangelical, where the John Birch Society, its chief rival, was secular.

Both groups, however, contended that the nation's unions, colleges, press and even clergy were controlled or strongly influenced by Communists, their dupes or their agents. Both accused the Supreme Court of aiding the Communists with its rulings and made similar charges about the UN. Whereas the Birch Society claimed sixty thousand members in 1962, Hargis said that his Crusade had more than one hundred thousand repeating contributors and that his monthly magazine reached five hundred thousand readers.

Billy James Hargis was a rotund, youngish man of thirty-six who weighed about two hundred fifty pounds and exhibited enormous energy. His degree of Doctor of Divinity came from a school operated by the late Gerald B. Winrod, a Kansas bigot, and he frequently acknowledged the debt he owed Winrod for help in beginning his anti-Communist radio crusade in the early 1950s. He had classed as a small time agitator until he attracted the help of L. E. (Pete) White, an Oklahoma public relations man who had previously built faith healer Oral Roberts into a

269

profitable business enterprise. By 1962, with White's assistance, Billy James had a million-dollar-a-year operation going out of Tulsa, Oklahoma. As he prepared to expand and move into national radio in the fall of that year, he also made a determined effort to coordinate the entire right wing movement. Among those attracted to this effort was Westbrook Pegler.

Because he was an authoritarian writing primarily for authoritarian personalities, Westbrook Pegler was by this time a great catch for a right wing fringe outfit. The theory of an authoritarian personality had been expounded in 1950 by a California team of social psychologists consisting of T. W. Adorno, Else Frankel-Brunswik, Max Borkheimer, Daniel Levinson and Nevitt Sanford, who had worked five years on their investigation.

The social scientists rated the persons they interviewed and the homes they studied (the home being the obvious crucible for the development of personality) on a graduated scale ranging from very high to very low, with the authoritarian at one end and the democratic personality, a flexible individual with a mind of his own capable of adjusting readily to new situations, at the other. The authoritarians, of course, would provide the new human material for groups with fascistic characteristics.

The California investigators concluded that perhaps 10 per cent of the men and women in the United States were authoritarian in some degree and that another 10 per cent carried the seeds within them which could be cultivated into authoritarianism.

An authoritarian frequently believed that his own group was free of scandal though he strongly distrusted others. One lesser sign of this type of personality was an intense distaste for sensuality. He held fixed beliefs about the natural inferiority of women, for example, and the inability of a "decent man" to marry an unchaste woman. He was likely to spend an inordinate amount of time ferreting out degeneracies and immoralities among the groups he suspected. He tried to exalt his own group in other ways. He was prejudiced against minorities and foreigners. He might possess brains, but if so, his thinking remained within narrow channels because of a conditioned rigidity of imagination. In politics he suffered from a false conservatism which in some cases produced a more destructive agitator than the radicals who worried him.

When Pegler wrote in his column that there were "millions" of Communists in the country whom the American people hated and would "exterminate" if they had their way, or when he roared that a group of NATO officials holding a quiet meeting in Georgia amounted to a "foreign-aid caucus trampling on our nationalism on American soil," or when he defined the fairly mild American inheritance tax as an opportunity for government to show "a snarling, sadistic joy in pouncing on horrified, stricken, lonely Americans in the worst calamity of life," he was stirring likeminded readers to similar ideological jitteriness.

According to the standards of the social scientists, Westbrook Pegler inflamed the potential xenophobia, populistic fear of conspiracy and hyperpatriotism which normally lie latent in the minds of many marginal authoritarians. He spread mischief like itching powder between the various layers of the population. His excessive vehemence and denunciatory hyperbole tended to create an hysterical national mood.

Pegler had a simple answer to this sort of accusation. His purpose, he said, was merely "to write the truth with clarity and emphasis." Wasn't that better than a "bland and milky form of writing" which confused the reader with lack of clarity and lack of emphasis? He asked the question in a manner which suggested that he was no longer open to conviction. He now referred occasionally to himself as the Crusader for Truth and the Right, in addition to his earlier self-conferred title of True Crusader of the Press. Nobody converts a Crusader, of course; it's the other way around.

Reaching out retroactively for an historic role, Westbrook Pegler divulged in his column some of his past efforts to influence events. In addition to bringing suspected subversives to the attention of the late Joe McCarthy, he revealed that he had undertaken various secret chores for the Junior Senator from Wisconsin. One of them was no less than an investigation of the income tax returns of Alexander Wiley, the Senior Senator from Wisconsin, whom McCarthy loathed. In return for access to confidential files of the House Un-American Activities Committee, Pegler often gave advice to the Committee. On one occasion in the late 1940s when the committee planned to call Charlie Chaplin as a witness, he dissuaded it in a private session, on the ground that the comedian might make the committee look ridiculous by putting on a baggy-pants routine.

When Richard Nixon, defeated for President by JFK in 1960, essayed a political comeback in the spring of 1962 and seemed to be backing away from the Birchites and others on the radical right, Pegler hit him between the eyes with a column charging

271

that Nixon, as a member of the House Un-American Activities Committee, had almost "torpedoed" the case against Alger Hiss because of his "desire to tip the committee's hand to the Dept. of Justice and expose its evidence to seizure and sabotage."

The column caused consternation in California, where Nixon was gathering his forces to run for Governor. After explanations and assurances, Pegler did a second column a week or so later reinstating the former Vice President of the United States as a hero and making the Dept. of Justice the prime enemy of the HUAC in the Hiss case—which in itself was an odd and debatable view. Nixon rewarded the columnist's renewed confidence. During the remainder of his campaign, he maintained an accommodation of sorts with the ultra-rightists—though he did not manage to defeat Gov. Brown in the November election.

As he coasted downhill toward the age of seventy, Westbrook Pegler found himself more isolated in his personal and professional relationships than ever before. The biggest blow was the death of his father early in March, 1961. According to the best available records, Arthur Pegler was ninety-nine when he died. For some years before he had been under care in a sanitarium outside Tucson, where his second wife had predeceased him in 1958. On the ground that his miserable extension of existence could hardly be called life, the veteran newspaperman often expressed a wish that he could have died a decade earlier. Except for his son Westbrook, who dropped around every so often in the evening "to my dear old Daddy-O's house," as he put it, "to read him the pick of the fan mail and talk a little shop," the world had forgotten him.

The night Arthur Pegler died, his son lay beside him on an adjoining bed, staring up at the ceiling. Then he went home, and in the morning they told him it was over. The Church of England man had turned Catholic at the end, and his Solemn Requiem Mass was celebrated in the Tucson Cathedral. "He was impatient to be gone," Westbrook wrote in a moving columnar account of the services, "now that nobody was left whom he had known as a full contemporary in St. Paul, Chicago or even New York."

Up to this point, whenever anything particularly exciting or pleasing happened to him, Pegler would think instinctively: "I must tell the Governor about that." Now the central point of reference in his life was gone and he was free also to realize how few contemporaries of his own were left.

272

A month or so after his father's death, he encountered Charles Coburn, the actor, in a Minneapolis hotel. Though Coburn had a glass eye, he was often mistaken for Westbrook Pegler. The look-alikes exchanged comments in a gay mood. Several days later, the columnist read in a newspaper that Coburn had died in New York. "Twilight is lowering," he wrote moodily in his column, "and good companions are thinning out."

He could tick them off in his mind, one by one: Frederick Tisdale, Jr., who died in 1957; Bill Corum, in 1959; Gene Fowler, in 1960; many, many others.

Domestic difficulties added to Westbrook Pegler's edginess. At one point in 1960, after he had been ordered by a judge to pay one thousand dollars a month temporary alimony pending trial of opposing suits, he and Pearl Pegler achieved a reconciliation. Both suits being withdrawn, they went back to living together at Casa Cholla.

Then new quarrels arose, new suits were filed and Mrs. Pegler established a separate residence in New York. During negotiations in 1961 for an amicable parting, Westbrook became so upset that he required treatment for bleeding ulcers in a hospital. For several days, his space in the New York *Journal-American* bore the extremely rare notice that he was ill. When a clean break with his wife was achieved, his health improved.

The divorce decree was signed on October 30, 1961, by Superior Judge Robert O. Roylston of Tucson after a brief trial during which Mrs. Pegler testified that her husband treated her cruelly. Under a prearranged settlement, she received thirty-five thousand dollars and thirty-five acres of valuable land in Pima County, Arizona.

On November 22, barely three weeks later, the sixty-seven-year-old columnist married for the third time. His bride was Maude Towart, forty-six, his former secretary, who noted on the marriage register that she was a native of Cannes, France. The marriage took place in St. Anne's Roman Catholic Church in Midland, Texas. Robert Stripling, oil man and former chief investigator of the House Un-American Activities Committee, who lived in Midland, served as best man in a ceremony witnessed by sixty persons. The Rev. J.T. Kennedy was able to perform the marriage in church, it was explained, because Pegler and his second wife had not been married by a priest.

For the next nine months, the columnist stayed close to his Arizona home. Periodically, he visited Stripling's district in Texas for further exploration of the Estes scandal and he made one short jaunt into Senator Barry Goldwater's summer vacation area in Southern California. Otherwise he and his third wife lived quietly at Casa Cholla on the edge of the desert.

Friends worried somewhat over his health, since in recent years he had been banged up in a taxi collision and had complained of a variety of minor ailments in addition to his ulcers. In letters to him, they joked that he must be suffering from a Southwest kind of agoraphobia, which kept him far from the Eastern marketplace in New York where the shears of editorial censorship were cutting paper dolls out of his copy.

Arthur Pegler's death had served indirectly to increase Westbrook's resentment against his employers. In the years since 1937 he and Julie (Julie had to be brought into it since she made the financial decisions) had spent one hundred fifty thousand dollars on the support of the old man and his second wife. Serving as his father's social security was his duty, Westbrook Pegler believed. Nevertheless, he could not help thinking—and sometimes saying in circumstances where his words would be repeated—that here was "the best rewriteman of his time anywhere, a great reporter and so manly and honorable that in his seventies the Hearst interests sawed him off with severance pay of thirty dollars a week —for six months!"

Hearst officials like Richard Berlin and J. D. Gortatowsky, who used to protect him (because they liked him or because they thought the way he did) and who had served to a certain extent to keep him in line, were either dead or assigned to other duties. Their supervisory role had been assumed by William Randolph Hearst, Jr. and a phalanx of bright young assistants whom Pegler derisively referred to in private as "Junior and his baby-sitters."

Though this muttering was undoubtedly relayed to New York, more than personalities were involved in the increasing censorship of Pegler columns.

King Features acted according to solid memos on policy from Hearst headquarters at Eighth Avenue and Fifty-seventh Street, New York. The cuts were so deep and frequent that the columnist was required to produce much more than his usual copy. During one four-month period, Pegler told Walter Winchell, who reported it later, 14 columns were killed. Occasionally, the New York *Journal-American*, his home paper, would turn his space over to somebody else like James Bishop or Charles Bartlett, without any explanation to the public. No wonder Pegler fumed. If a break came, he vowed, Junior and his baby-sitters would pay heavier than their predecessors paid his father.

Since George Spelvin was an excellent refuge from censorship trouble, Pegler's public often got an uninterrupted diet of Everyman columns for a week or more. These were never quite as successful as George Sokolsky and some other admirers thought, if only because they provided a lowbrow version of an already lowbrow writer. There was insufficient room between creator and puppet for real satire. Anybody who knew Westbrook Pegler, however, found one character in the Spelvin saga invariably fascinating—George's wife, known as Dreamie.

In the morning, George would bring the breakfast coffee into Dreamie's bedroom with a flower on the tray. When he arrived home in the evening, she would meet him "at the door like a frisky little puppy, though we have been wedded a long time now . . . She comes whipping at me like a good spring breeze and she lets out a squeal of joy and she calls me wonderful names . . ."

Though he had two subsequent wives, Westbrook Pegler seemed to be writing about Julie. One piece going back to his country squire days of the 1930s told how George Spelvin, who sometimes exclaimed, "Boy, am I idealistic about women!" allowed himself to be kissed on the verandah of the country club by a girl who drank martinis and sang limericks which were pretty broad-minded. Dreamie caught them. When she got her husband alone, she lectured him on the unscrupulous nature of some women. George promised never to stray again. Kissing him in forgiveness, she said with sudden passion, "You are mine, mine, mine and I am a killer, I will positively kill the next woman . . ." Thereafter she conscientiously quizzed him after absences as to whether he had been a "good little boy," but there was apparently no next woman so long as she lived.

One episode told of Dreamie cheering George up, when he was depressed, by "diving" at him, yanking his ears and roughhousing him into good nature. Another ended: "She said nobody knows how crazy I am about the most wonderful husband of all. Frantic, insane, frenzied. I said I know, I know, I know. And you know what she did? She cried . . ."

Every once in a while, Westbrook Pegler would realize that Dreamie was really dead, and his recollections would end on a jagged note. George, so thick-fingered and obtuse in every relation of life except marriage, was allowed to recall that he and

Dreamie had agreed to live together "until death do us part." That column ended: "And that's the way it turned out." Another time, the columnist retold a Greek fable of a man and his wife who "wished most that they might die together as they had lived, for neither could endure a life that would be unendurable alone."

Pegler's increasing ideological itch did not permit him to stop with domestic reminiscences. He soon had Dreamie arguing with George that "democracy is for bums . . . this country needs a dictator," and convincing him that she was right, too, on the ground that God himself was a dictator. In a similar incident, Dreamie exclaimed, "I wish I could make a speech and start a revolution!"

It was unfortunate. A relationship between George and Dreamie Spelvin which some day might have attracted scholars in search of data on one of the greatest love stories of all time was being spoiled for small propaganda purposes.

Westbrook Pegler was on edge when he arrived in Tulsa on Thursday, August 2, 1962, for the closed August 3-5 convention of Billy James Hargis' Christian Crusade. In an interview with John Drummond of the Tulsa *Tribune*, which carried his column, he promptly declared that the school integration decision of the Supreme Court was "anti-Constitution" and that former President Eisenhower committed "an act of violence against the State and the people" in sending troops to Little Rock, Arkansas, to enforce that decision. The federal government, he exclaimed, might just as well send troops "to shoot up a school [if] it had children saying the Lord's Prayer!"

Harry Ashmore, the former Little Rock newspaper editor, should never have received a Pulitzer prize for praising the Supreme Court decision and the sending of federal troops to Little Rock, Pegler continued. Pulitzer prizes should never go to editors, he declared.

"What reason have they found to hang a Pulitzer on them except their opinions agreed with the fellows who gave them?" This was getting dangerously close to his private contempt for the Pulitzer prize awarded in 1956 to William Randolph Hearst, Jr., and his Moscow task force. He was saving that for a Sunday speech at the convention, where he could say it safely, since attendance was by invitation only, with reporters banned.

"I was forced to suppress a column blasting Pulitzer prize procedures," he told the convention, "because after Junior and

276

his Baby Sitters interviewed Khrushchev, Junior immediately set up the petulant howl of a spoiled brat for a Pulitzer award."

In his best vein, the columnist went on to describe King Features Syndicate as "a subdivision of the Hearst empire dealing in comic strips, comic strip books, sweet powders to make soda pop, toys and a very ingenious variety of dingbats for the immature."

"Much of our daily press is now under a coercion as nasty and snarling and menacing as Hitler's was in the first years of his reign," he charged, "I will not speak of other newspapers, but of recent alarming experiences in the Hearst organization. I received insolent, arrogant warnings from King Features that nothing unfavorable to the Kennedy administration or offensive to any member of the Kennedy family will be allowed out of New York where the censors sit."

The columnist praised the late William Randolph Hearst as "the great founding genius" of the newspaper chain and added that control had "passed to his sons, who lack character, ability, loyalty and principle." He characterized William Randolph Hearst, Jr., and Frank Conniff, the Hearst national news editor, as a "pair of juvenile delinquents."

What Pegler and Billy James Hargis did not suspect was that the supposedly reliable guest list included a young woman who knew shorthand and who sent in occasional notes to *Newsweek*. This "stringer" got the speech down word for word. Frank Conniff in New York was soon being asked how he felt about it, since William Randolph Hearst, Jr., was in San Simeon, unavailable for comment.

Conniff broke out laughing. "How can he do that to me?" he demanded. Turning serious, he said: "The maximum tolerance is made in this organization for prima donnas, but this has become personal."

After *Newsweek* broke the story, the columnist came to New York without haste and in an entirely unrepentant mood. There were negotiations between lawyers. One Hearst adviser suggested that such a personal attack on an employer justified breaking the contract without compensation; but he was over-ruled. Newspapers guessed later that Pegler was paid $100,000 in the settlement. Actually, it was not half that; even so, it compared favorably with the seven hundred eighty dollars in severance received by Arthur Pegler in 1936.

On August 14, the New York *Journal-American* carried a

formal announcement on the page where Pegler's copy ordinarily appeared:

"King Features Syndicate and Westbrook Pegler announced jointly today that they had terminated the contract between them. Mr. Pegler's column will, therefore, no longer appear in the Hearst newspapers or be syndicated by King Features Syndicate.

"Too many irreconcilable differences on vital matters have existed between the parties to continue a workable relationship, and compensation under the contract, which had until March 1964 to run, was settled by mutual agreement."

Interviewed by Ray Erwin of *Editor & Publisher* at the Park Lane Hotel, Pegler objected immediately to the lead on the story about himself in the New York *Herald Tribune*, which read: "Westbrook Pegler, journalism's angry man, lost his job yesterday." He did not lose his job, he contended, since the contract had been broken by mutual agreement and he had been compensated.

"I have plans but cannot disclose them now as negotiations are under way and I don't want to scare the hen off the nest," he told Erwin. "I will be a journalist as long as I live. I will continue to write, perhaps not on a daily basis, as that has become onerous. I have a great deal of information which has been inapplicable until now because I couldn't get it published. This censorship has been going on a long time . . ."

The true crusader went on to charge the Kennedy administration with covering up the Billie Sol Estes scandal in Texas. "An innocent woman was arrested in Washington and held in a mental institution and yet they talk about civil rights. They talk about civil rights being violated and permit riots in Jackson, Mississippi, because somebody can't buy hot dogs. They ought to be glad they can't buy hot dogs—they give you ulcers!"

Time carried a lengthy article on the break, declaring among other things that it was a wonder Pegler had lasted so long. "The ultimate non-conformist, he came to hate almost everything he wrote about, from politics to literature to animals. Occasionally his tirades were hilarious; more often they were simply ridiculous. No columnist in American history has heaped so much abuse on so many people over so long a period.

" 'Liar,' 'Communist,' 'traitor,' 'parasite,' were words that Pegler commonly used to describe most of the people he disliked."

The magazine asserted that the columnist had confined him-

278

self in the last couple of years largely "to innocuous columns about George Spelvin." It continued: "George still has a small, eccentric following, and chances are that he (and Pegler) will be kept by some papers even though he has been dropped by Hearst. But the demand is likely to be small. By week's end, the Hearst papers had received only a handful of letters and a few phone calls protesting the loss of their onetime titan."

Westbrook Pegler had some strong defenders. William F. Buckley's *National Review* commented that he was "easily the greatest satirist in American journalism and probably in American letters . . . the most vigorous and sometimes the most amusing polemical journeyman in the country." And Murray Kempton, a determined but unpredictable liberal columnist for the New York *Post* who was due to become a roving editor for the *New Republic* in 1963, added: "He was true to us at the end, truer than we are to ourselves, because his last words were a curse on his employer for defiling the product."

Ultra-rightist propaganda sheets from the John Birch Society Bulletin to Common Sense raged in unison over Westbrook Pegler's dismissal. "The surviving manipulators of the brothelian press," wrote the *New Letter* of the Nationalist News Service of Los Angeles, "reached the place where their chameleonic minds could not absorb truth as sharp and fearless and dynamic as that which is put out by the great Pegler."

Pegler himself retired to Tucson to rest. "I am joyous over the achievement of my freedom," he wrote in September to his biographer in New York, "though it is a trial to me to realize that vicious whores of the Roosevelt cult believe that Junior, the great publisher, was my 'boss.' On the contrary, King Features was my agent and was dismissed for failure to live up to its obligations under the contract. The financial terms are satisfactory and I came out victorious in all respects."

The veteran found he could not arrange new syndication as easily as he had expected. The large syndicates proved reluctant to offer themselves as successor-agents to King Features, and the columnist himself was reluctant to deal with a small syndicate. He faced the choice of trying to handle his own syndication from Arizona, or of dropping, at long last, out of journalism. Inevitably it would be a hard choice. In 1963, he became a member of the speakers' bureau and a monthly columnist of *American Opinion*, a magazine owned and edited by Robert Welch, founder and leader of the John Birch Society. *American Opinion* appealed

279

only to a small group of ultra-rightists. It was a far cry from the national pulpit in journalism once enjoyed by Pegler. Tired and bitter though Westbrook Pegler might be, he was still vocal, still full of protest, still ready to do battle with his legion of enemies, whether or not they still paid any attention to him. Without newsprint he would be almost powerless—a True Crusader without a sword.

BIBLIOGRAPHY

Adorno, T. W., and others. *The Authoritarian Personality.* New York: Harper & Bros., 1950.

Alexander, Jack. "He's Against." *Saturday Evening Post,* December 14, 1940.

Allen, Robert S. *Our Fair City.* New York: Vanguard Press, 1947.

Allport, Gordon W. *The Nature of Prejudice.* Boston: Beacon Press, 1954.

Bagdikian, Ben H. "Pitchmen of the Press." *Providence Journal and Evening Bulletin,* 1950.

Beichman, Arnold. "America's Irrelevant Newspapers." *Columbia University Forum,* spring, 1960.

Bell, Daniel. *Work and Its Discontents.* Boston: Beacon Press, 1956.

Bingham, Robert K. "A Talk with Westbrook Pegler." *The Reporter,* March 28, 1950.

————. "Westbrook Pegler and 'That Man in the White House.'" *The Reporter,* August 17, 1954.

Brinton, Crane. *The Anatomy of Revolution.* Englewood Cliffs: Prentice-Hall, 1938.

Brush, Katharine. *Young Man of Manhattan.* New York: Farrar & Rinehart, 1929.

————. *This Is On Me.* New York: Farrar & Rinehart, 1939.

Calmer, Ned. "WCBS-TV Views the Press," August 19, 1962.

Casey, Robert J. *Such Interesting People.* Indianapolis: Bobbs-Merrill Co., 1943.

Crozier, Emmet. *American Reporters on the Western Front, 1914-1918.* New York: Oxford University Press, 1959.

Ebenstein, William. *Today's Isms.* Englewood Cliffs: Prentice-Hall, 1954.

Ernst, Morris. *The Best Is Yet . . .* New York: Harper & Bros., 1945.

Fisher, Charles. *The Columnists.* New York: Howell, Soskin, 1944.

Fowler, Gene. *Skyline.* New York: Viking, 1961.

Gauvreau, Emile. *My Last Million Readers.* New York: Dutton, 1941.

Goldman, Eric F. *Rendezvous with Destiny.* New York: Knopf, 1952.

Grover, John. "The Truth about Westbrook Pegler," *Los Angeles Mirror* series, August, 1954.

Hecht, Ben. *A Child of the Century.* New York: Simon & Schuster, 1954.

Hoffer, Eric. *The True Believer.* New York: Harper & Bros., 1951.

Jager, Henry. *Westbrook Pegler Unmasked.* Published by the author, 1947.

Kennedy, John B. "Square Peg." From *Moulders of Opinion.* Milwaukee: Bruce Publishing Co., 1945.

Kotlowitz, Robert. "Westbrook Pegler Revisited." *Esquire,* December, 1958.

Kramer, Dale. *Heywood Broun.* New York: A. A. Wyn, 1949.

Lens, Sidney. *The Counterfeit Revolution.* Boston: Beacon Press, 1952.

————. *The Crisis of American Labor.* New York: Sagamore Press, 1959.

Liebling, A. J. "Wayward Press." *New Yorker,* November 18, 1950.

Lundberg, Ferdinand. "The Values of Westbrook Pegler." *The New Leader,* January 1, 1934.

Mackaye, Milton. "Westbrook Pegler." *Scribner's Magazine*, October, 1938.

Marrow, Alfred J. *Living Without Hate*. New York: Harper & Bros., 1951.

Marshall, Margaret. "Columnists on Parade." *Nation*, March 5, 1938.

McCarten, John. "Tough-Guy Columnist." *American Mercury*, February, 1945.

McEvoy, J. P. "Tall, Tough and Truculent." *Who*, 1941.

Pegler, Westbrook. *'T Ain't Right*. New York: Doubleday, Doran, 1936.

————. *The Dissenting Opinions of Mister Westbrook Pegler*. New York: Charles Scribner's Sons, 1939.

————. *George Spelvin, American, and Fireside Chats*. New York: Charles Scribner's Sons, 1942.

————. Syndicated columns distributed by Chicago Tribune News Syndicate, United Features, and King Features, 1925-1962.

————. Biographical sketch, United Features, 1933.

Pilat, Oliver. "Inside Westbrook Pegler." *New York Post* series, May, 1950.

————. "Pegler and His Friends." *The New Leader*, August 9, 1954.

————. "Pegler the First." *The Reporter*, April 27, 1961.

Rovere, Richard H. *Senator Joe McCarthy*. New York: Harcourt, Brace & Co., 1959.

Smith, Robert. *Baseball*. New York: Simon & Schuster, 1947.

Straight, Michael. *Trial by Television*. Boston: Beacon Press, 1954.

Taylor, Tim. Unpublished article on Pegler, 1956.

Tebbel, John. *An American Dynasty*. New York: Doubleday, 1947.

Velie, Lester. "Las Vegas: The Underworld's Secret Jackpot." *Reader's Digest*, October, 1959.

Wysor, Andrew. "How Does Pegler See It?" Unpublished paper for New York University Scholarship Writing Contest, 1962.

INDEX

A

Adams, Franklin P., 150
Adams, Sherman, 227
Adler, Julius Ochs, 242
Albany *Times-Union*, 239
Aldrich, Winthrop, 8
America, 211
Atlantic Monthly, 83
American Mercury, 177
American Opinion, 279
Annenberg, Moses L., 163
Associated Press, 67, 79
Auchincloss, Gordon, 22

B

Baer, Bugs, 190-191, 221
Baker, Newton D., 79, 80
Baruch, Bernard, 206-207
Bayly, Lewis, 72-74
Bender, Robert J., 127
Berle, A. A. Jr., 2
Berlin, Richard, 274
Billingsley, Sherman, 104
Bourjaily, Monte, 117
Bovard, O. K., 64
Bridgeport *Herald*, 174
Bridges, Harry, 185, 204, 237
Brisbane, Arthur, 53, 124
Brett, George, 170
Brameld, Theodore, 8, 232-234
Bioff, Willie, 166-168
Broom, 205
Broun, Connie, 147, 216-217
Broun, Heywood, 3, 9, 75, 76, 85,
  101, 118-120, 122-123, 130, 136-
  137, 139-140, 146-148, 161-165,
  215
Broun's Nutmeg, 162, 163
Browder, Earl, 136, 205
Browne, George E., 167, 169
Brown, Irving, 242
Brownell, Herbert, 227
Brush, Katharine, 92-93, 103
Buckley, William, F. Jr., 221, 227,
  279
Bufano, Benjamin, 146, 147
Burns, William J., 67

Bye, George T., 161
Byrnes, James F., 7

C

Cantor, Eddie, 134
Capone, Al, 104, 112, 256
Carey, James B., 161, 181
Carey, Robert J., 26, 45
Carrozzo, Mike, 9, 180
Caruso, Enrico, 89
Chambers, Whittaker, 159
Chapin, William, 64
Chaplin, Charlie, 199, 271
Chicago *American*, 40, 46, 47, 49,
  56, 59
Chicago *Daily News*, 62, 118, 168
Chicago *Examiner*, 56
Chicago *Tribune*, 18, 44, 83, 106,
  108, 110, 132, 142, 149, 180, 248
Chicago *Tribune* News Syndicate,
  102, 106, 110
Christian Century, 183
Cleveland *Press*, 187
Coburn, Charles, 273
Coffelt, Leslie, 13
Cohan, George M., 76
Cohn, Roy M., 221, 224, 227, 247
Collazo, Oscar, 12
College Humor, 92
Collier's, 130, 161, 208, 215
Common Sense, 205, 279
Congressional Record, 15
Connecticut *Nutmeg*, 148, 162
Coolidge, Calvin, 88
Corum, Bill, 94, 273
Costello, Frank, 104, 255-259
Cox, John, 267
Creel, George, 75
Coughlin, Father, 133, 143
Conniff, Frank, 18, 240, 243-244,
  266, 277
Cox, Gardner, 88
Crawford, Kenneth, 170
Croly, Herbert, 53
Cross and Flag, 205, 236, 260
Curley, W. A., 220

D

Daily Worker, 132, 137, 205
Dallas, Texas, 65
Daniels, Josephus, 74, 82, 116
Darrow, Clarence, 112
Davenport, Walter, 130
Daybook, 62
Defender, 205
Delaney, Lawrence, 159
Dempsey, Jack, 103
Denver, Col., 65
Denver *Express*, 65
Des Moines, Iowa, 62-63
Deutch, Arthur James, 8
Dewey, Thomas E., 7, 170
Dies Committee, 155, 163
Disney, Walt, 151, 152
Doane, Pearl Wiley, 260-262, 273
Doolittle, Jimmy, 208
Douglas, Helen Gahagan, 7
Dubinsky, David, 7
Dunn, John, 266
Dyer, Patrick (Packy), 149

E

Ederle, Gertrude, 106-109
Editor & Publisher, 144, 165, 190, 207, 236, 278
Eisenhower, Arthur, 240
Eisenhower, Dwight D., 16-18, 224-226, 230, 240-241, 254-255, 266-269
Elwell, Joseph Browne, 85
Erskine, John, 148
Erwin, Ray, 278
Esquire, 266
Estes, Billie Sol, 266, 267, 278

F

Fadiman, Clifton, 3
Farley, James A., 130, 190
Ferguson, Fred, 66, 81, 84, 91
Field, Marshall, 186, 187
Fitzgerald, John F. (Honey Fitz), 23
Flegenheimer, Arthur (Dutch Schultz) 104
Ford, Henry, 65
Forrest, Wilbur S., 68-69
Forrestal, James V., 238
Forsythe, Robert, 131
Foster, William Z., 136

Fowler, Gene, 45, 103, 273
Fowler, Raymond P., 200, 201
Frankfurter, Felix, 256, 259

G

Gallico, Paul, 247
Gannett, Lewis, 170
Gauvreau, Emile, 124, 125
George, Lloyd, 83
Getty, Bob, 69
Gibbons, Floyd, 76, 82-83, 85, 90, 125
Gibson, William, 103
Gimbel, Bernard, 146
Goebbels, Joseph, 132
Gold, Mike, 132
Gonzales, Westbrook Pegler, 199
Gortatowsky, J. D., 220, 274
Grant, Percy Stickney, 86
Green Mountain Rifleman, 243
Green, William, 179
Greene, Ward, 220
Gruenther, Alfred, 242
Grynszpan, Herschel, 135
Guild Progressive, 159
Guild Reporter, 160

H

Harding, Warren G., 88
Hargis, Billy James, 269, 276
Harpman, Julie, 86, 88
Harrison, James Renwick, 94
Hart, Merwin K., 205
Hearst, William Randolph, 11, 22, 96, 116, 142, 155, 178, 239, 277
Hearst, William Randolph Jr., 220, 240, 242-244, 246, 274, 276-277
Hecht, Ben, 27, 61-62, 263
Hellinger, Mark, 98, 104
Henry, Charles, 217
High, Stanley, 148
Hillman, Sidney, 7
Hiss, Alger, 272
Hitler, Adolf, 131-132
Hoff, Boo Boo, 103-104
Hollywood *Daily Variety*, 166, 171
Hoover, Herbert, 111-112, 115-116
Hoover, J. Edgar, 2, 215, 236
Hope, Bob, 221-222
House, Edward M., 17-20, 84
Howard, Roy, 66, 74, 76, 80, 82, 84-

85, 87, 90, 118-120, 122, 130, 138, 140, 143, 156, 164, 183, 190, 220
Hume, Paul, 15-16
Hughes, Charles Evans, 65

I

Ickes, Harold L., 2-3, 130
International News Agency, 51
Irwin, Will, 76

J

Jacobs, Joe, 103
James, Edwin L., 76
James, Marquis, 64
Jenner, William, 21
Joliet *Herald*, 50
John Birch Society, 266-267, 269, 271
Johnson, Hugh, 139, 150, 171
Jordan, G. Racey, 221, 229

K

Kamp, Joseph P., 205, 230
Keen, Ed, 69, 74, 80, 82, 84
Kennedy, Jacqueline, 22
Kennedy, John F., 20-23
Kennedy, Joseph P., 20-21, 206
King Features (Scripps-Howard syndicate), 14, 18-19, 110, 118, 190, 207, 247-248, 278
Knox, Frank, 9, 118, 186-187
Kramer, Dale, 164, 203, 213
Kuhn, Fritz, 193

L

Ladies Home Journal, 181
LaGuardia, Fiorello H., 2, 119
Lamont, Corliss, 7-8
Larchmont, New York, 109
Lardner, Ring, 101
Lawrence, Jack, 72, 89
Lewis, Fulton Jr., 227, 239
Lewis, John L., 58, 140
Life, 161, 173, 230, 232
Liberty League, 11, 142, 178
Lingle, Alfred (Jake), 58
Lippman, Walter, 119, 241, 263
Liverpool, 81
London, 67
London *Daily Telegraph*, 24, 125
Long, Huey, 133, 143, 269

Long, Ray, 255-256
Look, 178
Lovestone, Jay, 242
Luce, Clare Booth, 7, 247
Luce, Henry, 2, 247
Lundberg, Ferdinand, 138

M

MacGregor, Daniel, 16
Macfadden, Bernarr, 96
Mann, Arthur, 69
Maragon, Johnny, 13, 237
Maragon, Louis, 102, 103
Matthews, J. B., 163
Maurice, Frederick F. M., 70, 83-84
Maxwell, Elsa, 2
McCarthy, Joseph, 20-22, 221, 223, 231, 236, 238-240, 243, 247, 260, 271
McCormick, Robert R., 11, 83, 85, 87, 115-116, 118, 142, 178, 184, 186
McGeehan, W. O. (Bill), 90, 101
McWilliams, Carey, 166, 169
Meany, George, 242
Mellett, Lowell, 69, 80, 82
Memphis *Commercial Appeal*, 86
Mencken, Henry L., 1, 10
Meyer, Eugene, 3
Millay, Edna St. Vincent, 102
Miller, Webb, 58-59, 69, 81, 84
Minneapolis *Daily News*, 34, 36-37
Minneapolis *Journal*, 28, 34
Montana *Standard*, 14
Montgomery, Robert, 135, 166-169
Mooney, Tom, 155
Moratille, Henriette, 76, 80
Morgenthau, Henry, 168-169, 158
Murphy, Frank, 7
Mussolini, Benito, 134

N

National Review, 279
Newark *Ledger*, 137
New Leader, 177
New Letter, 279
New Masses, 3, 131, 136
New Republic, 156, 161, 279
Newspaper Guild, 119, 130, 136-141, 144, 158-161, 163-165, 181
Newsweek, 277

New Yorker, 13, 139, 259
New York *Daily Mirror*, 96, 98, 124
New York *Daily News*, 13, 86-87, 96, 106, 108-109, 149, 207, 209
New York *Enquirer*, 193
New York *Graphic*, 96
New York *Herald Tribune*, 135, 177, 203, 205, 278
New York *Journal-American*, 208, 220, 248, 256, 275, 277
New York *Post*, 14, 150, 164, 170, 174-175, 279
New York *Sun*, 99
New York Times, 138, 224, 232, 234, 242
New York *Tribune*, 91
New York *World*, 24, 90, 125, 140, 263
New York *World Telegram*, 118-120, 136, 139, 148, 164, 171, 181, 187
Nixon, Richard, 261, 265, 271, 272
Nizer, Louis, 204-206, 212, 214-217
Nolan, Dennis E., 78-79, 83, 85
Norris, J. Frank, 97

O

O'Brien, Lucy, 249
O'Donnell, John, 13, 149, 220
O'Flaherty, Hal, 68-69
Owen, Blaine, 135

P

Page, Walter Hines, 70, 74, 83
Parrott, Ursula, 148
Patterson, Eleanor (Cissy), 239
Patterson, Joseph Medill, 87, 178, 184
Patterson, Robert P., 242
Patton, George, 78
Pattula, George, 80
Payne, Phil, 86
Pearson, Drew, 204, 224, 235-239, 246
Pegler, Arthur James, 24-35, 40, 45-47, 54, 59, 62, 90-91, 98-99, 124-125, 153, 199, 272, 274
Pegler, Arthur James II, 151, 185
Pegler, Frances Nicholson, 31, 34, 38, 41, 89, 123-124
Pegler, Frances, 41, 124

Pegler, James Westbrook, boyhood and youth, 28-30, 35-39, 41-45, 47-48; early newspaper employment, 49-51, 53, 56-62, 65; World War I correspondent for UP in England and France, 67-79; discredited as war correspondent for censorship violation, 80; enlists in Navy, 81; rehired by UP in New York on return from Europe, 87; marries Julie Harpman, 91; achieves prominence as sports writer in the '20s, 90, 95-105; employed by Chicago *Tribune* News Syndicate, 102; leans toward Hoover in '28 elections, 111; influenced by employer's beliefs, 111, 138, 142, 178, 184; levels first journalistic attacks on Prohibition, 112-113; denounces the rich in the first years of the depression, 114-115; buys home in Pound Ridge, New York, 116; hired by United Features Scripps Howard syndicate as news commentator, 118; condones California lynchers, 120-122; initial commitment to FDR, 117; espouses anti-fascism, 130; reports Winter Olympics in Nazi Germany, 131-135; attacked by Joseph Goebbels, 132; writes column on Nazi torment of Jewish children, 133; friendship with Roy Howard, 136, 138-140; opposes FDR tax program, 143; wins award from National Headliners Club for exposing income tax evasion, 144; joins and resigns from Newspaper Guild, 136-141; exposes labor racketeers, 145, 166-170, 180; voices anti-labor opinions, 14, 144-145, 179-181, 194-195; turns against New Deal, 144; defends Loyalist Spain, 156; his forceful attitudes hinder anti-Communist caucus in Newspaper Guild, 159-160; feuds and breaks with Heywood Broun, 149, 161, 163-164; Broun sketches Pegler at the height of his career, 162; develops own style as columnist, 154-156; unworried by his inconsistencies, 155; wins Pulitzer Prize for series on labor racketeers, 171; buys and remodels farm in Ridgebury, Connecticut, 172-176; adopts ultra-right position, 182; settles in Tucson, Arizona, 188; first supports then opposes war effort, 178, 182-187; dropped by Chicago *Daily News* because of his extremism, 187; Roy Howard breaks with Pegler over his anti-FDR virulence, 190; joins Hearst's King Features Syndicate, 190; Quentin Reynolds sues for libel, 203-206, 208-209, 212-218; receives Hearst's Banshee award, 219-222; criticizes Catholic trade unionists, 209-212; collaborates with Senator Joseph McCarthy, 223, 227-231, 238-239; hounds Theodore Brameld, 232-235; quarrels with Drew Pearson, 235-239; objects to Korean War, 207; pulls for Taft vs. Eisenhower in 1952, 240; disagrees with moderate policies of W. R. Hearst, Jr., 240, 242-244; Julie Harpman dies, 245-248; associates with Barry Goldwater, 252-254; drops investigation of Bioff murder, 250-254; remarries, 260-262, 273; supports ultra-right Constitution Party of California, 254-255; proposes Frank Costello arrange murder of Supreme Court Justice, 257; attends Billy James Hargis' Christian Crusade Convention, 276; opinions on racial and religious bigotry, 183, 192-193; peddles antisemitic "invisible government" theory for seven years, 19; Pegler's advocacy of violence, 6-7, 61, 122-123, 194-195, 243-244, 257, 265; the preferred spokesman for authoritarians, 195, 265-271; his column dropped by Hearst papers, 278; appointed columnist for *American Opinion,* 279

Pegler, John A., 29, 35, 41, 42, 47, 49, 59, 62, 85, 91, 124, 147, 151, 228

Pegler, Julie Harpman, 92, 105-109, 117, 120, 149, 152-153, 188, 196-199, 201, 214, 216, 222, 245, 249, 279

Peine, Virginia (Mrs. Quentin Reynolds), 203, 208, 209, 214, 217

Peress, Irving, 225

Pershing, John J., 75, 77-79, 82-84

Philadelphia *Bulletin,* 130

Philadelphia *Inquirer,* 163

Philadelphia *Public Ledger,* 83

Pilat, Oliver, 159

P. M., 174, 187, 193

Poetry, 59

Pope Pius XII, 209

Pound Ridge, New York, 116

Pravda, 242

Pyle, Ernie, 156

R

Randau, Carl, 138, 159

Reber, Miles, 224

Reber, Samuel, 224, 225

Reynolds, Quentin, 130-131, 146-147, 165, 203-205, 208-209, 212, 214-218, 247

Rice, Grantland, 90, 101

Richmond *Times-Dispatch,* 182

Riordan, Art, 170

Roberts, Oral, 269

Rockne, Knute, 101

Roosevelt, Eleanor, 11-12, 139, 150-151, 170, 184-185, 206

Roosevelt, Franklin D., 10-12, 19-20, 81-82, 88, 116-117, 143, 149-150, 158, 183-185

Roosevelt, Theodore, 52-53, 54, 57, 65, 88

Root, Elihu, 53

Ruark, Robert, 247, 248

Runyon, Damon, 76, 90

Ruth, Babe, 91-92, 97-98

Ryan, Seymour, 89

S

Sandburg, Carl, 62

Saturday Evening Post, 5, 25, 80

287

St. Louis *Post-Dispatch*, 24
Scalise, George, 169, 170
Schine, G. David, 224-225, 247
Schultz, Benjamin, 221, 227
Scripps, E. S., 118
Scripps Howard syndicate (see King Features)
Seldes, George, 78
Sims, William S., 72-74, 82-84, 116
Sinatra, Frank, 4-5, 22
Sioux City, Iowa *Times*, 23
Skolsky, Sidney, 104
Smith, Alfred E., 111
Smith, Gerald L. K., 17, 194, 205, 230, 236
Smith, H. Allen, 127
Social Justice, 183
Sokolsky, George, 275
Stars and Stripes, 76, 181
Stern, J. David, 158, 164
Stevenson, Adlai, 255
Stevenson, Robert Louis, 154, 155, 156
Stotesbury, Mrs. E. W., 130
Straton, John Roach, 96, 97
Stripling, Robert, 273
Sturm, Justin, 145
Sullivan, Ed, 104
Sullivan, Frank, 148
Sunday *Worker*, 135, 136
Syracuse *Post Standard*, 242, 243

T

Taft, William Howard, 52-53, 55, 57
Tampa *Morning Tribune*, 249
The Sign, 177, 211
Thomas, J. Parnell, 236, 237
Thomas, Lowell, 208
Thompson, Dorothy, 135
Time, 15, 24, 159, 184, 278
Tisdale, Frederick Jr., 149, 273
Torresola, Griselo, 12
Towart, Maude, 214, 249, 261, 273
Trohan, Walter, 149, 220
Truman, Harry S., 12-16, 84, 206, 207, 227
Truman, Margaret, 12, 15-16
Tucson, Arizona, 188
Tunney, Gene, 99, 103, 129, 146-147, 152, 196

U

Ungar, Arthur, 166, 169
United Features Syndicate, 117
United News, 90
United Press, 49, 50, 63, 66-67, 79

V

Van Loon, Hendrick Willem, 3-4, 147
Variety, 15
Vaughan, Harry, 13
Vidmer, Richards, 94

W

Wage Earner, 210
Wallace, Henry A., 6, 206
Walker, Edwin A., 265, 266
Walker, James J., 190, 191
Walton, Hick, 63
Warren, Earl, 256, 258-259, 269
Washington *Post*, 3
Washington *Times Herald*, 184
Ways, Max, 160
Welch, Joseph, 226
Welch, Robert, 266, 279
Welles, Orson, 5-6
White, L. E. (Pete), 269
White, William Allen, 84
Wiegand, Karl H. Van, 64
Wiley, Alexander, 271
Willard, Jess, 97
Williams, Wythe, 76
Wilson, Clarence True, 112
Wilson, Lyle, 149
Wilson, Woodrow, 54, 57, 65-66, 71, 88, 116
Winchell, Walter, 2, 104, 127-128, 171, 193, 236, 274
Winrod, Gerald B., 17-19, 205, 269
Wise, Stephen S., 134
Work, 210
Woollcott, Alexander, 76

Y

Yudain, Harold, 163-164

Z

Zwicker, Ralph, 225, 230

CPSIA information can be obtained
at www.ICGtesting.com
Printed in the USA
BVHW032050030722
641223BV00008B/143